# Contemporary Wales

# Volume 22

# CONTEMPORARY WALES

Volume 22

Edited by

**Paul Chaney (Cardiff University)**
**Elin Royles (Aberystwyth University)**
**Andrew Thompson (University of Glamorgan)**

*Published on behalf*
*of the University of Wales*

**Cardiff**
**University of Wales Press**
**2009**

*www.uwp.co.uk*


**British Library Cataloguing in Publication Data**
A catalogue record for this book is available from the British Library.




ISBN 978-0-7083-2251-2
e-ISBN 978-0-7083-2252-9
ISSN 0951-4937

Original cover design by Marian Delyth
Cover photograph: Ian Homer
Printed in Wales by Dinefwr Press, Llandybïe

# CONTENTS

# FIGURES AND TABLES

## FIGURES

## TABLES

# CONTRIBUTORS

**Dave Adamson** is Professor of Community and Social Policy at the University of Glamorgan.

**Simon Brooks** is a lecturer in the School of Welsh at Cardiff University. His work explores tensions between conservatism and liberalism, as they affect literature, politics and the history of ideas in minority language communities.

**Jane Bryan** is Research Associate in the Welsh Economy Research Unit, Cardiff Business School.

**Penny Byrne** is a member of Programme for Community Regeneration, University of Glamorgan.

**Patrick Carlin** is a PhD candidate at the Department of International Politics at Aberystwyth University. His thesis deals with language planning in subregional authorities in the Basque Country, Catalonia and Wales.

**Anwen Elias** is a lecturer at the Institute of Welsh Politics, Aberystwyth University. Her research interests include: European integration; nationalism; devolution in the UK; and French and Spanish political systems.

**Alan Felstead** is Research Professor at Cardiff School of Social Sciences. He is principal investigator on a project entitled, Learning as Work: Teaching and Learning Processes in the Contemporary Work Organization.

**Rhian Siân Hodges** is a final year Welsh-medium Sociology and Social Policy PhD student, studying at Bangor University.

**William Housley** is senior lecturer at Cardiff School of Social Sciences. His research interests include culture and identity; culture, community and regeneration; interaction, decision-making and organizations; and, interaction, the public sphere and democratic communication.

**Martin Jephcote** is senior lecturer at Cardiff School of Social Sciences. His research interests include the contested and evolutionary nature of the construction of pedagogic discourse and the ways in which policies are made and implemented.

**Stuart Jones** is lecturer in Community Regeneration at the University of Glamorgan. His major focus of research is continuing developments in the fields of poverty and social exclusion, youth, community dynamics, substance misuse and the environment.

**Jennifer Maher** is a doctoral student, part-time criminology lecturer and researcher at the University of Glamorgan.

**Laura McAllister** is Professor of Governance at University of Liverpool Management School.

**Kate Moles** is employed on the Wales Rural Observatory at Cardiff School of City and Regional Planning.

**Gareth Rees** is Professor at Cardiff School of Social Sciences, Cardiff University and, Associate Director, ESRC Research Centre on Skills, Knowledge and Organizational Performance.

**Neil Roche** is a researcher associate at the Welsh Economy Research Unit, Cardiff Business School.

**Jane Salisbury** is senior lecturer at Cardiff School of Social Sciences. Her research interests include: post compulsory education and training; further education sector in Wales; differential attainment; ethnography and qualitative methods; teacher education and socialization.

**Diana Silvia Stirbu** is a final year PhD student at the University of Liverpool Management School and researches on institutional and constitutional design in Wales and on the development of Welsh devolution.

**Robin Smith** is a PhD student at Cardiff School of Social Sciences. His thesis comprises of a multi-modal qualitative study of the regeneration of Cardiff Bay.

**Morton Warner** is Visiting Professor at the Welsh Institute for Health and Social Care, University of Glamorgan.

**Richard Williams** is Professor of Mental Health Strategy at the University of Glamorgan.

# 1. THE RHETORIC OF CIVIC 'INCLUSIVITY' AND THE WELSH LANGUAGE

*Simon Brooks*

## ABSTRACT

*This article examines the discourse of inclusivity following political devolution, as it impacted on Wales' autochthonous Welsh-speaking minority language community. Devolution in 1999 led to the strengthening of civic identity in Wales. The post-devolution political elite adopted buzzwords such as inclusivity to underpin the vision of a new democracy and citizenship open to all. Paradoxically, however, admirable as the goal of inclusivity was, the term was problematic for the minority language community. Post devolution, claims were made of a shift from ethnic to civic nationalism. In this new paradigm, minority language discourse was often imagined as ethnic, and normative majority language discourse as civic. As a result, inclusivity could be used in an ideologically loaded way in public discourse. Minority language discourse could be implied to be exclusive, monocultural and intolerant, and majority language discourse as inclusive, multicultural and open. The rhetoric of inclusivity thus tended to delegitimize cultural claims made by some players in the minority language community, and impacted negatively on their public policy contribution. Drawing on examples from other European minority communities, it is argued that inclusivity is a form of universalism which suppresses cultural difference. The article concludes by showing how inclusivity has been used to criticize some Welsh language cultural institutions.*

## INTRODUCTION

This article is about an apparent paradox regarding the development of civic notions of inclusivity; namely that in some political contexts, the use of the rhetoric of civic inclusivity can legitimize the marginalization of some minority groups. The article proposes that this may hold true if a minority group is autochthonous, i.e. indigenous to a particular territory, and has been imagined in political discourse as 'ethnic' or 'ethno-linguistic' in character, and if that minority group has used the rhetoric of self-determination or nationalism in order to gain democratic, cultural or linguistic rights within the state. In such circumstances the minority group may be open to criticism from concepts of civic inclusivity that perceive the cultural or linguistic norms of the hegemonic culture of the state to be empty of ethnicity, and therefore by definition both civic and inclusive, while simultaneously deriding the cultural claims of the minority community as ethnic, communitarian or essentialist.

This article examines this contention by studying the use of the civic buzzword 'inclusivity' as it developed in Wales before and after devolution in 1999, and its use as a rhetorical device when discussing the Welsh language, a minoritized language. In Wales, intellectuals from the minority language community had established the movement for self-determination, and campaigns for minority language rights were often linked in the public mind with Welsh nationalism. The Welsh-language community had for many decades been portrayed by some of its detractors as ethnically closed and intolerant (Brooks, 2006a), while the majority English language community was perceived by its supporters to be open and international in character. The implication being that minority and majority language communities were on opposite sides of an ethnic–civic divide whilst some used inclusivity to marginalize the discourse of minority language rights in post-devolution Wales. This in turn had an effect on public policy debate and policy development in the newly established National Assembly for Wales.

## THE WELSH LANGUAGE AND THE MEANINGS OF 'INCLUSIVITY'

The term inclusivity was not invented in Wales. The term became prominent in British political debate in the mid-1990s as part of a New Labour discourse on 'social inclusion'. The term was imported into Wales as rhetoric during the internal pre-1997 Labour Party debate on devolution, and was employed by Ron Davies and others to argue that any future devolved government in Wales should be representative and include an element of proportionality in its electoral system (Chaney and Fevre, 2001a).

Revealingly, the term was not originally used to suggest that the Welsh language and 'Welshness' were 'exclusive' – given the political realities of Welsh marginalization during the 1979–97 Conservative Governments, to do so would have been inopportune. Indeed, a major beneficiary of proportionality was Plaid Cymru, whose electoral strength at the time was concentrated in mainly Welsh-speaking communities in north and west Wales. This initial use of the word 'inclusion' in pre-devolution Welsh political discourse thus identified the Welsh-speaking community as being one among a number of communities marginalized within the decision-making process in Wales. Nor were the terms 'inclusivity' and 'inclusiveness' used in pre-devolution Wales to project concerns regarding the inappropriateness of a language rights agenda. Indeed, following the election of the Labour government in 1997, the new Secretary of State for Wales, Ron Davies, met the Welsh Language Society, Cymdeithas yr Iaith Gymraeg, in the name of 'inclusivity' (Chaney and Fevre, 2001a). This early discursive context, the 'cult of inclusiveness', as Chaney and Fevre call it, was about the validation of liberal political values and was sufficiently undefined not to have marginalized vested interests later identified as 'exclusionary', such as the Welsh language lobby.

The meaning of 'inclusivity' in Welsh political discourse seems, however, to have mutated following the devolution referendum held in September 1997, and to have begun to develop undertones of antipathy towards 'exclusive' language-based identities. The referendum was won by the narrowest of margins: 50.3 per cent/49.7 per cent. Furthermore, the differential voting patterns in various identity-based groupings in Wales suggested that the 'Yes' vote contained ethno-cultural and ethno-linguistic traces. Strong Welsh-identifiers voted 'Yes' in greater numbers than those who identified only weakly or not at all with Welsh identity. Welsh-born residents were more likely to have voted 'Yes' than English-born residents. Fluent Welsh speakers voted for a Welsh Assembly by a margin of almost four to one, while English monoglots had opposed devolution by about three to two (Jones and Trystan, 1999).

The Welsh devolution referendum result thus suggested an interesting paradox for the minority language and civic concepts of national identity. Although the Welsh language had been politically marginalized in Wales prior to devolution, and had indeed faced institutionalized discrimination until quite late in the twentieth century (Davies, 2000), many in Wales – both inside and outside the Welsh-language community – perceived the minority language to be the central element of Welsh identity. The narrowness of the devolution result, and the associated identity-based patterns of differential voting, gave sustenance to those who argued that the emphasis on the Welsh language as central to national identity had not helped the cause of devolution. The rhetoric of inclusivity thus began to be used to reconfigure the symbolic markers of Welsh identity in a way that would more easily tally with the non-Welsh-speaking identity of the majority of the population, and thus better support the project of civic nation-building represented by the devolution project.

According to Ron Davies, post-referendum debates about citizenship concentrated on the issue of:

> how you create the idea of Wales and Welsh identity [. . .] devising new ways of reaching out, not only in terms of conventional social inclusiveness, but the new ways that we have to devise to attract or encompass those people that are excluded by the traditional ways. [. . .] it is vital for the construction of a more inclusive society that the new spirit of confidence and assertiveness is owned by all the people of Wales, not just those born here and those able to speak the native language. (Quoted in Chaney and Fevre, 2001a, pp. 30–1)

This was to become the dominant meaning conveyed by the word inclusiveness and its synonyms in post-devolution Wales. Here, Ron Davies implies that an autochthonous minority language community, which does things in the 'traditional ways', might be exclusive. Davies does not himself argue that the minority language should be marginalized on the grounds that it is exclusive; rather he focuses on developing Welsh identities which are not language-based. Yet it can be a short step from suggesting that particular identities are exclusionary to one of opposing such identities for this reason. For while the development of a new civic concept of Welshness is both necessary and inevitable, it does contain the potential within itself to drive out older identity-based attachments, many of which remain important for the minority language community, and for minority language reproduction.

Inclusivity was also problematic for the Welsh language because of the Cinderella status of language in public policy debate in other parts of the United Kingdom. Concepts of inclusion and inclusivity have often been developed in England, and then adopted in Wales with little idea as to how this might play out for the minority language community. Downplaying language as an equal opportunities issue reflects a UK model of inclusiveness. In Wales this ignores the power inequalities between the English and Welsh languages, while simultaneously opening the door to the possibility that the minority language might be identified as a barrier to the social inclusion of certain marginalized groups.

The recommendation by the 1997–8 National Assembly Advisory Group (NAAG) that the Assembly establish an equal opportunities committee 'with a remit including the three strands of gender, race and disability as a minimum' (NAAG, 1998, p. 36) placed the three big UK equality strands at the centre of the post-devolution agenda. This institutionalized the secondary status of language – as well as some other equality claims pertaining to religion, sexuality and age – in relation to the politics of inclusiveness. Although the 1998 and 2006 Government of Wales Acts require the Assembly to function 'with due regard to the principle that there should be equality of opportunity for all people', various Assembly committees and documents have often approached language equality in a rather ad hoc way. Language has been treated as part of the equality agenda in some documentation (see for example WAG, 2003), yet ignored in others. The Assembly Government's 2007 document on 'Inclusive Policy Making' for example excludes language, and makes no reference to the statutory responsibilities placed on public bodies in Wales to treat the Welsh and English language on the basis of equality:

> Over the last thirty years successive legislation has been introduced that is designed to protect people against unfair discrimination and in recent years public bodies have been placed under statutory duties to promote equality. Disadvantaged people are often categorised into six equality strands or groups, these relate to: gender identity; disabled people; minority ethnic people; older and younger people; gay, lesbian or bisexual people; people with religious or other beliefs, or no belief. (Welsh Assembly Government, 2007, p. 1)

Such public policy omissions regarding the minority language have remained largely unscrutinized as the dominant discourse in theoretical and sociological writing tends to position Welsh-language identity, and associated concepts of 'Welshness', as 'exclusive' in either implicit or explicit ways (see for example Day, 2002; Williams, 2005b; Smith, 2007).

## WELSH: AN EXCLUSIVE LANGUAGE?

The core problem for the relationship of the Welsh language with the concept of inclusivity is that while autochthonous minoritized languages are often marginalized by everyday political power and discourse, they remain powerful within symbolic orders of national or ethnic identity. This is certainly true of the Welsh language in Wales. This is an unusual situation, because when markers of national identity are powerful within a symbolic order, they are normally also powerful within political structures. An example might be unexamined concepts of whiteness which have been criticized as being both hegemonic symbolically in terms of assumptions that to be Welsh is to be white, and also hegemonic politically, as ethnic minorities have been under-represented in Wales at a political level (Chaney and Williams, 2003). The politics of inclusion has been positive in Wales for ethnic minority communities; both because it has fore-grounded public acknowledgment of black and Asian identities in Wales as Welsh identities, and also because it has led to greater representation of ethnic minorities at a political level, thus improving the position of ethnic minorities in both symbolic and 'real' orders of power.

In the post-devolution Welsh context it was because the minority language remained powerful as a symbol of national (and nationalist) identity that the social movement campaigning to normalize the minority language in everyday life could be criticized as exclusive. The tendency to criticize Welsh-language cultural nationalism was in part a continuation of a pre-1997 academic discourse that had equated 'a nation-building project based on language' with 'notions of exclusive ethnicities and cultural supremacy', typified in Europe by the politics of the New Radical Right with its use of cultural essentialism to achieve racist ends (Williams, 1995, p. 126). But although tabloid journalists and others linked language campaigning with racism during the Assembly's first term (McGuinness, 2003; Brooks, 2006a), sociological criticism in post-devolution Wales was subtler. It placed the Welsh language lobby outside the realm of civic inclusivity, an accusation both less serious, but also more wide-ranging, than the refrain of racism (see for example Day, 2002).

Such an interpretation of inclusivity assumed a link between the Welsh language agenda and nationalism, and between nationalism and ethno-cultural intolerance. This is well illustrated in 'Welsh Nationalism and the Challenge of "Inclusive" Politics', which argues that the *raison d'être* of Welsh nationalism 'often appeared to be the vehement defence of a language group and its culture and it might be difficult to imagine how such a movement could respond positively to the idea of inclusiveness' (Chaney and Fevre, 2001b, p. 232).

The keyword 'inclusivity' positioned the Welsh language on the wrong side of a supposed ethnic–civic divide. The logic of this appropriation can be seen in many texts, of which a few examples will suffice. Jonathan Bradbury's examination of 'An Inclusive Identity?', for example, offers a definition of 'inclusivity' that exiles the Welsh language from the civic to the ethnic sphere:

> Commentators have frequently questioned the inclusiveness of Welsh identity, suggesting that it is basically a white identity, or indeed specifically a white Welsh-speaking identity. On the other hand, many of devolution's proponents have argued that it would foster a new inclusive civic Welshness which would overcome this. (Bradbury, 2004/5, p. 70)

The problem here is not the critique of hegemonic and racially exclusive whiteness, but the positioning of the language as central to a white monoethnic entity. Juxtapositions which presume a link between the Welsh language and whiteness inevitably imply that the minority language is exclusive and resistant to diversity (Houlihan, 2005; Williams, 2005a), and largely ignore the attempts of language activists to argue that the Welsh language should be no barrier to inclusivity; for example in claims that the majority Welsh-speaking communities of *Y Fro Gymraeg* should be 'a multi-racial and inclusive region whose particular and proper language is Cymraeg' (Webb, 2005, p. 66).

Indeed, in many ways the post-devolution use of the word 'inclusivity' has involved a reconfiguration of the Welsh language debate from a 1960s to 1980s discourse in which the Welsh language 'struggle', with its appeal to linguistic equality and civil rights, enjoyed largely positive connotations in progressive circles to a more critical discourse in which increased emphasis on the language is seen as problematic and connected to ethnicized exclusions. In this discourse, minority cultural claims can be pitched against each other, with ethnic minority cultures encouraged in an inclusive Wales and yet the autochthonous minority language depicted as a barrier to inclusivity (Davies, 2004).

However, the suggestion that (nationalist) minority language communities are monoethnic, and somehow at odds with multiculturalism, is both theoretically problematic and empirically unexamined. The Romany, for example, provide one historical example of ethnic and cultural diversity within the context of rural Welsh-language culture (Jarman and Jarman, 1991). Groups and individuals from non-Welsh ethnic backgrounds that have participated in Welsh-language nationalist discourse include political refugees, first generation immigrants, and second-generation writers exploring their hybrid ethnic identities (see for example, Bosse-Griffiths, 1941; Griffiths, 2004; Fitzgerald, 1969; Apolloni, 2004). This is not to deny the presence of Welsh ethnocentricism in some Welsh-language discourse (Brooks, 2006b). Presumably too, members of migrant groups are more likely to learn the language of the state than a non-hegemonic language such as Welsh. However, it is empirically incorrect to suggest that minority languages such as Welsh, even when associated with nationalistic social move-ments, are only spoken by particular ethno-linguistic groups, i.e. that Welsh in Wales is only spoken by the (ethnically) Welsh. Yet the keyword 'inclusive' is often used to suggest this, often in quite explicit ways:

There is a Patagonian version of Welsh culture that is inclusive in ways unlike Welsh-language culture in Wales. Of the twenty-seven of our interviewees who were the most involved in local Welsh cultural activities, nine spoke no Welsh, and three of those had no Welsh ancestry at all. Many ethnic groups – even including the indigenous Mapuche – were represented among those taking Welsh lessons, singing in Welsh choirs and competing in the eisteddfod. (Trosset et al., 2007, p. 242)

The revealing comment here is not the ethnic diversity of the Welsh-language community in Patagonia, but rather the assumption that this is not true about Welsh-language culture in Wales.

## THEORETICAL REASONS FOR EXCLUSIVE 'INCLUSIVITY'

What then are the theoretical reasons which have enabled the concept of 'inclusivity' to be used to criticize autochthonous minority language communities as monocultural, despite the existence of empirical evidence that this is not the case? How did 'inclusivity' move from being an expression of a desire to develop a plurality of Welsh identities to one which sought to criticize the minority language as being incapable of incorporating diversity?

In many ways inclusivity is a continuation of the eighteenth-century Enlighten-ment rhetoric that positioned minority languages as being outside the rational order (Williams and Morris, 2000). The belief that the majority language is rational and universal, while the minority language is emotional and insular, lies behind many of the metaphors historically used in Wales to delegitimize the Welsh lan-guage. In early twentieth-century Wales, for example, socialism identified English as the language of internationalism and rationalism, and Welsh was reduced to a patois of parochialism. It could be argued that 'inclusivity' is a new name for this discursive formation in that it imagines the majority language as being universal by virtue of its assimilating rationalism. If the minority language stands outside the rational order of majority discourse, it becomes that which rejects, and therefore excludes, reason.

Welsh is not the only autochthonous minority language to have been excluded by universalist Enlightenment thought in this way. France, in particular, has historically defined concepts of political citizenship and equality in terms of com-pulsory inclusion within one linguistic space. This egalitarian reduction of difference claims for the French language universality, while the state's minori-tized languages such as Breton, Corsican, Catalan or Basque have been marked out as elitist and undemocratic (Brooks, 2004). The break up of the Soviet Union has seen newly independent nations conduct debates between the inheritors of state socialism and minority nationalism not dissimilar to those in Wales. In postcolonial Ukraine, for example, the Ukrainian language has been imagined by some as insular and exclusive, while the Russian language community, with its claims to universality, has used rhetoric based on ideas of inclusion to resist Ukrainian language cultural claims (Riabchuk, 1996).

In Scotland, the rhetoric of inclusivity has also been used against the autochthonous minority language community. Myths of ethnic harmony similar to those in Wales propagate the idea 'that Scottish people in general are more tolerant and accommodating than their English cousins' (Maan, 1992, p. 205). Civil society is more firmly entrenched in Scotland than in Wales, and Scottish nationalism is celebrated as a civic rather than ethnic phenomenon. Despite this, the Gaelic language community has fewer rights than its Welsh-language counterpart, even in those parts of the Highlands and Islands where Gaelic speakers form a majority or sizeable minority of the local population. In recent debate about the establishment of designated Gaelic-medium primary schools on the Isle of Skye, opponents have employed metaphors of social exclusion. 'If a dedicated Gaelic school is given the green light', writes one supporter of English-medium education, 'it will create in the village [of Portree] an insular, separate Gaelic community which could conceivably have a negative effect on the Gaelic language, making it less inclusive and in fact marginalising the Gaelic-speaking community' (Hammond, 2008). 'It's an exclusion or inclusion argument' says the group opposed to a Gaelic-medium school in another part of the island (BBC News, 2006).

Evidently too, Enlightenment universalism can be used to position other non-normative identities outside the rational order, and is not necessarily restricted to language-based identity. German scholars have traced the under-researched theme of anti-Semitism on the German Left to a rationalist fear of the particularism of Judaism in leftist German Enlightenment thought (Kneer, 2007). Historical case studies position the rhetoric of universalism and rationalism as the means by which left wing thinkers from hegemonic majorities can exclude minorities, and yet remain true to their own self-image that they themselves are inclusive and therefore 'good' (Brosch et al., 2007). It is not accidental that much of the opposition to the Welsh language in Wales has come from the Left.

In many ways then, inclusivity and exclusivity are nomenclature that identify discursive statements as being either inside or outside the body of political discourse acceptable to a particular polity at a particular time. The same could be said of that discourse in post-devolution Wales which appropriates to language ideologies the attributes of 'civic' or 'ethnic' nationalism. Indeed, in this context, the terms civic and inclusive, and ethnic and exclusive, are often interchangeable. This discourse has identified Welsh nationalism as being on a journey from pre-devolution ethnic to post-devolution civic nationalism, while simultaneously holding that exclusive Welsh-language ideologies are a marker of ethnic national-ism. By comparison, undeclared ideologies of English monolingualism are presumed to be civic. This suggestion that civic nationalism has somehow freed itself of the attributes of the hidden universalizing ethnicity that justifies its cultural norms could be much criticized. It has been argued by some, for example, that 'even in cases of apparent "civic" nationalism what is really taking place is the imposition of the culture of the dominant ethnicity – whose ethnicity is rendered invisible by assumptions of universal validity – over subordinate ethnicities' (Breuilly, 2008, p. 22). In Wales, the tendency has been for civic nationalism to act as cover for the continued hegemony of the English language, albeit with a veneer of thin bilingualism, and an acceptance of Welsh-language cultural autonomy in certain defined fields, such as statutory education and broadcasting.

It could be argued then that the binary opposition between civic/inclusive and ethnic/exclusive cultural discourses is a false one (Thomas, 1999; Jones, 2007). These terms are questionable in the sense that all in Wales are civic by virtue of their residence and/or citizenship, and all are ethnic because all possess an ethnicity or ethnicities. Repeated examinations and criticisms of 'exclusionary' and 'ethnic' Welsh-language nationalism, although useful in terms of opening up Welsh-language discourse to the Other, has the discursive effect of allowing supposedly civic and ethnically blind non-nationalist Welsh identities to remain unscrutinized. It has permitted a discourse in the field of historical studies, for example, which unfavourably compares 'linguistically exclusive "Welshness"' with the laudable actions of 'a "collectivist, universalist" working-class who promoted "an inter-meshing of class and community solidarities whose horizons were truly international"' (Williams, 2006, p. 82). In effect, universalism has let the advocates of culturally normative ideologies off the hook, and perpetuates myths of Welsh tolerance correctly criticized by Charlotte Williams and others (Williams et al., 2003).

## THE PUBLIC POLICY IMPACT

The concept of 'inclusivity' was not merely problematic in Wales at a theoretical level. It also fed into public policy debate and policy development in post-devolution Wales in a way that delegitimized claims made by some members of the minority language community. In her study of Welsh civil society during the Assembly's first term, the political scientist Elin Royles sought to ask 'whether the Assembly's "inclusive" structures achieved the aim of promoting engagement opportunities for civil society organisations' and if 'the supposed "inclusiveness" of the Assembly was realized in practice' (Royles, 2007, pp. 7–9). The study analysed a variety of organizations, including those connected with Welsh-language political activism (Cymdeithas yr Iaith Gymraeg and Cymuned) which, because they were located 'outside the "consensus" of the new Welsh politics, provided an opportunity to investigate the extent to which the Assembly's rhetoric of "inclusiveness" became reality' (Royles, 2007, p. 81). The study concluded that while other voluntary sector and minority rights groups had been encouraged to engage productively with the Assembly, the more radical Welsh-language pressure groups had been discouraged from doing so and given 'outsider' status. For Royles, this demonstrated that in the case 'relating to the Welsh language' there were 'limits to the Assembly's "inclusiveness"' (Royles, 2007, p. 149). Indeed, Royles was not the only observer to criticize the Assembly for a lack of 'inclusiveness' when faced with controversial Welsh-language issues. The constitutionalist Rawlings made the same accusation when questioning the decision (later reversed) of the Assembly's Education committee in May 2001 not to consider controversial evidence on Welsh-medium higher education after one AM described it as xenophobic (Rawlings, 2003).

Royles does not advance theoretical reasons for the exclusion of radical Welsh language cultural claims from the 'wide tent' of post-devolution inclusivity. However, it is the contention of this article that this came about because of the concept of inclusivity itself. In theoretical terms, inclusivity is an attempt to divide the ethnic from the civic, and to ensure that politics is based on the civic alone. In this context, the false binary that describes minority and majority language discourses as respectively ethnic and civic has empowered those politicians who oppose minority language promotion. As inclusivity rejects the ethnic as closed, some of the more radical viewpoints on the Welsh language could therefore be excluded from the political process.

Indeed, this logic had further implications for public policy-making. In particular, inclusivity is problematic for institutions which have normalized the use of the minority language. For many advocates of inclusivity, monoglot Welsh-language spaces are expressions of a singular and ethnic identity, and are therefore to be challenged in a way that monoglot English-language spaces are not. The National Eisteddfod of Wales for example has been critiqued by politicians and journalists using metaphors of inclusion and exclusion to suggest that a monoglot Welsh-language festival might have the potential to exclude (Pugh, 2006; Manning, 2008).

Another case in point is that of Welsh-language broadcasting. Criticism has been levied that it should 'move away from essentialist constructs of Welsh identity tied to language' and that a more 'inclusive media in Wales' should be embraced (Mackay and Ivey, 2004, p. 153). Others have argued that S4C's recent decline in audience share provides 'an opportunity for S4C to make a virtue out of necessity with a shift to bilingual programming [. . .] and a more inclusive, broader identity' (Thomas and Lewis, 2006, p. 39). Such comments have been accompanied by calls from elected politicians such as Labour MP Chris Bryant for S4C to take on a bilingual remit (Tryhorn, 2007). No similar policy push has been made for majority-language television channels to include the minority language, as the majority language is of itself somehow assumed to be inclusive of diversity. In this example, the rhetoric of inclusivity has been used to argue for the reduction of minority language space.

## CONCLUSION

The shift towards civic concepts of national identity in post-devolution Wales, and the subsequent emphasis on inclusivity, identified many minority language discourses as ethnic rather than civic. On the wrong side of the ethnic–civic divide, Welsh-language demands could be portrayed as theoretically problematic, and language rights discourse as exclusive and intolerant. As a result, certain public policy interventions to support the minority language community were delegitimized and marginalized. The language of inclusivity was used to exclude from the political process radical viewpoints arguing for state intervention in favour of the minority language.

Inclusivity has worked towards the exclusion of certain minority discourses in post-devolution Wales. A similar phenomenon can be identified in other countries, such as Scotland. This is deeply problematic for the concept of inclusivity itself. Is the rhetoric of inclusivity indeed a Trojan horse for the carriers of hegemonic majoritarian cultural power, as some Welsh language commentators have claimed (Jobbins, 2001/2)? Perhaps a new terminology should be found to better express the values of plurality and respect required by the various citizens of a bilingual and multi-ethnic Wales.

## REFERENCES

Apolloni, D., *Roma – Hen Wlad fy Nhad* (Llanrwst: Gwasg Carreg Gwalch, 2004).
BBC News, 'Row over Skye Gaelic-only school' (2006), *http://news.bbc.co.uk/1/hi/scotland/4695954.stm* (accessed 16 October 2008).

Bosse-Griffiths, K., *Anesmwyth Hoen* (Llandebie: Llyfrau'r Dryw, 1941).

Bradbury, J., 'An inclusive identity?', *Planet*, 168, 70–4 (2004/2005).

Breuilly, J., 'The historical conditions for multiculturalism', in J. Eade, M. Barrett, C. Flood and R. Race (eds), *Advancing Multiculturalism, Post 7/7* (Newcastle: Cambridge Scholars Publishing, 2008), pp. 7–28.

Brooks, S., *O Dan Lygaid y Gestapo: Yr Oleuedigaeth Gymraeg a Theori Lenyddol yng Nghymru* (Cardiff: University of Wales Press, (2004).

Brooks, S. 'The idioms of race: the "racist nationalist" in Wales as bogeyman', in T. Chapman (ed.), *The Idiom of Dissent* (Llandysul: Gomer Press, 2006a), pp. 139–65.

Brooks, S., '"Yr hil": ydy'r canu caeth diweddar yn hiliol?', in O. Thomas (ed.), *Llenyddiaeth mewn Theori* (Cardiff: University of Wales Press, 2006b), pp. 1–38.

Brosch, M., Elm, M., Geißler, N., Simbürger, B. and Wrochem O. (eds), *Exclusive Solidarität: Linker Antisemitismus in Deutschland* (Berlin: Metropol Verlag, 2007).

Cardús, S., 'Multikulturelle Gesellschaft in Katalonien – Aufzeichnungen für eine Analyse der gegenwärtigen katalanischen Gesellschaft', in R. Sevilla, M. Gygax and J. Lligé (eds), *Katalonien – Tradition und Moderne* (Bad Honnef: Horlemann Verlag, 2004), pp. 194–202.

Chaney, P. and Fevre, R., 'Ron Davies and the cult of "inclusiveness": devolution and participation in Wales', *Contemporary Wales*, 14, 21–49 (2001a).

Chaney, P. and Fevre, R. 'Welsh nationalism and the challenge of "inclusive" politics', *Research in Social Movements Conflict and Change*, 23, 227–54 (2001b).

Chaney, P. and Williams C., 'Inclusive government for excluded groups: ethnic minorities', in P. Chaney, T. Hall and A. Pithouse (eds), *New Governance: New Democracy?* (Cardiff: University of Wales Press, (2001), pp. 78–101.

Chaney, P. and Williams C., 'Getting involved: civic and political life in Wales', in C. Williams, N. Evans and P. O'Leary (eds), *A Tolerant Nation? Exploring Ethnic Diversity in Wales* (Cardiff: University of Wales Press, 2003), pp. 201–19.

Chaney, P., Hall, T. and Dicks, B., 'Inclusive governance? The case of "minority" and voluntary sector groups and the National Assembly for Wales', *Contemporary Wales*, 13, 203–29 (2000).

Davies, C. A., 'Researcher positioning and "the problem of Wales"', *Contemporary Wales*, 17, 206–13 (2004).

Davies, G. P. 'The legal status of the Welsh language in the twentieth century', in G. H. Jenkins and M. A. Williams (eds), *'Let's do our best for the Ancient Tongue' The Welsh Language in the Twentieth Century* (Cardiff: University of Wales Press, 2000), pp. 217–48.

Day, G., *Making Sense of Wales* (Cardiff: University of Wales Press, 2002).

Fitzgerald, J., *Cadwyn Cenedl* (Pontypridd: Cyhoeddiadau Modern Cymreig, 1969).

Griffiths, J. (ed.), *Teithiau'r Meddwl: ysgrifau llenyddol Kate Bosse-Griffiths* (Tal-y-bont: Y Lolfa, 2004).

Hammond, J., 'Portree Gaelic School can only divide the community', *West Highland Free Press*, 26 September 2008, 13 (2008).

Houlihan, M., 'Social history: closed for reconstruction', *Social History in Museums*, 30, 5–8 (2005).

Jarman, E. and Jarman, A. O. H., *The Welsh Gypsies: Children of Abram Wood* (Cardiff: University of Wales Press, 1991).

Jobbins, S., 'Dreyfus Cymru a'r wlad newydd', *Barn,* 467/468, 36–9 (2001/2002).

Jones, R. W., *Rhoi Cymru'n Gyntaf: Syniadaeth Plaid Cymru* (Cardiff: University of Wales Press, 2007).

Jones, R. W. and Trystan D., 'The 1997 Welsh referendum vote', in B. Taylor and K. Thomson (eds), *Scotland and Wales: Nations Again?* (Cardiff: University of Wales Press, 1999), pp. 65–93.

Kneer, M., 'Rationalistischer Antijudaismus im 19. Jahrhundert', in M. Brosch, M. Elm, N. Geißler, B. Simbürger and O. Wrochem (eds), *Exclusive Solidarität: Linker Antisemitismus in Deutschland* (Berlin: Metropol Verlag, 2007), pp. 27–47.

Maan, B., *The New Scots: The Story of Asians in Scotland* (Edinburgh: John Donald Publishers, 1992).

Mackay, H. and Ivey D., *Modern Media in the Home* (Trieste: John Libbey Publishing, 2004).

Manning, J., 'Having a maes time at Welsh fest' (2008), *http://news.bbc.co.uk/1/hi/wales/7544896.stm* (accessed 7 August 2008).

McGuinness, P., '"Racism" in Welsh politics', *Planet,* 159, 7–12 (2003).

Morgan, B., 'Eisteddfod sermon, Cardiff, August 2008' (2008), *www.churchinwales.org.uk/structure/bishops/sermonsb/b32.html* (accessed 7 August 2008).

National Assembly Advisory Groupm *National Assembly Advisory Group Recommendations* (Cardiff: NAAG, 1998).

Pugh, A., 'Minister congratulates Eisteddfod for broadening its appeal' (2006), *http://wales.gov.uk/news/archivepress/localgovculpress/locgovpress2006/1086478/?lang=en* (accessed 7 August 2008).

Rawlings, R., *Delineating Wales: Constitutional, Legal and Administrative Aspects of National Devolution* (Cardiff: University of Wales Press, 2003).

Riabchuk, M., 'Ukraine without Ukrainians?', in R. Lindheim and G. Luckyj (eds), *Towards an Intellectual History of Ukraine* (Toronto: University of Toronto Press, 1996), pp. 400–3.

Royles, E., *Revitalizing Democracy? Devolution and Civil Society in Wales* (Cardiff: University of Wales Press, 2007).

Smith, D., 'Review symposium: postcolonial Wales', *Contemporary Wales,* 19, 276–83 (2007).

Thomas, N., 'Never say ethnic: the political culture of devolution', *Planet,* 136, 35–8 (1999).

Thomas, J. and Lewis, J., '"Coming out of a mid-life crisis"?: the past, present and future audiences for Welsh language broadcasting', *Cyfrwng,* 3, 7–40 (2006).

Trosset C., Thornton J. and Caulkins D., 'Perceptions of Welshness in Patagonia', *Contemporary Wales,* 19, 234–48 (2007).

Tryhorn, C., 'Call for more English on S4C' (2007), *www.guardian.co.uk/media/2007/oct/29/television.welshassembly* (accessed 5 August 2008).

Webb, T., 'Y Fro Gymraeg declaration', *Planet,* 169, 63–7 (2005).

Welsh Assembly Government, *Wales: A Better Country: The Strategic Agenda of the Welsh Assembly Government* (Cardiff: Welsh Assembly Government, 2003).

Welsh Assembly Government, 'Inclusive policy making' (2007), *http://new.wales.gov.uk/caec/publications/equality/inclusivepolicy/ipmpart1e.pdf?lang=en* (accessed 16 October 2008).

Williams, C., ' "Race" and racism: some reflections on the Welsh context', *Contemporary Wales*, 8, 113–31 (1995).

Williams, C., 'Passports to Wales? Race, nation and identity' , in R. Fevre and A. Thompson (eds), *Nation, Identity and Social Theory: Perspectives from Wales* (Cardiff: University of Wales Press, 1999), pp. 69–89.

Williams, C., 'Can we live together? Wales and the multicultural question', *Transactions of the Honourable Society of Cymmrodorion 2004*, 11, 216–30 (2005a).

Williams, C., 'Problematizing Wales: an exploration in historiography and postcoloniality', in J. Aaron and C. Williams (eds), *Postcolonial Wales* (Cardiff: University of Wales Press, 2005b), pp. 3–22.

Williams, C., Evans N. and O'Leary, P. (eds), *A Tolerant Nation? Exploring Ethnic Diversity in Wales* (Cardiff: University of Wales Press, 2003).

Williams, D., 'Back to a national future?', *Planet*, 176, 78–85 (2006).

Williams, G., 'Blaming the victim', *Contemporary Wales*, 17, 214–32 (2004).

Williams, G. and Morris, D., *Language Planning and Language Use: Welsh in a Global Age* (Cardiff: University of Wales Press, 2000).

Žižek, S., 'Multiculturalism, or, the cultural logic of multinational capitalism', *New Left Review*, I/225, 28–51 (1997).

# 2. WELSH LANGUAGE USE AMONG YOUNG PEOPLE IN THE RHYMNEY VALLEY

*Rhian Hodges*

## ABSTRACT

*Education has long been seen as an effective tool of Welsh language production in Wales, and much importance has been attached to the sector in helping to realize the targets of the Welsh government's language strategy, Iaith Pawb.¹ The surge in the number of Welsh speakers aged between 3–15 years in south east Wales has been attributed to the success of Welsh-medium education in the area over the past thirty years. However, there is concern among policy makers that the language learned by young people in school is not being transferred to actual use with friends, family and the community at large. The aim of this paper is to look in depth at the use made of the Welsh language by a sample of eight former students of a Welsh-medium secondary school in south east Wales, aged 22 at the time of the study, all of whom attended Welsh-medium education until the age of 18, and who then went onto study at universities located outside the local area. It assesses their experiences of using Welsh within the family, education, community, and the workplace.*

## INTRODUCTION

The aim of this paper is to give a brief overview of Welsh language use within a south Wales valley – the Rhymney Valley – and subsequently to place these findings within a wider corpus of research fields such as family language transmission and the construction and maintenance of social networks. Language use in south Wales is still a relatively unexplored field of research and therefore this study aims to address existing lacunae. It differs from the current body of research due to its geographical focus. Studies of education and the Welsh language are often conducted in the Welsh language 'heartlands' of Gwynedd, Anglesey and Carmarthenshire. An example of such a study is the Bilingualism Project centred on Anglesey (Lyon, 1996). Notable studies examining Welsh-medium education in south Wales have focused on the reasons why parents chose Welsh-medium education for their children, such as research in the Rhondda by Williams, Roberts and Isaac (1978); Bush (1979, 1981) in Gwent; Aitchison and Carter (1988) and Packer and Campbell (1997) in Cardiff; and Gruffudd (1996) in Swansea.

The present case study area, the Rhymney Valley is a location that has been traditionally under-researched in terms of its patterns and processes of Welsh language use. It has often been overlooked in favour of higher profile Valley regions, such as the Rhondda Valleys or ultimately within south Wales, Cardiff. Previous studies have essentially ignored the Rhymney Valley's significant contribution to Welsh-medium education and Welsh language. This is the first study of its kind to qualitatively assess Welsh language use by past pupils of Welsh-medium education within the Rhymney Valley region. However, it must be noted that the Rhymney Valley has featured within sociolinguistic research by Siân Rhiannon Williams (1992) and historical research on Welsh-medium education by Ben Jones and Lily Richards (in Wyn Williams, 2003).

The aim of this paper is to map out current language use patterns within the study area by using the four main language transmission spheres (family, education, community and work) as 'signposts' or indicators for understanding language use. It is structured in the following way. First, the paper sets out the wider context to the study by reference to the current status of the Welsh language within Wales and draws upon 2001 Census statistics to highlight the prominent role of education in maintaining and developing the Welsh language in the case study area. Second, consideration is given to the linguistic profile and history of education provision in the Rhymney Valley. Third, the study's methodological and theoretical underpinnings are described. Four, 'pen pictures' or vignettes of the study group are then provided. These are accompanied by a discussion of the main research findings in relation to each language transmission sphere. The paper concludes with recommendations for future Welsh language policy development.

It is commonly acknowledged that the number of people who actually use a minority language is often considerably less than the numbers who are able to speak it and this pattern is especially prevalent among young people. This trend has been described not only in the context of Welsh (WLB, 2004),[2] but also for other European minority languages.[3] Consequently, young people have been a specific target group for the Welsh Assembly Government's *Iaith Pawb*, the National Action Plan for a Bilingual Wales (WAG, 2003). It states:

The Assembly Government is acutely aware that if Welsh is to flourish young people in particular need to develop a sense of ownership for the language and to see it as their language and not simply the language of school and culture. (WAG, 2003, para 4.38)

According to the 2001 Census, 582,368 people aged 3+ years in Wales could speak Welsh; 20.8 per cent of the population, and an increase of almost 2 percentage points since the 1991 Census. However, the percentage of young people aged 5–19 years who could speak Welsh was 37.4 per cent, with the main surge in the percentage of young Welsh speakers being found in south east Wales. It is generally held that the increase in the percentage of these young speakers can be attributed to the establishment and development of Welsh-medium education in the area.[4] A milestone was the founding in 1951 of the first voluntary, Saturday morning, Welsh-medium school in Rhymney; but it was not until 1981 that Ysgol Gyfun Cwm Rhymni, a Welsh-medium secondary school, was established. Indeed, the opening of the school hailed an exciting new era for Welsh-medium education in the locality.

## THE CASE STUDY AREA

The Rhymney Valley is a post-industrial valley that stretches sixteen miles from Rhymney in the north to Bargoed in the centre and then a further eight miles south to Caerphilly. Caerphilly lies approximately eight miles north of Cardiff. The percentage of Welsh speakers in the area is low – in 2001, the Census figures showed that in the whole of Caerphilly County Borough, just over 11 per cent of the population spoke Welsh fluently, while 16 per cent had some knowledge of the language; some 19,000 and 28,000 respectively, out of a total population of approximately 170,000. Obviously, the low percentage of speakers means that the opportunities for using Welsh in the community are limited. There is only one designated Welsh-medium comprehensive school within the Rhymney Valley; this is the only option for pupils wanting to study through the medium of Welsh at 11–16 years as well as sixth form level. At Community College level, there are various accredited courses to learn Welsh, including GCSE and A level Second Language Welsh.

As noted, Ysgol Gyfun Cwm Rhymni was established in Aberbargoed in 1981, much to the delight of the hard campaigning parents of the Welsh-medium primary schools, who were themselves mostly non-Welsh-speaking. However, the establishment of the school was not without some local opposition (Pierce, 1990,

p. 81). When the school first opened it had just 156 pupils, but by 1996, there were 920 pupils in attendance; by 2005, it had grown to over a thousand, highlighting the success of the school and the demand for Welsh-medium education in the area.

## METHODOLOGY

The present research sample is drawn from among past pupils of Ysgol Gyfun Cwm Rhymni. It comprises four males and four females, who were aged between 21–23 years at the time of the study in 2006. The purposive sample was drawn on a basis of age, gender, home language background and location of higher education institution. The sample was drawn from one class within a specific school year of twenty-four pupils, thus representing a quarter of that year group. The purposive nature of the sample was such that it gave a fair representation of that particular school year. Each member of the study group was interviewed separately, using a semi-structured interview schedule; this allowed the participants to elaborate on their responses as they wished.

The interview data were recorded and transcribed verbatim (where possible) and the computer software package NVivo 2 was subsequently used in order to code the data and create analytic themes, including family, community, education and work. The research adhered to the principles of the Data Protection Act (1998). Respondent data was securely stored and participant anonymity and confidentiality was maintained throughout. Thus, for the purpose of the paper, respondents have been given fictional names.

## THEORETICAL BACKGROUND

This study draws upon Bourdieu's 'cultural capital' theory with its emphasis on the skills, knowledge, education and advantages that a person possesses in order to gain a higher status in society (Bourdieu, 1986). According to Bourdieu, the main function of the educational system is cultural reproduction and reproduction of the dominant culture; therefore, according to this perspective, education is merely a tool in which to enforce the values and power of the higher classes. As Bourdieu (1991, p. 167) noted, 'the culture which unifies is also the culture which separates and which legitimates distinctions by forcing all other cultures to define themselves by their distance from the dominant culture'. Indeed, it could be argued that parents provide children with 'cultural capital' by transmitting knowledge

needed to succeed in the educational system and beyond. Indeed, parents choosing Welsh-medium education for their children, within an increasingly Anglicized area, are arguably partaking in the reproduction of 'cultural capital'.


## THE STUDY GROUP

Alex is from a non-Welsh-speaking background, and both his parents come from the Rhymney Valley. None of his grandparents speak Welsh. He has two older brothers who can speak Welsh. As a child, Alex attended an English-medium chapel, and he was also a member of Urdd Gobaith Cymru.[5] He studied religious studies at Bangor University and now works in Cardiff.

Buddug comes from a 'mixed language'[6] home, with her father coming from north Wales and her mother from England. Buddug has spoken Welsh since she was a toddler. She comes from Caerphilly but is at present working in London in an investment bank, after spending three years at university in that city. She has a younger sister who has also followed a Welsh-medium education route. Buddug used to regularly attend the Welsh-medium chapel in Caerphilly.

Dafydd is from a non-Welsh-speaking background. He studied in London before returning to the area recently. He uses Welsh regularly in his job as a translator. His parents are from the Rhymney Valley, neither speaks Welsh, and the only Welsh speaker in his family was his great grandmother on his father's side. He has a sister who teaches at a local Welsh-medium primary school. He attended the Urdd regularly and is now a member of a Welsh-medium drama group and Welsh choir.

Elizabeth is from a non-Welsh-speaking background, and has just returned to the area after attending university in England. Her mother attended Welsh lessons, but is not a fluent speaker. She has two grandparents who can speak 'tipyn bach' (a little bit) of Welsh, one from her mother's side and one from her father's. Elizabeth came into Welsh-medium education later on in her school career, and has two siblings who are presently in Welsh-medium education. Currently, she works through the medium of Welsh on a local authority education scheme.

Hywel is an only child, who has always spoken Welsh at home. Both his parents come from west Wales originally. He used to attend the Welsh-medium chapel and the Urdd regularly and now plays football with a Welsh club. He graduated in Welsh and works for the National Assembly for Wales.

Lliwen has just returned to the area after studying at Oxford University. As a child, she attended the Welsh-medium chapel, a Welsh-medium youth club, and received piano and harp lessons through the medium of Welsh. She comes from

a non-Welsh-speaking background. Her mother is from the Rhymney Valley and her father is from England. One of her grandmothers could speak Welsh. Lliwen works through the medium of Welsh for a private sector company in Cardiff. She sings with a Welsh choir. She has an older brother who can also speak Welsh.

Meleri comes from a Welsh-speaking family background, with her father from north Wales and her mother from the Rhymney Valley area. Her mother is herself the product of a Welsh-medium education, and also taught for a number of years. Meleri has an older sister (who sends her child to a Welsh-medium school) and younger brother; they have all had Welsh-medium education. She attended the Welsh-medium chapel, and was a member of the Urdd and local Welsh choir. She has just returned to the Rhymney Valley after spending four years in England studying. She is presently looking for work.

Rhun is on the last year of his university course, studying art. He is from a non-Welsh-speaking background, with a mother from England and father from the Rhymney Valley. The majority of his father's family have chosen Welsh-medium education for their children. However, none of his grandparents speak Welsh. He has an older sister who lives abroad. He used to attend the Urdd regularly when he was in school.

Having introduced the study group, we will now focus our attention on their specific language use patterns within contrasting language transmission spheres.

## LANGUAGE USE WITHIN THE FAMILY, EDUCATION, COMMUNITY AND WORK

As noted, the sample's Welsh language use patterns were analysed according to four language transmission spheres (Hodges, 2006) that emerged from the primary data collection. They are: the family, education, the community and the workplace.

### Family

*Iaith Pawb* recognizes the importance of the family in terms of language transfer: 'We see family language transfer as a key element of our language strategy' (WAG, 2003). Twf (Transfer of Welsh in Families) is a project funded by the Welsh Language Board. It was established in 2001 in order to achieve WAG's policy aims and increase Welsh language transmission within the family, thereby acting as a valuable revitalization tool for the Welsh language (Edwards and Newcombe, 2003). Existing work shows how the family is central to the 'intergenerational transmission' of minority languages (Fishman, 1991). It is the informal context

of the family which provides a solid foundation in order to master the conversational aspects of a mother tongue (Williams and Morris, 2000, p. 63). Jones and Morris (2007, p. 52) summarize the primary factors affecting a child's Welsh language socialization as: interactive practices with Welsh speaking parent; involvement of Welsh speaking grandparents; language background; language values and language practices of parents and their extended families. Moreover, the importance of family language transmission in Wales is accentuated by ongoing research by organizations such as The Welsh Language Board and the ESRC Bilingualism Centre, Bangor University.[7]

As the foregoing vignettes suggest, the members of the study group came from quite different home language backgrounds, and not unexpectedly their use of Welsh within the family varied according to the abilities of other family members. Accordingly, the sample was distributed into three different categories: families where both parents speak Welsh (WL), where only one parent speaks Welsh (ML), and where both parents are non-Welsh-speaking (NWL).

Two members of the sample belonged to WL families. These were families which had two Welsh-speaking parents who had originally moved into the Rhymney Valley from the Welsh language 'heartlands', such as Gwynedd, Anglesey and Carmarthenshire. Only one Welsh-speaking parent in the sample was a local person. Despite the high level of Welsh language ability, it was apparent that the use of Welsh within the WL families was very low. The reluctance of Welsh-speaking siblings to use the Welsh language with each other was also evident, possibly resulting from peer pressure to assimilate to the norms of an anglicized area. This confirms the pattern highlighted in a study by the Welsh Language Board (2006) which indicates that a fifth of WL families speak 'English mainly' at home. This obviously has implications for the future reproduction of the Welsh language in the area, although, it should be noted that at the same time, the WL families possessed a high level of 'Welsh cultural awareness' and were supporters of chapels, choirs and other local Welsh-medium events.

Five out of the eight members of the sample came from NWL families, with most of the parents being native to the Valley itself. The fact that so many had sent their children to a Welsh-medium school indicates the level of support from those who do not themselves possess the language. A number of the mothers in these families had made some attempt to learn Welsh, one in particular gaining an A Level in Welsh, but none of the fathers in the sample had done so. Despite this, the majority of NWL families were generally extremely supportive of the Welsh language and their enthusiasm was on a parallel with WL families. In terms of NWL sibling language choice, only Dafydd regularly spoke Welsh to his sister.

Others did not, because of what they termed 'bad habits' and 'not wishing to isolate non-Welsh speaking parents'. Alex's parents thought it was unacceptable to speak Welsh in the home in front of them ('disrespectful'), but Lliwen, Elizabeth, and Dafydd's parents urged their children to do so, and expressed how they loved hearing the language spoken so fluently by their children. However, although the siblings generally spoke English together, they tended to use Welsh with each other when using SMS messaging and e-mail.

Only one member of the study group came from an ML family, Buddug, who had a Welsh speaking father and a non-Welsh speaking mother. In order not to isolate the mother within the home, the concept of 'language courtesy' was adopted and English was used as the dominant family language. 'Language courtesy' was also present in research conducted by Jones and Morris (2007, p. 61), who stated that there was a tendency for Welsh speaking parents to use English out of politeness to include their non-Welsh speaking partners, even when the non-Welsh speaker did not mind them speaking Welsh in their company. Moreover, this study found that among the group as a whole, English was the dominant household language, even among the Welsh speakers of the family. As Buddug noted, 'it's not really fair to speak Welsh in front of Mam . . . I even speak English mostly with Dad now, out of habit.'

The latter finding affirms the 2001 Census figures that reveal that Welsh language transmission within ML families in some parts of Wales can be as low as 19.0 per cent. For example, this is evident in Newport, and surprisingly the figure is only 55.7 per cent in Welsh language 'heartlands' such as Gwynedd.[8] This pattern could threaten the future of a minority language such as Welsh.

Generally, the study group did not use the language on a daily basis with their families in the home, but rather it was used on occasion, for example, when visiting Welsh-speaking relatives. Therefore, Welsh language use appeared to be contextual.

**Education**
Generally, the study group felt that their experience of Welsh-medium education had been a valuable, multidimensional experience. However, some of the members had reservations about their parents' choice of Welsh- medium schooling for them – for example, Elizabeth felt that the Welsh- medium education system was, 'too elite, with an immense pressure to conform to the perfect image of a Welsh speaker' (Elizabeth, NWL member). Lliwen, on the other hand, took a completely different view. She felt that her experience of school had been, 'an enriching, rather than elitist experience, receiving another language, and the language of Wales is a priceless gift' (Lliwen, NWL member).

Not unexpectedly, the group's use of Welsh increased as they progressed through the education system, from their days at nursery school, the 'Ysgol Feithrin', where they were immersed in the Welsh language, to a peak at their primary school. Baker (2003) suggests that the establishment and expansion of Welsh-medium education and the introduction of Welsh as a compulsory subject in the National Curriculum is a key factor in language survival. However, in Ysgol Cwm Rhymni, their use of Welsh decreased outside the classroom, although another increase was apparent in the group's use of Welsh when they reached the sixth form. There seemed a heightened awareness and increased ownership of the Welsh language and its cultural and educational value, especially among those who had studied Welsh as an A level. This is an alternative outcome to Baker's (1985) theory of a decline in Welsh language use as students become older. However, as Gruffudd (2000) points out, research evidence suggests that while pupils may use Welsh within the classroom, they make very little use of the language outside school. This scenario was confirmed by the present study, and indeed it was found that even within some WL families, the young people increasingly used English as they grew up, especially with their peers and on certain occasions with family members. For instance, both Hywel (WL member) and his father had increasingly spoken English to each other and with friends, as they both played football and cricket for local teams where English was the norm. Also Meleri and her siblings spoke both Welsh and English to each other at home now, as opposed to solely Welsh when they were younger. The sample felt that English was the status language, whereas Welsh was firmly locked within the educational sphere.

There was also evidence of a gender split in the group's language use patterns, as well as in their choice of A level subjects. The girls were more likely to choose arts subjects, and to discuss academic matters in Welsh – as Elizabeth, Meleri, Lliwen and Buddug confirmed. The boys on the other hand tended to discuss schoolwork in English. They also avoided using Welsh when playing sports – Hywel and Dafydd in particular noted that English is the universal language for sport. Despite being a well-recognized phenomenon, it is not known whether this trend is widening or declining, however Census figures over the past twenty years have indicated the marked difference between the increased usages of Welsh by females as opposed to males. As of yet, this is an under-researched area.

The study participants' transition to higher education saw a sharp pattern of decline in Welsh language use. However, it should be emphasized that there is limited opportunity available to study degree subjects through the medium of Welsh in a number of Welsh universities. Indeed, during 1996/7, the percentage of Welsh speakers studying courses (part or full time) through the medium of Welsh varied from 2.4 per cent in Aberystwyth University to 6.2 per cent in Bangor

University and 18.4 per cent in Coleg y Drindod, Carmarthen (WLB, 1999, p. 3). During their time at university, it appears that the Rhymney Valley group became less and less confident in their use of Welsh and had a tendency to use English in social activities in higher education; they stopped using Welsh every day unlike during their period of compulsory phase education.

**Community**
All the members of the sample described the Rhymney Valley as a disadvantaged area, experiencing social problems, yet possessing a sense of optimism for regeneration and a new post-industrial identity. Although the area is not Welsh speaking, there is a strong sense of 'being Welsh' and of 'belonging to Wales'. However, the sample had a mixed opinion on the situation of the Welsh language in the area. Both Rhun and Hywel talked of the negative attitudes they faced because they attended the Welsh-medium school – being taunted as "Welshies" by local pupils who attended the local English-medium comprehensive school. However, positive attitudes were also evident as some of the sample helped their English-medium school friends with their Welsh homework.

The Welsh language is not heard on the streets of the Rhymney Valley, and it is essentially an 'educational phenomenon' and a 'school language'. There is a clear paradox between the formality and compulsory nature of the academic sphere and the informality of the community where the Welsh language does not exist to the same extent. There are some Welsh-language activities within the community such as the Urdd Youth Group, Welsh Chapels, 'Côr Cwm Ni' Choir, and coffee mornings run by Menter Iaith Caerphilly,[9] which impact positively upon Welsh language use in the area. Indeed, Menter Iaith Caerphilly has been instrumental in increasing language use opportunities within Caerphilly County Borough. For example, in partnership with the TWF initiative and Urdd Gobaith Cymru, Menter Iaith provides an extensive range of activities through the medium of Welsh ranging from 'clybiau carco' (after school care clubs for children aged 4–11 years old) to Welsh-medium girls football clubs (school years 4–6) and Clwb CIC (a Welsh-medium youth group for school years 7–8).

Some of the group still took part in Welsh language activities. While they were at school, every member of the study group had been active within the Urdd, although nobody continued to compete in the Urdd Eisteddfod at university. These activities underline the limited opportunity to socialize locally through the medium of Welsh. They also emphasize the stark contrast between the Rhymney Valley and Welsh language 'heartland' areas where comprehensive community Welsh language network contacts are in existence, such as neighbours, people involved in service delivery (shopkeepers, post, milk), sports clubs and social clubs (Morris 2007, p. 447). Moreover, Morris (2007, p. 452) notes the high levels of Welsh language interaction in the social networks of those who lived in the tightly knit Welsh language communities of north-west Wales; however, this social and community aspect is not yet possible to any large extent in the Rhymney Valley, as the present study highlights. Instead, the Welsh speakers in the area need to make a conscious decision to make Welsh language contacts and attend Welsh language activities, as these do not happen readily within everyday life.

Dafydd, Lliwen, Hywel and Meleri still attended Welsh chapels regularly in their home towns, even travelling up from Cardiff in order to do so. 'Côr Cwm Ni' Choir, which was established with the aim of providing school leavers with an opportunity to be involved in the Welsh language music scene after leaving school, was set up after the present study group left school. Dafydd, Lliwen and Meleri were all involved in Côr Cwm Ni.

Most of the study group's present leisure time was taken up with English-medium activities. However, Buddug, Dafydd, Lliwen, Hywel and Meleri also spent some time socializing in Cardiff's Welsh language scene: at Clwb Ifor Bach, and a couple of Welsh pubs, the Cayo Arms and Y Mochyn Du. When Buddug (ML member) attended Ysgol Gyfun Cwm Rhymni she travelled to Cardiff to work in the Cayo Arms pub and still frequents it when she returns to Wales from London, where she is living at present. By contrast, three members of the group, Alex, Elizabeth and Rhun, had not taken part in any Welsh language activities since leaving school.

Family language background did not appear to play a significant part in the group's choice of Welsh-medium leisure activities after leaving school. Indeed, this outcome differs from research done by Morris (2007, p. 447) on young people's social networks and language use which specified a link between home language and that of community activities. Indeed, when the home language was Welsh, a high percentage of community activities were conducted through the medium of Welsh, but when the home language was English there was a high tendency for social activities also to be in English.

The group's consumption of the Welsh-medium press and media was generally low, with the local community newspaper, *Tua'r Goleuni* and the weekly magazine *Golwg*, being the only exceptions. Dafydd, Lliwen, Hywel, Meleri and Rhun read *Tua'r Goleuni*, and all – except Hywel – also regularly read *Golwg*.

Just four of the group watched the Welsh-medium television channel S4C (Sianel Pedwar Cymru) – Dafydd, Lliwen, Hywel and Meleri. The group had mixed feelings about S4C and the whole issue of 'Welsh' programmes. Some mentioned that they watched Welsh-medium programmes occasionally but only to follow a specific interest; it was not their preferred channel when it came to daily viewing programmes such as the news and current affairs shows. Indeed, Hywel noted that he watched S4C mainly to watch European football on 'Sgorio' and Elizabeth noted that she only watched S4C for the American sitcoms. Only Alex felt there was cultural value to the channel and 'its increasing importance as a means to hear the Welsh language outside education'. Generally, the consensus was that the Welsh mass media had very little relevance to the young people of the Valley; they could not 'take ownership' over the medium and felt almost estranged from it.

At the same time, their consumption of the English-medium 'Welsh' media was also low, with few listening to stations such as Radio Wales. This seeming irrelevance of the mass media in Wales to the group indicates support for the idea that young people from non- or limited-Welsh speaking backgrounds attending Welsh-medium schools possess a 'psychological tension' within their identity. According to Thomas (in Edwards 2003, p. xiv), 'they do not "belong" to a traditional first language Welsh culture, but neither do they belong to the English medium culture of their families, friends and neighbours.' This is possibly why a number of past pupils from Welsh-medium schools opt to only use the English language in their daily lives, as an identity marker, rather than continuing with the Welsh language and feeling almost 'in limbo' between two different cultures (Thomas in Edwards 2003, p.xiv). According to this view it is easier to follow the majority language culture than make the conscious decision to follow the minority language culture. However, there are many past pupils who manage to achieve a balance between the two.

## Work

The group's occupations were varied: Buddug (investment banker, London); Alex (telesales, Cardiff), Dafydd (translator in local government, Cardiff), Elizabeth (LEA Language Support Assistant, Rhondda), Lliwen (political consultant, Cardiff), Rhun (student and part-time shop assistant, Swansea), Hywel (information officer, The National Assembly for Wales, Cardiff), and Meleri (currently unemployed). Buddug, Alex and Rhun mainly/ always used English at work, while Dafydd and Lliwen used mainly Welsh, and Elizabeth and Hywel used both languages equally.

The workplace appeared to be the one place that gave the group the opportunity to use the Welsh language since leaving formal full-time education. This finding differs to research conducted by Williams and Morris (2000, p. 129) who note that there is evidently a relationship between the status of minority languages and access given to minority languages within the labour market and that within Wales governmental policies have limited Welsh language access, particularly within the public sector. In terms of the Rhymney Valley research, both education and the workplace are similar spheres in their formal and structured nature in which to hone a complete set of Welsh linguistic skills. Indeed, this confirms Giggs and Pattie's (1992) theory that within the south Wales valleys, Welsh speakers have a clear advantage in the workplace over monolingual English speakers. However, securing jobs which need Welsh language skills does not necessarily imply that the post holder will use Welsh often, as a lot depends on the Welsh language abilities of their work colleagues (WLB, 2006). It should also be noted that a number of the sample said that they welcomed the chance to use Welsh again where they felt comfortable with it, within a formal sphere. Moreover, Elizabeth, who is employed by the Local Education Authority in Rhondda, Cynon, Tâf stated:

> Had it not been for my current occupation, travelling around Welsh-medium schools assessing literacy levels of the pupils, I would not be using the Welsh language at all. However, it has come back to me very quickly, and I feel a lot more confident with my Welsh language skills now.

However, as this suggests, a key element of language use is confidence, and not all of the group were as confident in their ability to work through the medium of Welsh in a formal setting. According to Alex, who works in Telesales in Cardiff, 'although I'm confident enough to use the Welsh language, I would not want to deal with formal work matters through the medium of Welsh, especially if I was under pressure.'

Once again, it was found that family language background had little influence on the group's choice of occupation. Interestingly, Dafydd, Elizabeth and Lliwen who use Welsh in their work on a daily basis, come from a NWL background. This is a positive outcome in terms of Ysgol Gyfun Cwm Rhymni's production of Welsh speakers who use the Welsh language regularly. Hywel's post as an Information Officer at the National Assembly for Wales means using the Welsh language on a daily basis, especially when conducting tours around the Senedd building in Cardiff Bay. Therefore, his occupation merely strengthens the language of his home.

It can be seen that most of the use made of the Welsh language in the workplace is done in the public sector. Three-quarters of the group who use Welsh on a daily basis in the workplace are employed by the public sector – local government, local education authority, the Welsh Assembly Government and The National Assembly for Wales (in addition, Lliwen is employed by a private political company that also works closely with the Welsh Assembly Government). Those respondents who were working daily through the medium of Welsh felt that this allowed linguistic confidence to flourish and helped them maintain their use of the language.

It was notable that most of the group who worked through the medium of Welsh worked in Cardiff. The city's increasing importance as a governmental and business centre means that there are growing opportunities for highly skilled Welsh-medium employment in the city, for example in the Welsh Assembly Government, Millennium Centre, S4C and various translation companies. This drift to find work in Cardiff and elsewhere means that the young people who have learned Welsh through the educational system in Caerphilly County Borough do not generally remain in the area. The migration of young people to Cardiff has been previously remarked upon, and figures from the 2001 Census show that young Welsh speakers are more likely to move to Cardiff than their non-Welsh speaking counterparts. Indeed, H.M. Jones' analysis of moves in 2000, the year preceding the 2001 Census, highlights that young Welsh speakers living in traditionally Welsh-speaking areas, the Welsh Language 'heartlands' such as Gwynedd, Anglesey and Carmarthenshire, are leaving these areas and migrating to Cardiff. As Jones (in Morris, 2009 forthcoming) notes, 'the bright lights of Cardiff and its environs are drawing Welsh-speakers of all classes.' Thus, 15 per cent moved to Cardiff and the comparable figure for those with no skills in Welsh was 10 per cent (author's analysis of Census SMS tables in Morris, 2009 forthcoming).

In the case of Caerphilly County Borough, this drift exacerbates the limited use of Welsh in the community. In 2001, just 11.2 per cent of the population could speak Welsh, and although the Welsh-medium educational system is producing large numbers of fluent speakers, if they do not stay to work in the area, it will mean that it will become increasingly difficult to extend the use of Welsh outside the educational sphere. Both Caerphilly County Borough Council and Menter Iaith Caerphilly are trying to tackle this issue at present and it is obvious that this work needs to continue if the language imbalance in the community is to be addressed in the future.

## WHAT IS THE FUTURE OF THE WELSH LANGUAGE IN THE RHYMNEY VALLEY?

The sample had a mixed opinion regarding the future of the Welsh language within the Rhymney Valley. Some noted that the Welsh language would continue to exist and be used occasionally, but that it would fail to capture the imagination of the local inhabitants. Buddug stated, 'the Welsh language will remain a static feature of this area; it will not progress and develop.' Moreover, Rhun noted the need to take ownership of the Welsh language locally, 'the Welsh language is progressing slowly, however, it will not be able to be fully integrated until our generation decides to fully embrace it and take ownership of it, as *our* own.' A more optimistic response was that the Welsh language would continue to develop through the education system, but as Lliwen stated, 'the turning point will be if our generation decide to speak Welsh to our children at home, therefore our children will become first language Welsh speakers.'

Indeed, follow-on transmission within families is crucial if Welsh is to flourish in the area (Gruffudd, 2000, p. 180). The respondents also felt that collaborative, multi agency work would be useful to increase the community use of Welsh, and they recognized the contribution of the National Assembly for Wales and the Welsh Assembly Government in increasing the political status of Welsh and employment value associated with the Welsh language. According to Dafydd:

> We need further collaborations between institutions such as the County, Council, Bwrdd yr Iaith, Menter Iaith, the Urdd, MYM (Mudiad Ysgolion Meithrin) a RHAG (Rhieni Dros Addysg Gymraeg) Parents for Welsh-medium education in order to develop a variety of opportunities to use the Welsh language, 'natural' opportunities will sustain the language.

They all felt that there needed to be continuing pressure and campaigning to increase the status of the Welsh language within every language transmission sphere, and that a stronger Welsh Language Act which reinforced the status of the Welsh language within the public, private and voluntary sectors was needed, and this included private bodies providing public services. Indeed, this reflects the recommendations for a new Assembly Measure[10] on the Welsh Language put forward in a recent report (Jones, Eaves and Ioan, 2007, p. 136) that states that Welsh speakers should have their rights strengthened when dealing with public service providers by giving them the right to correspond in Welsh; speak Welsh with the organization's staff on the phone; receive face-to-face services through the medium of Welsh; and receive written information through the medium of Welsh.

## CONCLUSIONS

Whilst it is recognized that the present small sample size limits the extent to which any wider claims can be made, nevertheless this study provides an insight into Welsh language use among a small group of former pupils of Ysgol Cwm Rhymni in the under-researched area of the Rhymney Valley in south east Wales.

As expected, Welsh language use among the sample varied according to the different spheres of language use. It was anticipated that the respondents would not use Welsh very much outside school and the research project proved it to be so. Even those from a WL background increasingly used English with peers. The one area where some members of the sample regularly used Welsh was within the workplace, but this was due to the nature of their employment (public sector) and its associated Welsh Language Scheme requirements. Thus, a key finding was that the past pupils in the study needed the formal framework provided by the workplace to use the language on a daily basis; in this sense the workplace could be said to have taken over the role formerly provided by the structure and formality of the educational system which hitherto sustained daily language use outside the home.

Although it is recognized that it is difficult for school leavers to get the opportunity to use the Welsh language after leaving compulsory phase education, it was also noted that they did not always take up Welsh-medium activities even when these were available. However, given the limited nature of Welsh-medium activities in the Rhymney Valley (chapel and choir) for those who had left school, it is perhaps not surprising that the take-up was low. The lack of a Welsh language scene for young people in the area led to a geographical dislocation whereby it appears inevitable that Cardiff will be a more attractive locality for using the language on a social basis. This is, of course, compounded by the fact that many of the Valley's young Welsh speakers also work in Cardiff.

At present, therefore, it can be seen that Ysgol Cwm Rhymni and the other Welsh-medium schools in the area are successfully producing young people with good Welsh language abilities; individuals who are comfortable to use the language within formal spheres. However, as there is insufficient support in the local community and in the workplace for this to be applied in regular use, it has in turn has weakened the small percentage of Welsh language families in the Valley who have attempted to transmit Welsh in the home environment.

This suggests a clear need to turn Welsh language competence into regular usage within all four language transmission spheres. One possible policy response to this would be the creation of more Welsh-medium public sector employment within Caerphilly County Borough and also further provision of courses where staff can learn Welsh. Another response would be to further develop Welsh language awareness training for private sector companies, helping them realize the statutory requirements of the Welsh Language Act within the workplace (Eaves, 2007). Another possible response would be to extend the present Welsh Language Act to cover elements of both the private and voluntary sectors, which would result in increased demand for Welsh in the workplace and an associated increase in its status locally. Furthermore, the voluntary sector together with the Welsh Language Board could undertake initiatives to increase choices for young people to socialize through the medium of Welsh in the area. Indeed, there is a need for a multidisciplinary approach from Menter Iaith Caerphilly, Urdd Gobaith Cymru, Caerphilly County Borough Council and the Welsh-medium schools of the Rhymney Valley to provide further opportunities, not only for young people of school age – but for adult learners to speak Welsh. This approach also recognizes the role of parents and grandparents in learning the Welsh language (WLB, 1999, p. 3.2.3) and the development of Welsh-medium schools in providing community classes to encourage the learning of Welsh outside the educational sphere. Such a response is important if the Welsh Assembly Government's bilingual strategy, as articulated in *Iaith Pawb,* is to be translated into reality with growing numbers of people of all ages being able to speak Welsh. Some of our sample had studied in England for over three years and had lost fluency, and ultimately confidence in speaking Welsh, therefore there is also a need for bodies such as Menter Iaith to provide Welsh language refresher courses for such adults as well as activities such as leisure and art/craft clubs so that language use can ultimately progress and develop generationally and naturally within the community. Social resources are priceless in terms of constant language use; based on the present findings there needs to be investment in centres where the Welsh language can be integrated in society.

In little over half a century, Welsh-medium education in Caerphilly County Borough has now become a realistic option for parents. Indeed, it could be said that parents choosing Welsh-medium education for their children underline Bourdieu's 'cultural capital' theory as they want to accrue the necessary cultural capital for their children to succeed in the educational system – and ultimately in life in general – in a bilingual country. This links to the findings of the earlier study of bilingual education in the Rhondda by Williams et al. (1978) that found that parents chose Welsh-medium education for their children in order to gain upward social mobility.

The gift of being bilingual is a valuable asset for the individual and society and Welsh-medium education has delivered this within the Rhymney Valley. Caerphilly, as a local authority, has the greatest number of Welsh-medium schools in south Wales, and to further consolidate this position, an additional Welsh-medium primary school opened in September 2008 and another is expected to open in September 2009. The ability to speak Welsh means opening the door on a rich, multidimensional and unique culture, but language use across the range of spheres in a local community is vital in maintaining this ability. The present study points to the need for innovative policies in the Rhymney Valley – and beyond – that will help to secure a higher level of language use among the next generation of Welsh speakers.

## NOTES

1  The document produced by the Welsh Assembly Government in March 2003, which is a National Action Plan for a Bilingual Wales. The aim of this policy is to ensure that the Welsh language can be used freely in social, leisure and business activities throughout Wales and that the number of people in Wales able to speak Welsh continues to increase.

2  See, for example, *2004 Welsh Language Use Survey*, Welsh Language Board

3  For example, Euromosaic study (1996) See: *www.uoc.edu/euromosaic/web/homean/index1.html*

4  See the Welsh Language Board's Education and Training Strategy (2004) for an analysis of Welsh in the education system in Wales.

5  'A movement for children and young people with development officers working across Wales on a full programme of activities such as sport, music and crafts. It gives the young people of Wales the chance to live vibrant lives through the medium of Welsh, learning at the same time to respect each other and people around the world' (*www.urdd.org*, accessed 10 October 2008).

6  'Mixed language' refers to one Welsh-speaking parent and one non-Welsh-speaking parent.

7  *www.bilingualism.bangor.ac.uk/news/documents/Group2.1.pdf* (accessed 5 November 2008).

8  'Trosglwyddo iaith o fewn cartrefi lle mae dau oedolyn ond un yn unig sy'n gallu siarad Cymraeg', Bwrdd yr iaith Gymraeg/ Welsh Language Board Mawrth/March 2006.

9  'A Menter Iaith or Language Initiative is a local organisation which offers support to communities to increase and develop their use of the Welsh language. A Menter Iaith usually services a whole county, and it reflects the wish of local people to make more use of the language' (*www.mentrau-iaith.com*, accessed 10 October 2008).

10  Assembly Measures are primary legislation for Wales passed by the National Assembly akin to Acts of the UK and Scottish Parliaments.

## REFERENCES

Aitchison, J. and Carter, H. (1988). *The Welsh Language in the Cardiff Region: A Survey of School Children and their Parents*, A report prepared for *Y Byd ar Bedwar* (HTV Wales), Aberystwyth: University College of Wales, Department of Geography, Rural Surveys Research Unit.

Baker, C. R. (1985). *Aspects of Bilingualism in Wales*, Clevedon: Multilingual Matters.

Baker, C. R. (2003). 'Language planning: a grounded approach', in J. M. Dewaele, A. Housen and Li Wei (eds), *Bilingualism: Beyond Basic Principles*, Clevedon: Multilingual Matters.

Baker, C. R. and Jones, M. P. (1999). *Continuity in Welsh Language Education*, Cardiff: The Welsh Language Board.

Bourdieu, P. (1986). 'The forms of capital', in J. G. Richardson (ed.), *Handbook for Theory and Research for the Sociology of Education*, London: Greenwood Press.

Bourdieu, P. (1991). *Language and Symbolic Power*, J. Thompson (ed.), Gino Raymond and Matthew Adamson (trans.), Cambridge: Polity Press.

Bush, E. (1979). 'Bilingual education in Gwent: parental attitudes and aspirations', unpublished M.Ed. thesis, Cardiff: University of Wales.

Bush, E., Atkinson, P. and Read, M. (1981). *A Minority Choice: Welsh Medium Education in an Anglicised Area – Parents' Characteristics and Motives*, Cardiff: Sociological Research Unit, Department of Sociology, University College, Cardiff

Eaves, S. (2007). 'Cyfraniad hyfforddiant ymwybyddiaeth am yr Iaith Gymraeg at gynllunio ieithyddol a'r broses o greu Cymru newydd', *Contemporary Wales*, 20, 82–105.

Edwards, H. T. (ed.) (2003). *Yn Gymysg Oll i Gyd*, Llandysul: Gwasg Gomer.

Edwards, V. K. and Newcombe, L. P. (2003). *Evaluation of the Efficiency and Effectiveness of the Twf Project, Which Encourages Parents to Transmit the Language to their Children*, Cardiff: The Welsh Language Board.

Fishman, J. A. (1991). *Reversing Language Shift: Theoretical and Empirical Foundations of Assistance to Threatened Languages*, Clevedon: Multilingual Matters.

Giggs, J. and Pattie, C. (1992). 'Wales as a plural society', *Contemporary Wales*, 5, 25–63.

Gruffudd, H. (1996). *Y Gymraeg a Phobl Ifanc*, Swansea: University of Wales Press.

Gruffudd, H. (2000). 'Planning for the use of Welsh by young people', in C. H. Williams (ed.), *Language Revitalisation*, Cardiff: University of Wales Press.

Hodges, Rh. (2006). 'Cymoedd y De: Defnydd o'r Gymraeg ar ôl Cyfnod Ysgol? Astudiaeth o Bobl Ifanc yng Nghwm Rhymney', unpublished MA thesis, Bangor: University of Wales.

Jones, H. M. (2008). 'Siaradwyr Cymraeg ac Allfudo', in D. Morris (ed.), *The Welsh Language in the 21st Century*, Cardiff: University of Wales Press.

Jones, K. and Morris, D. (2007). 'Welsh language socialization within the family', *Contemporary Wales*, 20, 52–70.

Jones, K., Eaves, S. and Ioan, G. (2007). *Creating a Truly Bilingual Wales: Opportunities for Legislating and Implementing Policies*, Newcastle Emlyn: Cwmni Iaith.

Lyon, J. (1996). *Becoming Bilingual: Language Acquisition in a Bilingual Community*, Clevedon: Multilingual Matters.

Morris, D. (2007). 'Young people's social networks and language use: the case of Wales', *Sociolinguistic Studies*, 1, 3.

Morris, D. (ed.) (2009 forthcoming). *The Welsh Language in the 21st Century*, Cardiff: University of Wales Press.

Packer, A. and Campbell, C. (1997). 'Parental choice in the selection of Welsh-medium education', in P. W. Thomas and J. Mathias (eds), *Developing Minority Languages: The Proceedings of the Fifth International Conference on Minority Languages*, Llandysul: Gwasg Gomer.

Pierce, G. (1990). *Nabod Cwm Rhymni*, Llandysul: Gwasg Gomer.

Welsh Assembly Government (2003). 'Iaith Pawb: the National Action Plan for a Bilingual Wales', Cardiff, Welsh Assembly Government.

The Welsh Language Board (1999). *Welsh for Adults Strategy*, Cardiff: Welsh Language Board.

The Welsh Language Board (2006a). *2004 Welsh Language Use Survey*, Cardiff: The Welsh Language Board.

The Welsh Language Board (2006b). *Young People's Social Networks and Language Use*, Cardiff: The Welsh Language Board.

Williams, C. (ed.) (2000). *Language Revitalization: Policy and Planning in Wales*, Cardiff: University of Wales Press.

Williams, G. and Morris, D. (2000). *Language Planning and Language Use: Welsh in a Global Age*, Cardiff: University of Wales Press.

Williams, G., Roberts, E. and Isaac, R. (1978). 'Language and aspirations for upward social mobility', in G. Williams (ed.), *Social and Cultural Change in Contemporary Wales*, London: Routledge & Kegan Paul.

Williams, I. W. (ed.) (2003). *Our Children's Language: The Welsh-Medium Schools of Wales 1939–2000*, Aberystwyth: Y Lolfa.

Williams, S. Rh. (1992). *Oes y Byd i'r Iaith Gymraeg*, Cardiff: University of Wales Press.

# 3. ARE JOBS IN WALES HIGH SKILLED AND HIGH QUALITY? BASELINING THE *ONE WALES* VISION AND TRACKING RECENT TRENDS

*Alan Felstead*

## ABSTRACT

*The 'One Wales' government[1] has an ambitious vision of a Welsh economy based on high skilled and high quality jobs. This article presents evidence on which future progress towards this goal may be judged. It tracks the skills requirements of jobs using a variety measures, analyses the alignment of qualifications supply and demand, and examines several different aspects of job quality. These issues are investigated using large-scale surveys of those employed in Britain as a whole. These surveys were carried out in 1992, 1997, 2001 and 2006. The results they produce for Wales are compared with other parts of Britain. The article therefore provides baseline measures on which to judge a central plank of the 'One Wales' government's skills and employment strategy.*

## INTRODUCTION

The *One Wales* vision for skills and employment is for an economy based on high skill, high quality jobs (Labour Party Wales and Plaid Cymru, 2007: chapters 4 and 6). This vision is at the heart of the skills and employment strategy which provides the framework for the Assembly government's actions over its four year term (Welsh Assembly Government, 2008). This, then, is an appropriate juncture at which to benchmark the current skill level and quality of Welsh jobs and track how this has changed over recent years. Such an approach also serves to focus attention on the demand side of the economy, on which there is far less evidence in contrast to the wealth of data that exist on the skills and qualities of the Welsh workforce.

Furthermore, *Contemporary Wales* is an ideal forum in which to discuss these issues, not least because it complements the annual statistical profile of the Welsh economy which is an established feature of the journal (e.g. Bryan et al., 2007; Brooksbank, 2006) and the occasional articles which focus in more detail on the state of the Welsh labour market (e.g. Jones et al., 2004).

For many years, the skills debate has seen more than its fair share of inquiries often prompted and undertaken by different government departments. The lead department for the latest UK-wide enquiry – the Leitch Review of Skills – was HM Treasury and it was commissioned by the, then, Chancellor of the Exchequer, Gordon Brown. Lord Leitch's final report was published in December 2006, but it was not until Gordon Brown moved from Number 11 to Number 10 Downing Street that the implementation plan for England was presented to Westminster in July 2007 (DIUS, 2007).

In both Wales and Scotland the implementation plans have taken longer to materialize – elections have intervened and new governments have been installed. In Wales, for example, the Webb Review of post-14 years provision was only published in December 2007 and consultation on the Welsh Assembly Government's skills and employment strategy was issued in January 2008, with the strategy published in July 2008. Careful reading of the Welsh and English documents suggests that there are some subtle differences in the approach to skills policy such as the rejection of 'arbitrary targets for skills attainment', recognition that 'a "mass" education and training response will not suffice' and acceptance that 'there is no evidence that a generally more skilled workforce will automatically drive the economy forward' (Welsh Assembly Government, 2007, pp. 6–12). Yet there is a desire to increase both the employment rate and the quality of jobs above and beyond their skill content. In the area of skills and employment policy, then, is it possible to detect – to use Rhodri Morgan's classic 2002 analogy – some 'clear red [and green] water' between the Senedd and Westminster. The data presented in this article suggest that such a differential approach to the UK evidence is justified given the current skills and employment make-up of Welsh jobs and the direction of travel.

While there are many research papers on 'skills' – see, for example, those listed in Learning and Skills Observatory Wales (2007) – most are either based on *employers' views* of the skills of their workers or focused on *skills supply* as reported by individuals according to measures such as the possession of basic skills and the highest level of qualification held. While neither of these approaches is illegitimate, they need to be complemented by data which give the *workers' views of the skills demanded* by the jobs they carry out. However, the regularity and size of employer surveys commissioned in Wales, Scotland and

England are in stark contrast to the relative infrequency and less widely canvassed studies of the views of workers. Recent employer skills surveys, for example, have gathered data from around 7,000 employers in Wales, almost 25,000 employers in Scotland and nearly 75,000 employers in England (Futureskills Wales, 2005; Futureskills Scotland, 2007; Learning and Skills Council, 2006). This dwarfs individual-level surveys of skills carried out in 1986, 1992, 1997, 2001 and 2006 which, at best, muster responses from approaching 8,000 workers from across the UK.

Nevertheless, the results of such surveys do provide a valuable addition to the evidence base by giving voice to workers' views on the skills, qualifications and quality of their jobs. This article outlines some of these results (for Britain, see Felstead et al., 2007b). Where possible, the results for Wales are against other parts of 'outer' Britain/UK and the more prosperous London and the South East in order to set a baseline against which future judgments can be made (for other earlier regional/national contrasts, see Felstead, 2002 and 2005).[2] It is hoped that this will highlight the scale of the challenge of meeting the *One Wales* vision of an economy based on high skills and high quality jobs as well as providing a set of benchmarks against which to judge the Assembly Government's progress towards meeting these goals.


**DATA**


The evidence presented in this article is based on data collected for the 2006 Skills Survey which contained a Welsh boost as well as data collected for the 2001 and 1997 sweeps of the same survey, in addition to data collected for similar surveys carried out in 1992 and 1986. All of the data reported here have been weighted to account for the sampling techniques used and the slight under-representation of men in each of the surveys (Felstead et al., 2007b: 15). Each generated high quality, large and representative samples of individuals aged 20–60 years old working in Britain. All interviews were conducted in people's homes and lasted around one hour. The sample sizes are: 4,047 in 1986; 3,855 in 1992; 2,467 in 1997; 4,470 in 2001; and 7,787 in 2006 (this also included Northern Ireland and the 61–65-year-olds for the first time). Welsh sample sizes vary accordingly. However, in 2006 the Welsh sample was boosted by additional funding from Futureskills Wales. The sample sizes for Wales are 208, 155, 224 and 407 in each of the four surveys containing Welsh data (the 1986 survey did not include Wales). The Welsh analysis is therefore based on small samples, although they are representative of the occupational, industrial and demographic make-up of the country. The Welsh comparisons must, therefore, be treated with caution, but nevertheless can be taken as indicative of variation and difference from other parts of 'outer' Britain/UK and the more prosperous London and the South East.

Unlike the much larger employer skills surveys, individual-level skills surveys gather information on the *skills used at work via questions directed at workers themselves*. By making comparisons across five (four for Wales) separate, but comparable, surveys carried out in 1986, 1992, 1997, 2001 and 2006 we are able to analyse how skills have changed over time. Furthermore, these data sources also allow us to compare work skills in Wales with those found in other parts of the UK (or for trend analysis, other parts of Britain).

## SKILL CHANGE

A common way of measuring skills is to examine the stock of qualifications held by the workforce. Data sets such as the Labour Force Survey and their equivalents in other countries make this type of analysis possible on a regular basis. One aspect of the skills debate, therefore, has been to compare the qualifications of the British workforce with those of competitor nations. According to this type of research, the strength of the British educational system lies in the production of graduates – approaching a quarter of the population now have qualifications above National Vocational Qualification (NVQ) level 3, a proportion which has more than doubled over the last decade. However, the UK has proportionately more people with low qualification levels than many of its major comparators and is ranked 18th across the Organisation for Economic Co-operation and Development (OECD) on this measure. Five million people have no formal qualifications at all. It also has a smaller than average proportion of people with intermediate-level qualifications, which puts it twentieth out of the thirty countries in the OECD (HM Treasury, 2005, pp. 40–3). Performance in Wales is poorer still with a higher proportion of adults without qualifications compared to England or Scotland and fewer people with high level qualifications (Welsh Assembly Government, 2008: Table 1). However, such an approach focuses exclusively on the supply of skills as proxied by qualifications.

The surveys reported in this article, on the other hand, ask respondents about the skills demands of their job. The series collects data on three broad skill dimensions of jobs. These are:

• the qualifications required to get the job;
• the length of training for the type of work undertaken;
• the time taken to learn to do the job well.

Each of these dimensions is considered in turn and based on this evidence the substantive question of how skills have changed in Britain is addressed.

In all of the surveys reported here, each respondent was asked to judge what qualifications would be required to get his or her current job in today's labour market. They were asked: 'If they were applying today, what qualifications, if any, would someone need to *get* the type of job you have now?' A range of qualification options was given. To maximize comparability with previous surveys, relatively new qualifications such as NVQs and GNVQs were integrated as far as possible into this coding framework without lengthening it unduly. In the analysis which follows, the highest qualification level ranked by NVQ equivalents is derived. Hence, the responses are grouped into five categories. As a summary measure of the entire scale, the Required Qualifications Index is calculated ranging from zero to four, corresponding to the five qualification levels.

According to this measure, the required levels of skills used at work have increased over the last two decades (see Figure 3.1). In 1986, a fifth of jobs (20 per cent) required a level 4 or above on entry, but by 2006 the figure had risen

**Figure 3.1**
**Trends in broad skills: Required highest qualification, Britain, 1986–2006**

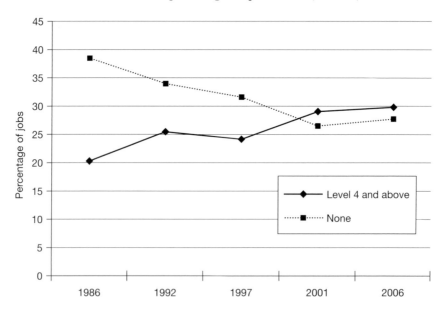

**Figure 3.2**
**Trends in broad skills: Training time, Britain, 1986–2006**

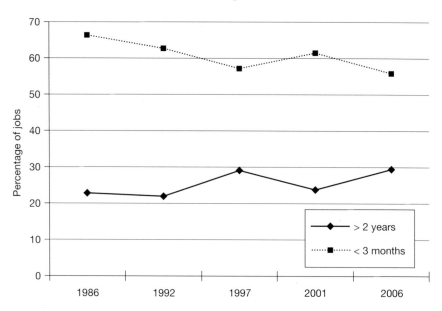

to three out of ten (30 per cent). At the other end of the scale, around a quarter (28 per cent) of jobs in 2006 did not require any qualification to enter, but in 1986 the proportion was much higher, approaching two-fifths (38 per cent).

Our second broad skill measure is based on responses to a series of questions on the length of training time required for the particular type of work carried out by respondents. It is based on the premise that the training time required for different jobs reflects various ability levels and knowledge demanded by contrasting types of work. Respondents were asked: 'Since completing full-time education, have you ever had, or are you currently undertaking, training for the type of work that you currently do?' If 'yes', 'How long, in total, did (or will) that training last?' If training was still on-going respondents were asked to estimate how long it would take. For the purposes of presentation, we examine the proportions reporting 'short' (less than three months) and 'long' (over two years) training times, i.e. the points at either end of the continuum. Later, we will also use a summary measure of the complete range of options allowed, ranging from zero to six, entitled the Training Time Index. Responses to this survey question show that jobs have become more skilled – the time it takes to train for jobs has lengthened. For example, 22 per cent of jobs in 1986 took longer than two years to train for compared to 30 per cent of jobs two decades later. At the other end of the scale, the proportion of jobs comprising skills that require little training (less than three months) fell by 10 percentage points over the same period (see Figure 3.2).

The third broad skill measure is similarly constructed and conceived. Respondents were asked: 'How long did it take for you after you first started doing this type of job to learn to do it well?' If they answered 'still learning', they were asked: 'How long do you *think* it will take?' Again, for the purposes of presentation, we examine the proportions at either end of the continuum – 'short' learning time denoting less than one month and 'long' denoting over two years. The Learning Time Index is a summary measure of all the answers given, ranging from one to six. The results show that jobs which can be picked up very quickly (less than one month) have become less prevalent, falling from 27 per cent in 1986 to 19 per cent in 2006 (see Figure 3.3).

**Figure 3.3**
**Trends in broad skills: Learning time, Britain, 1986–2006**

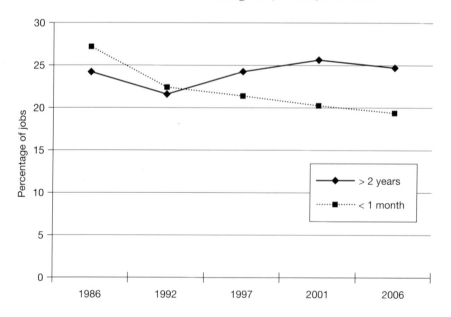

Table 3.1
Broad skills in Wales, 'outer' UK and London and the South East, 2006

| | Percentages/scores | | |
|---|---|---|---|
| | **Wales** | **'Outer' UK (excluding Wales and London and the South East** | **London and the South East** |
| *Qualifications required for current job* | | | |
| Level 4 or above | 25.6 | 27.2 | 38.4 |
| No qualifications | 31.8 | 30.1 | 21.9 |
| Required qualification index | 1.93 | 1.99 | 2.35 |
| *Training time for current type of work* | | | |
| Over two years | 27.2 | 30.3 | 27.0 |
| Less than three months | 59.6 | 55.9 | 56.7 |
| Training time index | 2.85 | 3.10 | 3.05 |
| *Learning time required for current job* | | | |
| Over two years | 25.6 | 28.0 | 24.7 |
| Less than one month | 19.1 | 19.2 | 18.1 |
| Learning time index | 3.66 | 3.66 | 3.69 |

However, it is increasingly being suggested that aggregate analyses of the British or UK economies fail to capture differential processes at work in different parts of the country (Rees, 2007; Felstead, 2002). In particular, the situation in London and the South East may be very different to what is happening in 'outer' parts of the country. The data presented above have therefore been re-analysed: first, by painting a picture of skills used at work in 2006 in Wales, the rest of the 'outer' UK, and London and the South East; and second, by analysing how skills have changed in these different parts of Britain over the last fourteen years (the switch between the UK and Britain reflects in inclusion of Northern Ireland in the 2006 data set and its absence from earlier other data sets).[3]

The analysis suggests that in 2006 Wales had proportionately fewer 'high skilled' jobs and proportionately more 'low skilled' jobs than other parts of the UK, especially compared to London and the South East. So, for example, around a quarter of jobs in Wales (26 per cent) required a level 4 or above qualification on entry compared to approaching two-fifths (38 per cent) of jobs in London and the South East. On this measure, jobs in Wales in 2006 were significantly less skilled than those in and around the English capital (p <0.01). Similarly, jobs in

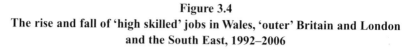

**Figure 3.4**
**The rise and fall of 'high skilled' jobs in Wales, 'outer' Britain and London and the South East, 1992–2006**

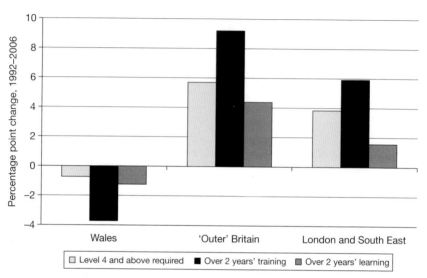

Wales, on average, required shorter periods of training than jobs elsewhere – the Training Time Index was lower Wales than in either the rest of the 'outer' UK or London and the South East. However, the required skills of jobs as measured by learning time differed little across the UK (see Table 3.1).

While the evidence suggests that the skills content of jobs in Wales may be of a poorer quality than jobs elsewhere in the UK (and hence may help to account for the greater prevalence of low pay in Wales compared to the UK as a whole, Sloane et al., 2005), the trend data suggests that the skill level of Welsh jobs may actually be falling at a time when it is rising elsewhere. This finding is based on a comparison of the proportion of jobs recorded in each of the top broad skill categories in 1992 with the proportion of jobs in each of these categories fourteen years later. Figure 3.4 presents the percentage point change for Wales, the rest of 'outer' Britain and London and the South East. What is immediately striking is the *fall* in the proportion of jobs in Wales that we might regard as 'high skilled' compared to the *rise* in the proportion of such jobs in London and the South East (as we might expect) and the rest of 'outer' Britain.

On the other hand, 'low skilled' jobs have become *more* prevalent in Wales over the last fourteen years, while they have become *less* prevalent in other parts of Britain. In Wales, jobs needing no qualifications on entry have grown by almost 12 percentage points, those requiring training periods of less than three months have risen by seven points and those jobs that can be done well in under a month have expanded by a couple of points. This compares to falls of between five and eight percentage points in the proportions of jobs in other parts of 'outer' Britain characterized as 'low skilled' according to these measures. The falls in London and the South East have been a little less dramatic, but the proportion of 'low skilled' jobs has fallen nonetheless (see Figure 3.5).

However, these comparisons should be treated with some caution because of the sampling sizes involved. While the evidence for upskilling outside of Wales is reinforced by statistical tests (see Table 3.2), the evidence for the opposite trend of deskilling in Wales is confirmed for only one of our three measures. Furthermore, over the last decade these different trajectories have become more muted and over the last five years the divergence has come to a halt. For example, between 2001 and 2006, these three measures of skill in Wales have moved more

**Figure 3.5**
**The rise and fall of 'low skilled' jobs in Wales, 'outer' Britain and**
**London and the South East, 1992–2006**

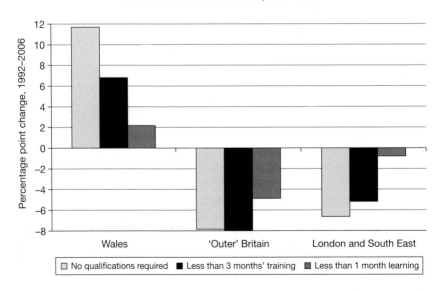

**Table 3.2**

**Trends in broad skills, Wales, 'outer' Britain and London/South East,
1992, 1997, 2001 and 2006**

Percentages/scores

| | Wales | | | | 'Outer' Britain (excluding Wales and London and the South East) | | | | London and the South East | | | |
|---|---|---|---|---|---|---|---|---|---|---|---|---|
| | 1992 | 1997 | 2001 | 2006[1] | 1992 | 1997 | 2001 | 2006 | 1992 | 1997 | 2001 | 2006 |
| *Qualifications required for current job* | | | | | | | | | | | | |
| Level 4 and above | 26.1 | 19.8 | 24.7 | 25.4 | 21.8 | 24.0 | 27.1 | 27.5* | 34.7 | 26.4 | 36.0 | 38.6 |
| No qualifications | 20.0 | 33.8 | 33.8 | 31.8* | 37.7 | 32.6 | 28.2 | 29.9* | 28.2 | 27.8 | 20.3 | 21.6* |
| Required qualification index | 2.36 | 1.77 | 1.95 | 1.92* | 1.79 | 1.87 | 2.02 | 2.00* | 2.23 | 2.02 | 2.35 | 2.36 |
| *Training time for current type of work* | | | | | | | | | | | | |
| Over two years | 31.0 | 27.6 | 24.1 | 27.3 | 21.2 | 29.9 | 23.6 | 30.4* | 21.3 | 26.2 | 23.3 | 27.2† |
| Less than three months | 52.8 | 59.9 | 64.8 | 59.7 | 64.1 | 56.6 | 60.9 | 55.7* | 61.2 | 57.5 | 60.9 | 56.1‡ |
| Training time index | 2.81 | 2.48 | 2.04 | 2.37 | 2.12 | 2.55 | 2.28 | 2.60 | 2.28 | 2.51 | 2.27 | 2.55† |
| *Learning time required for current job* | | | | | | | | | | | | |
| Over two years | 26.5 | 30.0 | 29.3 | 25.3 | 23.3 | 28.6 | 27.4 | 27.7* | 22.8 | 24.3 | 29.5 | 24.4 |
| Less than one month | 17.2 | 18.8 | 24.7 | 19.4 | 23.9 | 21.1 | 19.6 | 19.1* | 18.6 | 20.5 | 17.8 | 17.9 |
| Learning time index | 3.81 | 3.75 | 3.62 | 3.64 | 3.36 | 3.60 | 3.65 | 3.66* | 3.50 | 3.54 | 3.71 | 3.70† |

*Notes:*

1. The 2006 figures in Tables 3.1 and 3.2 are slightly different from one another. This is because the former covers 20–65-year-olds, while the latter restricts the focus to 20–60-year-olds in order to make comparisons over time.

\* 2006 significantly different from 1992 at p<0.01 level.
† 2006 significantly different from 1992 at p<0.05 level.
‡ 2006 significantly different from 1992 at p<0.10 level.

or less in line with their trajectory in other parts of 'outer' Britain and London and the South East. So, in common with patterns elsewhere, both the required qualification and the Learning Time Index have barely moved over the last five years, while the Training Time Index has risen in step with the more prosperous London and the South East (see Table 3.2). This is also corroborated by evidence which suggests that the changes in the occupational make-up of Wales between 2001 and 2006 broadly reflects the pattern of change across the UK (Revell, 2007).

More positively still, measures of the importance of activities performed at work suggest that in the last five years the rate of upskilling in Wales has surpassed rates achieved elsewhere in Britain (see Table 3.3). Considerable attention has been placed on the proposition that several identifiable 'generic' skills have risen in importance in the modern workplace. This has led to a policy focus on 'key skills', namely: 'communication skills', the 'application of number', 'information technology skills', 'problem-solving skills', 'working with others', and 'improving one's own learning and performance'. Despite their assumed importance, these skills are not easily quantified. However, the 1997 Skills Survey attempted to do

**Table 3.3**
**Trends in generic skills, Wales, 'outer' Britain and London/South East, 1997–2006**

| Generic skills | Change in generic skills scores | | | | | |
|---|---|---|---|---|---|---|
| | 1997–2001 | | | 2001–6 | | |
| | Wales | 'Outer' Britain* | London and the South East | Wales | 'Outer' Britain* | London and the South East |
| Literacy | −0.07 | +0.15 | +0.15 | +0.25 | +0.07 | +0.06 |
| Physical skills | +0.08 | +0.05 | +0.06 | +0.09 | −0.02 | −0.03 |
| Number skills | −0.11 | +0.12 | +0.17 | −0.01 | +0.01 | −0.06 |
| Technical know–how | −0.06 | +0.12 | +0.18 | +0.11 | −0.03 | −0.08 |
| Influence skills | +0.03 | +0.15 | +0.11 | +0.20 | +0.13 | +0.16 |
| Planning skills | +0.04 | +0.13 | +0.11 | +0.18 | +0.05 | +0.06 |
| Client communication skills | −0.10 | +0.06 | +0.06 | +0.14 | +0.07 | +0.07 |
| Horizontal communication skills | +0.02 | +0.12 | +0.07 | +0.04 | +0.07 | +0.12 |
| Problem-solving skills | −0.09 | +0.13 | +0.06 | +0.01 | −0.02 | −0.07 |
| Checking skills | −0.12 | +0.11 | +0.07 | +0.09 | +0.05 | +0.04 |

* Excluding Wales and London and the South East.

so. It drew on job analysis techniques in order to select and formulate questions designed to measure a wide range of activities used in a variety of jobs (Felstead and Gallie, 2004).

Respondents were asked a series of questions about particular activities that their job might involve. This section of the questionnaire was prefaced by the following: 'You will be asked about different activities which may or may not be part of your job. At this stage we are only interested in finding out what types of activities your job involves and how important these are.' Respondents were then asked: 'In your job, how important is [a particular job activity].' Examples of the activities included 'caring for others', 'dealing with people', 'using a computer', 'analysing complex problems' and 'planning the activities of others'. The questionnaire covered thirty-five activities designed to span the tasks carried out in a wide range of jobs. The response scale ranged from 'essential' to 'not at all important', with 'very important', 'fairly important' and 'not very important' in between. Both the 2001 and 2006 Skills Surveys subsequently repeated these questions (and asked some others focused on, for example, managerial skills; see Felstead et al., 2002, pp. 38–40, 53–4, and aesthetic and emotional skills, see Felstead et al., 2007b, pp. 29–32, 47–50).

The analysis which follows adopts the following approach: scores are awarded to each respondent according to how important each activity is in their job – the higher the score, the more important the skill. Scores of 4, 3, 2, 1 and 0 respectively are allocated according to an individual's response, so that those responding 'not at all important' score 0 whereas those reporting the activity to be 'essential' score 4. By subtracting the average scores for 2001 from those recorded for 2006 for each set of activity and by repeating this process for 1997 from 2001, we can track how skills demand have changed in the early and latter part of the last decade.[4] The results of these calculations are shown in Table 3.3.

These results show that in the period 1997–2001 the rate of upskilling in Wales fell short of rates achieved elsewhere. For example, according to six out of ten measures the generic skills of jobs in Wales were *falling* in the period 1997–2001, whereas on all ten measures the skill levels of jobs were on the *rise* in both 'outer' Britain and London and the South East (see Table 3.3). However, since 2001 the skill content of jobs in Wales has risen rapidly with the rate of increase outstripping the pace of change elsewhere in Britain on eight out of ten generic skill measures. Even so, the skill content of Welsh jobs remains below levels found in London and the South East on six out of ten generic skills measures and below the levels recorded in 'outer' Britain in four out of ten cases (results not shown here). This finding corroborates results presented earlier in this article (cf. Table 3.1), which suggests that there is still some way to go before it can be claimed that the Welsh economy is based on high skilled jobs. However, over the last five years there has been some movement in this direction.

## ALIGNMENT OF QUALIFICATIONS SUPPLY AND DEMAND

One of the major advantages of the Skills Surveys is the focus on the measurement of skills actually used in the workplace. Although it is possible to track accurately the qualifications held by those actually in employment (using the Labour Force Survey, see Sloane et al., 2005), the mismatch between the qualifications held by jobholders and the qualifications they require is only possible using data sets which collect both types of information. The five data sets reported here contain both of these elements. The analysis which follows allows us to reveal the extent, pattern and form of qualification mismatch: first, for Britain as a whole in 2006 (see Felstead et al., 2007a); second, for Britain at each data point over the last two decades; and finally, for Wales for 2006 compared to the rest of the 'outer' UK and London and the South East.

Evidence from all five surveys is used to derive a 'qualification demand and supply balance sheet'. Using evidence drawn from the corresponding Labour Force Survey, estimates of the qualification levels of the economically active are derived. Data from each of our five surveys are used to estimate the number of jobs requiring a particular level of qualification on entry. These proportions can, then, be grossed up to provide national or sub-national estimates. To these estimates, we add the number of vacancies as estimated by the Vacancies Survey for the relevant months of the survey (ONS, 2007; Williams, 2004). The total number of estimated vacancies is apportioned according to the qualifications requirements reported by new recruits to the relevant Skills Survey. This produces two columns of data – one estimates qualification demand, while the other estimates qualification supply – both of which are measured according to worker reports. Comparing the columns shows where in the qualification hierarchy demand and supply are broadly equal and where there are deficiencies or excesses in demand.

For Britain as a whole, the expansion of the education sector, rising participation rates and the drive to increase qualification levels has seen the numbers of people with no qualifications decline. In 2006, only 2.5 million economically active individuals (aged 20–65 years old) in Britain had no qualifications to their name (Felstead et al., 2007b, Table 3.6). However, for around 7.4 million jobs in Britain no qualifications were needed on entry. At the other end of the spectrum, 8.8 million had a level 4 or above and of these just over 6 million had a first or

**Figure 3.6**
**Qualification mismatch in Britain, 1986–2006**

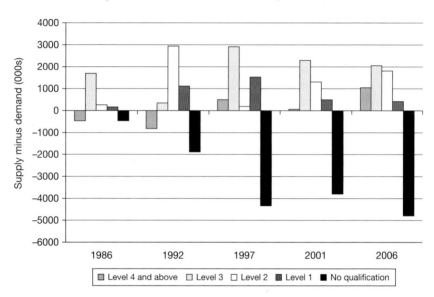

higher degree. On the other hand, 7.7 million jobs had entry requirements that stipulate level 4 or above qualifications were needed.

A comparison of the 'demand' and 'supply' columns of data – calculated as outlined above – is illustrated in Figure 3.6. It shows where in the qualification hierarchy demand and supply are broadly equal and where there are deficiencies or excesses in demand. In 2006, there were 1.1 million more degree-holders than there were jobs requiring these qualifications. Supply also exceeded demand at levels 3, 2 and 1, the differences being respectively of the order of 2.1, 1.8 and 0.5 million. Correspondingly, there were many more low qualification entry jobs than lowly qualified people. Here, the gap was 4.9 million.

The phenomenon of large excess numbers of jobs for people with no qualifications requirements has emerged over the last two decades. This excess arose, not because the numbers of jobs that do not require any qualifications rose, but because the number of people holding no qualifications fell substantially. The number of people with no qualifications fell by 5.5 million between 1986 and 2006, reflecting successful expansion of the education system and the growth of qualifications over this period. Meanwhile, the British economy saw the number of jobs requiring no qualifications for entry fall by 1.2 million. Figure 3.6 also shows that the differences between the supply of qualifications at levels 1, 2 and 3 and the numbers of jobs at these levels have fluctuated over the years. However, over the whole period the differences at levels 2 and 3 were still higher in 2006 than in 1986, even though they have been falling at level 3 since 1997.

The most notable change in recent years has taken place at graduate level (see Figure 3.7). The difference between the supply of graduates and the numbers of jobs requiring graduates for entry into them, standing at 1.1 million people in 2006, was less than 300,000 in 1986. This change is largely the result of the supply of graduates outpacing the growth of jobs where degrees are perceived by jobholders to be required for entry. Despite these results, graduates still earn a premium in the labour market. However, evidence is emerging of greater differentiation in these returns according to type of degree, the awarding institution and length of time since graduation. Furthermore, although there has been a rise in the proportions of graduates who report themselves as 'formally over-qualified' (i.e. graduates in jobs that do not require a degree on entry), the rise in the extent to which they are unable to use these skills at work has been more muted (Green and Zhu, 2007). Although this provides some reassurance, the policy message is

**Figure 3.7**
**Graduate mismatch in Britain, 1986–2006**

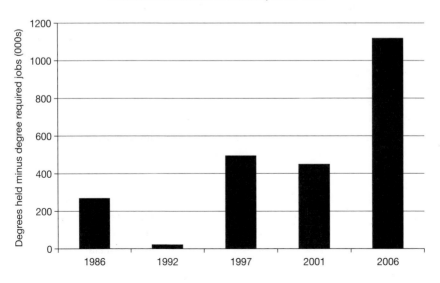

that more needs to be done on the demand side of the labour market to increase the skills quality of the jobs on offer in line with the increasing output of the education and training system.

The pattern in Wales is, if anything, a little more pronounced, with qualification mismatches greater than in other parts of the 'outer' UK and London and the South East. While comparison of the absolute figures may be of some interest, comparison of the percentage point differences are more meaningful since these results provide a comparative analysis which takes into account the different sizes of the three economies. These results confirm the findings of other studies which suggest that Welsh workers, on average, are poorer qualified than their counterparts elsewhere. For example, in 2006 approaching one in eight (12 per cent) Welsh workers had no qualifications to their name compared to one in ten (10 per cent) of those working in other parts of the 'outer' UK and one in twelve (8 per cent) of those working in and around the English capital. Similarly, in 2006 graduates were less prevalent in Wales than in either of these areas – they accounted for 19 per cent of workers in Wales, 20 per cent of those working in other parts of the 'outer' UK and 29 per cent of those in London and the South East.

The novel contribution of the analysis presented here, however, is that it reveals the differential levels of qualification *demand* across the UK. While these rankings follow a similar pattern to that of supply, the differences in qualification demand are even more exaggerated, and hence the qualification mismatches are greatest in the 'outer' UK and especially Wales. Figure 3.8 presents the results for the top and bottom of the qualification hierarchy. It shows that there is a six percentage point qualification gap at degree level in Wales compared to a gap of four points in the rest of the 'outer' UK and a three point gap in London and the South East. At the other end of the scale, the 'outer' UK as a whole has a larger mismatch than London and the South East. In 2006, the gap between the demand and supply of jobs/people in the 'no qualifications' category in the 'outer' UK was in the order of 20–21 percentage points compared to a smaller gap of 14 percentage points in London and the South East.

The policy implication is that while the education system has successfully equipped the Welsh workforce with higher qualifications, the Welsh economy has not upskilled sufficiently to keep pace with a rising supply of qualified labour (even though Wales has a poorer qualified workforce, on average, than elsewhere). The evidence from the 2006 Skills Survey suggests that while there are more qualified workers in Wales than in the past, they may not be being used as effectively as they might. Moreover, while a similar pattern is evident in the UK as a whole, it is more pronounced in Wales. These findings, therefore, highlight the importance of an 'economic pull' dimension to the skills and employment

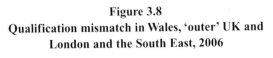

**Figure 3.8**
**Qualification mismatch in Wales, 'outer' UK and**
**London and the South East, 2006**

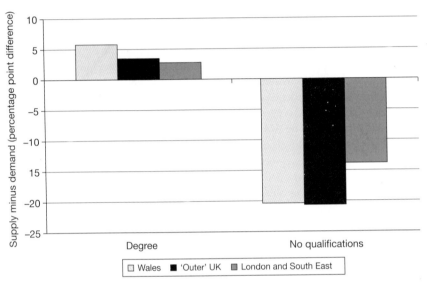

strategy consultation since there is 'no evidence that a generally more skilled [qualified] workforce will automatically drive the economy forward' (Welsh Assembly Government, 2007: 12). For that to happen, action has to taken on the skills quality as well as the quantity of jobs. In order to track the effectiveness of such actions solid individual-level evidence (such as Welsh boosts to future Skills Surveys) is needed to track movements in the demand for skills (including proxies such as qualifications) alongside their supply. In addition, this would put the Welsh findings in a UK context and provide insights not always available from employer-levels surveys (such as those carried out by Futureskills Wales and the Learning and Skills Council).

## JOB QUALITY

Despite historically low levels of unemployment in Wales – currently, in summer 2008, below the UK average – the *One Wales* vision is for an economy also based on high quality jobs. While the quantity of jobs is relatively easy to count and record, the concept of 'job quality' is contested and more difficult to measure (see Brown et al., 2007; Beatson, 2000). This is because individuals value different aspects of work differently. The value they place on work attributes may depend on their personal circumstances (such as age, gender and family composition) and outlook on life. In addition, 'quality' indicators tend to be more attitudinal and perceptual in nature. Large quantitative surveys commissioned by government tend not to focus on these issues, concentrating on more objective indicators instead (for example, job tenure is sometimes used as a proxy for job security, Gregg and Wadsworth, 1999). Evidence on 'job quality' therefore tends to come from less frequently conducted surveys such as the Skills Surveys reported in this article.

This section focuses on two aspects of job quality: the level of effort expended at work and associated levels of discretion exercised at work; and the employment security of jobs and the associated risk of unemployment. Commentators regularly focus on the 'downward' trajectory of both of these features of the labour market and in particular the suggestion that work intensity is rising and job insecurity is growing since they reflect some of the fundamental ways in which the quality of work life may be changing.[5]

It is often argued that skills are closely linked to levels of task discretion for employees – that is to say greater control over the detailed execution of the job. This is thought to reflect the need to motivate employees who are carrying out more complex work and greater difficulties in externally monitoring more skilled work. Discretion offers the potential productive advantages of flexibility, together with better use of employees' judgment and skill (cf. Felstead et al., 2007a).

The Skills Survey data series includes four questions that assess how much personal influence people have over specific aspects of their work. Respondents were asked: 'How much influence do *you personally* have on how hard you work?' The options were: 'a great deal'; 'a fair amount'; 'not much'; and 'none at all'. The same question format was used to determine employee influence on: 'deciding what tasks you are to do'; 'deciding on how you are to do the task'; and 'deciding the quality standards to which you work'. These questions were asked of the entire sample, but in this article we report only on the results for employees since they, by definition, have less control over their working environment.

These questions were asked in an identical way of respondents to the 1997, 2001 and 2006 Skills Surveys as well as in a comparable survey carried out in 1992. We therefore have a common benchmark on which to make comparisons over time. To provide an overall picture from the different items measuring task discretion, a summary index was constructed by giving a score ranging from 0 (no influence at all) to 3 (a great deal of influence) and then taking the average of the summed scores. Statistical tests confirm that the resulting measure captures a large part of the inter-correlation between the four-item index (the Cronbach's alpha is 0.78).[6] We use this summary index to examine the pattern of task discretion among jobs in Wales, make comparisons with the situation elsewhere and track changes over time.

The results show that in 2006 workers in Wales enjoyed a little less discretion in the way they carried out their tasks than those working elsewhere (see Table 3.4). Over time, autonomy exercised at work has fallen across Britain. However, in Wales the fall has been particularly sharp. As an illustration, job-holders in Wales exercised *more* autonomy in 1992 than other parts of 'outer' Britain or London and the South East, but in 2006 they exercised *less*. In other words, in Wales the task discretion index fell from 2.51 in 1992 to 2.11 in 2006, while in other parts of 'outer' Britain the fall was more modest, 2.43 to 2.18 over the same period. However, the direction of travel is unambiguously downward with statistically significant falls ($p < 0.01$) in task discretion for those working in Wales, 'outer' Britain and London and the South East.

Work effort can be divided into two components: (a) the amount of time spent at work – so-called extensive effort; and (b) the pace at which these activities are carried out – so-called intensive effort (Green, 2001). The evidence we have on each of these aspects of work effort is uneven.

Hours of work have been measured and monitored for many years and show an overall decline. This has been further prompted in recent times by legislative change such as the Working Time Directive, which limits hours of work to a maximum of forty-eight hours (averaged over seventeen, twenty-six or even fifty-two weeks) and provides workers with the right to three weeks paid annual leave. On this score, average working hours have remained stable over the last couple of decades following a long period of decline. In 1870, annual hours worked per person stood at 2,984; by 1998 this figure had fallen to 1,489 (Lindsay, 2003).

Important though it is (not least for compliance with the Working Time Directive) the length of the working week is one aspect to the work effort debate. It also happens to be the easiest to measure (cf. Revell, 2007). Changes in work intensity, on the other hand, are more difficult to identify since the concept is less clear-cut. It includes enhancements or reductions in the pace and/or quality of labour exerted in any given hour of work. To measure these aspects of effort, respondents were asked to indicate the strength to which they agreed or disagreed with the statement that they worked very hard. The results suggest an upward movement in the percentages strongly agreeing with this statement across all parts of Britain (see Table 3.4). However, in Wales, effort levels have increased the most.

Table 3.4
Trends in job quality, Wales, 'outer' Britain and London/South East, 1992, 1997, 2001 and 2006

| | Percentages/scores | | | | | | | | | | | |
|---|---|---|---|---|---|---|---|---|---|---|---|---|
| | Wales | | | | 'Outer' Britain (excluding Wales and London and the South East) | | | | London and the South East | | | |
| | 1992 | 1997 | 2001 | 2006 | 1992 | 1997 | 2001 | 2006 | 1992 | 1997 | 2001 | 2006 |
| Task discretion[1] | 2.51 | 2.36 | 2.22 | 2.11 | 2.43 | 2.23 | 2.17 | 2.18 | 2.44 | 2.27 | 2.22 | 2.16 |
| Work effort[2] | 32.0 | 33.9 | 34.0 | 45.6 | 29.4 | 38.6 | 36.9 | 40.1 | 31.7 | 38.1 | 38.3 | 41.7 |
| Work intensity[3] | 10.0 | NA | 21.0 | 26.0 | 18.2 | NA | 26.3 | 26.1 | 16.8 | NA | 25.1 | 25.0 |
| Job insecurity[4] | NA | 22.6 | 16.7 | 16.2 | NA | 22.4 | 17.0 | 18.0 | NA | 25.1 | 17.8 | 20.4 |

*Notes:*

1 Respondents were asked: 'How much influence do *you personally* have on . . . how hard you work; deciding what tasks you are to do; deciding how you are to do the task; and deciding the quality standards to which you work?' The options were: 'a great deal'; 'a fair amount'; 'not much'; and 'none at all'. Task Discretion Index reported here allocates scores of 3, 2, 1 and 0 to these responses respectively. This is summed and average is taken produce this Index with a range of 0 to 3.

2 Percentage reporting that they 'strongly agree' with the statement that: 'My job requires that I work very hard'.

3 Respondents were asked: 'How often does your work involve working at very high speed?'. The table reports the percentage who reported 'all of the time' or 'almost all of the time'.

4 Respondents were asked: 'Do you think there is any chance at all of you losing your job and becoming unemployed in the next twelve months?'. The table reports the percentage who said 'yes'.

For example, in 1992 effort levels in Wales and London and the South East were on a par with one another at 32 per cent, but by 2006 they were significantly different at 46 per cent and 42 per cent respectively ($p < 0.1$).

Similarly, workers in Britain as a whole are required to work at high speeds more frequently now than in the past, and this trend is even more marked in Wales. In 1992, one in ten employees in Wales reported that they worked at very high speed all or almost all of the time. By 2006 this proportion had risen to over a quarter (26 per cent). Rises elsewhere in Britain were more gradual (see Table 3.4).

However, fears of job loss have fallen more quickly in Wales than in other parts of 'outer' Britain and they have remained below insecurity levels felt in London and the South East. Table 3.4 shows the percentage who reported that they thought that there was a chance that they might lose their job in the next year (subsequent questions asked them to rate this possibility, see Felstead and Gallie, 2004). In Wales, this proportion has fallen from 23 per cent to 16 per cent in the space of fourteen years, whereas in other parts of 'outer' Britain it has fallen from a similar starting point in 1992 to 18 per cent in 2006. Job insecurity, on the other hand, is higher in London and the South East and the gap has widened over time, making these jobs *relatively* less attractive compared to jobs elsewhere.

## CONCLUSION

The *One Wales* agreement sets out a vision for employment and skills which frames government policy-making in this area. The vision is of 'a strong and enterprising economy with full employment based on high-quality, highly-skilled jobs' (Welsh Assembly Government, 2008: 1). However, this vision is not turned into measurable objective targets against which to judge the efforts of those tasked to turn the vision into reality. This article starts to do so. More specifically, by benchmarking the skills and quality of Welsh jobs, the article has provided evidence on the size of the challenge, and by tracking past trends, it has outlined the direction of travel so far.

The 'skills' and 'quality' content of jobs are not readily measurable concepts since the concepts themselves have a number of dimensions and the measurement instruments adopted vary. The article has therefore sought to provide evidence on the various dimensions of these concepts and the ways in which they can be measured in individual-level surveys. Despite this multiple source approach, the findings presented here tend to reinforce one another and therefore give validity to the overarching messages that emerge.

One of the most significant finding is that, according to this evidence, the skills content of jobs in Wales are of a poorer quality than jobs elsewhere in the UK. This may, of course, help to explain the greater prevalence of low pay in Wales and lower average rates of pay. Furthermore, the trend data suggest that the skill content of Welsh jobs has fallen over the last fourteen years, while it has risen elsewhere. However, between 2001 and 2006 the skills of jobs in Wales have risen at or above rates achieved in other parts of Britain.

Moreover, the qualification level of the Welsh workforce has risen over the last fourteen years. However, the demand from employers for qualified staff (as measured by workers' reports) has not increased at a similar pace. This has resulted in high levels of qualification mismatch and large proportions of individuals who report having qualifications above those required to get the jobs they currently occupy. This suggests that more needs to be done to raise the expectations of employers, so that workers' skills are used more effectively since, as is recognized: 'Skills will make the biggest difference to the prosperity of Wales when they are used effectively in the workplace' (Welsh Assembly Government, 2008, p. 2).

Wales also has some way to go before it can claim to be based on high quality jobs. Average pay in Wales, for example, is around 90 per cent of the UK average and it has the second highest proportion of low paid workers among the eleven regions/nations of the UK (Bryan et al., 2007, pp. 266–7; Sloane et al., 2005, Table 4.1). To this, one we can now add is that: levels of discretion are lower in Wales and have fallen quicker than elsewhere; very hard work is more prevalent now than in the past and this applies especially to Wales; and the speed with which jobs are performed has risen particularly sharply in Wales. In short, work intensification and reduced levels of autonomy have affected jobs in Wales most.

An economy which is based on high skill and high quality jobs is an admirable policy goal. Within the space of four years, this may be easier said than done. Nevertheless, a start in the right direction has been made. Most notably, the declining skill level of jobs in Wales has come to a halt and has recently been reversed. However, in order to track future progress and pinpoint where any action may need to be taken in the years ahead, we need 'the right intelligence to underpin our decision-making and provide accurate information' (Welsh Assembly Government, 2008, p. 11). Investment in surveys such as those reported here is urgently required, so that the new skills and employment strategy for Wales can be judged against the type of benchmarks used in this article. In the absence of such data it will be difficult to say with certainty how far we have come and how much further we need to go to achieve the economic objectives set out in the *One Wales* agreement.

## ACKNOWLEDGEMENTS

The 2006 Skills Survey on which this article is partly based was supported by grants from the Economic and Social Research Council, the Department for Education and Skills, the Department of Trade and Industry, the Learning and Skills Council, the Sector Skills Development Agency, Scottish Enterprise, Futureskills Wales, Highlands and Islands Enterprise, East Midlands Development Agency, and the Department for Employment and Learning, Northern Ireland. I would also like to thank the two anonymous referees who made some insightful comments and suggestions. However, none of these individuals nor the sponsoring organizations or their representatives can be held responsible for the analysis reported here.

## NOTES

1   'One Wales / Cymru Un' is the name of the coalition government's policy agenda.
2   The concept of 'outer' Britain is taken from my colleague Gareth Rees who argues that to the extent that the 'knowledge-based economy' exists, it is concentrated in London and the South East (Rees, 2007 and 2008). For this reason, the findings for Wales are set alongside the rest of 'outer' Britain (and, where the evidence allows, the 'outer' UK) and London and the South East.
3   In addition, the 2006 data when presented in isolation cover those aged 20–65 years old, whereas the 2006 data are restricted to 20–60-year-olds when presented alongside data from previous years.
4   The thirty-five activities were grouped into ten generic skills by using factor analysis to select those activities with the highest loadings. Then, an additive index was calculated (see Table 3.3; Felstead et al., 2007b: 27–9).
5   Other measures of job quality include: job satisfaction; stress levels at work; the type of employment contract; and psychological health and well-being. The Skill Surveys series contains some evidence on these other aspects of job quality, but for reasons of space these are not reported in Table 3.4. However, other research suggests that the quality of Welsh jobs may also differ in these respects (Jones and Sloane, 2004).
6   Cronbach's alpha is a measure of reliability, as to how well a set of variables captures a single latent construct with one dimension; a coefficient above 0.70 is typically considered acceptable for most purposes.

## REFERENCES

Beatson, M. (2000). 'Job "quality" and job security', *Labour Market Trends*, 108, 10, 441–9.
Brooksbank, D. (2006). 'The Welsh economy: a statistical profile', *Contemporary Wales*, 18, 275–97.

Brown, A., Charlwood, A., Forde, C. and Spencer, D. (2007). 'Job quality and the economics of New Labour: a critical appraisal using subjective survey data', *Cambridge Journal of Economics*, 31, 6, 941–71.

Bryan, J., Munday, M. and Roche, N. (2007). 'The Welsh economy: a statistical profile', *Contemporary Wales*, 19, 248–75.

DIUS (2007). *World Class Skills: Implementing the Leitch Review of Skills in England*, Cm 7181, Norwich: The Stationery Office.

Felstead, A. (2002). 'Putting skills in their place: the regional pattern of work skills in late twentieth century Britain', in K. Evans, P. Hodkinson, and L. Unwin (ed.), *Working to Learn: Transforming Learning and the Workplace*, London: Kogan Page.

Felstead, A. (2005). 'The geography of work skills: a focus on Wales', *Briefing Paper No. 6 for the Rees Review*, Cardiff: Welsh Assembly Government.

Felstead, A. and Gallie, D. (2004). 'For better or worse? Non-standard jobs and high involvement work systems', *International Journal of Human Resource Management*, 15, 7, 1293–316.

Felstead, A., Gallie, D. and Green, F. (2002). *Work Skills in Britain, 1986–2001*, London: Department for Education and Skills.

Felstead, A., Fuller, A., Jewson, N., Kakavelakis, K., and Unwin, L. (2007a). 'Grooving to the same tunes? Learning, training and productive systems in the aerobics studio', *Work, Employment and Society*, 21, 2, 189–208.

Felstead, A., Gallie, D., Green, F. and Zhou, Y. (2007b). *Skills at Work in Britain, 1986 to 2006*, Oxford: ESRC Centre on Skills, Knowledge and Organisational Performance.

Futureskills Scotland (2007). *Skills in Scotland 2006*, Glasgow: Futureskills Scotland.

Futureskills Wales (2005). *Future Skills Wales 2005: Sector Skills Survey – Summary Report*, Bedwas: Futureskills Wales.

Green, F. (2001). '"It's been a hard day's night": the concentration and intensification of work in late twenthieth-century Britain', *British Journal of Industrial Relations*, 39, 1, 53–80.

Green, F. and Zhu, Y. (2007). 'Overqualification, job dissatisfaction and increasing dispersion in the returns to graduate education', Manpower Human Resources Lab, London School of Economics, *Discussion Paper MHRLdp005*, November.

Gregg, P. and Wadsworth, J. (1999). 'Job tenure, 1975–98', in P. Gregg and P. Wadsworth (eds), *The State of Working Britain*, Manchester: Manchester University Press.

HM Treasury (2005). *Skills in the UK: The Long Term Challenge – Interim Report*, London: HM Treasury.

Lindsay, C. (2003). 'A century of labour market change: 1900 to 2000', *Labour Market Trends*, 111, 3, 133–44.

Jones, M. K., Jones, R. J. and Sloane, P. J. (2004). 'An overview of the Welsh labour market', *Contemporary Wales*, 16, 1, 150–77.

Jones, R. J. and Sloane, P. J. (2004). 'Regional differences in job satisfaction: why are the Welsh so happy at work?', *WELMERC Discussion Paper 05*, Swansea: Swansea University.

Labour Party Wales and Plaid Cymru (2007). *One Wales: A Progressive Agenda for the Government of Wales*, Cardiff: Labour Party Wales and Plaid Cymru.

Learning and Skills Council (2006). *National Employers Skills Survey 2005: Main Report*, Coventry: Learning and Skills Council.

Learning and Skills Observatory Wales (2007). 'Learning theme: the skills divide', December, Cardiff: Arad Consulting, *www.learningobservatory.com/uploads/publications/500.pdf* (accessed 18 April 2008).

Machin, A. (2003). 'The vacancy survey: a new series of National Statistics', mimeo, *www.statistics.gov.uk* (accessed 26 November 2006).

ONS (2007). *Virtual Bookshelf – Labour Market Statistics First Release Historical Supplement*, London: Office of National Statistics, *www.statistics.gov.uk* (accessed 11 January 2008).

Rees, G. (2007). 'The view from "outer Britain"', *Adults Learning*, September.

Rees, G. (2008). 'Devolved economies: labour markets and the importance of place', paper presented to NIACE Dysgu Cymru, National Assembly for Wales, Cardiff, 17 April.

Revell, J. (2007). 'Statistics on job quality in Wales, 2001 to 2006', *Statistical Article*, 25 October, Cardiff: Welsh Assembly Government.

Sloane, P. J., O'Leary, N. and Watson, D. (2005). 'The long tail of low skills in Wales and the UK – a review of the evidence', *Report to the Economic Research Unit, Welsh Assembly, Tender Contract No 99/2005*.

Welsh Assembly Government (2007). *Promise and Performance: The Report of the Independent Review of the Mission and Purpose of Further Education in Wales in the Context of the Learning Country: Vision into Action*, Denbighshire: Welsh Assembly Government.

Welsh Assembly Government (2008). *Skills that Work for Wales: A Skills and Employment Strategy*, Cardiff: Welsh Assembly Government.

Williams, D. (2004). 'Sources of data for measuring labour demand', *Labour Market Trends*, 112, 9, 375–83.

# 4. THE WELSH ECONOMY: 2008 UNDER REVIEW

*Jane Bryan and Neil Roche*

## INTRODUCTION

This article examines Wales's economic performance using the most up-to-date information available for 2008. In the last Economic Review in *Contemporary Wales* (Bryan and Roche, 2008), there was much discussion of the 'credit-crunch' precipitated by disturbances in the US sub-prime market, and it was already clear by then that reluctance among banks to lend to each other was likely to have serious ramifications. The observation was also made that the debt 'market' had become over-complex and had undermined the flow of credit. The last few months of 2007 saw lenders cutting back mortgages and in December the Bank of England delivered a surprise cut in the interest rate. However, the first Monetary Policy Committee (MPC) decision of the New Year was to hold steady, in the face of rising fuel and food costs. Indeed, 2008 was a year in which oil prices peaked at $135 per barrel in July, dropping back to below $40 in December providing a powerful barometer of the global turmoil.

Throughout the year extraordinary and alarming events continued to unfold, with unprecedented levels of government support deemed necessary to underpin the banking system. The effect of this bled rapidly into other sectors, including automotives as they suffered constricted credit and turned to the state for support.

From the beginning of 2008, global investors started to cash in their financial interests in a serious way. In the US the Federal Reserve began a reduction in interest rates. In the UK the mortgage market tightened leading to sluggish sales and a general reduction in consumer demand, and as the year progressed retail and construction firms started to feel the pinch. From April to September 2008 the MPC kept UK interests rates stable at 5.0 per cent facing the inflationary pressure of rising oil and commodity prices (which should have provoked a rise in interest rates) while at the same time being alerted to severely reduced consumer demand (which should have provoked a drop in interest rates). Sitting in the middle of this paradox, the MPC appeared to be in a state of inertia (see also Minford, 2008).

Throughout the spring and summer, a number of US financial giants were showing signs of strain, and from September 2008 onwards Fannie Mae and Freddie Mac went under, Lehman Brothers posted losses and eventually filed for Chapter 11 bankruptcy protection, Merrill Lynch agreed to be taken over by the Bank of America, and AIG Insurers were nationalized. In the UK Bradford and Bingley was nationalized, and the Lloyds TSB potential merger with HBOS seemed doomed never to make progress. Throughout the autumn of 2008, a tranche of major government bailouts across the globe showed that no one was immune; China set out a two-year $586bn economic stimulus package. By the end of the year, the US was officially in recession, with the UK soon to follow. The UK news media continues to report a succession of creeping banking nationalizations. However, there is a new preoccupation with reporting failures in the retail and construction sector, and with monitoring large-scale unemployment. So far, ailing big names include Woolworths, Corus, Adams, Viyella, Zavvi, Wedgwood, Royal Worcester and MFI. These companies will have been brewing their difficulties for some time.

Against this increasingly dismal and highly volatile unfolding future, this article seeks to provide commentary on Wales's performance relative to the UK and at the local level, with reference to data from Government Office Regions of the UK, Unitary Authorities, and, where appropriate at the NUTS3 level (output).[1] It should be noted that local level data are less reliable than aggregate data, and that the full extent of the economic gloom will not be reflected in these data, except for unemployment and housing data which are fairly current.

## OUTPUT, INCOME AND EXPENDITURE

Table 4.1 provides provisional data on Gross Value Added (GVA) per head of population for 2007 for the UK nations and regions, with Table 4.2 giving similar information for 2006 for the sub-regions of Wales – this being an example of an unfortunate time lag. Despite this, the old story remains clear. During periods of relatively strong economic growth, Wales is still not able to grow as fast as the rest of the UK and therefore remains at the bottom of the rankings. What is most distressing is the fact that the gap is actually widening over time, and at an accelerating rate. In 2005 Wales's GVA per head was just over one fifth lower than the UK average. In the following year this gap had widened by 1 percentage

**Table 4.1**
**Regional accounts**

|  | GVA per head 2007[1] | | Household disposable income per head 2006 | | Individual expenditure per head[2] 2006–7 | |
|---|---|---|---|---|---|---|
|  | £ | % of UK | £ | % of UK | £ | % of UK |
| London | 30,385 | 152 | 16,900 | 123 | 11,279 | 112 |
| South East | 22,624 | 113 | 15,400 | 112 | 11,378 | 113 |
| East | 20,524 | 103 | 14,600 | 106 | 10,899 | 108 |
| South West | 18,195 | 91 | 13,700 | 99 | 10,733 | 107 |
| East Midlands | 17,698 | 89 | 12,900 | 93 | 9,178 | 91 |
| West Midlands | 17,161 | 86 | 12,500 | 91 | 8,965 | 89 |
| North West | 17,433 | 87 | 12,700 | 92 | 9,173 | 91 |
| Yorkshire and Humber | 16,880 | 85 | 12,500 | 91 | 9,355 | 93 |
| North East | 15,688 | 79 | 11,800 | 86 | 8,663 | 86 |
| England | 20,463 | 103 | 14,000 | 102 | 10,156 | 101 |
| Scotland | 19,152 | 96 | 13,100 | 95 | 10,020 | 100 |
| Northern Ireland | 16,170 | 81 | 12,000 | 87 | 9,090 | 90 |
| *Wales* | *14,877* | *75* | *12,300* | *89* | *9,032* | *90* |
| *United Kingdom* | *19,956* | *100* | *13,800* | *100* | *10,057* | *100* |

Source: ONS
*www.statistics.gov.uk/pdfdir/gva1208.pdf*
*www.statistics.gov.uk/downloads/theme_social/Family_Spending_2007/FamilySpending2008_web.pdf*
*www.statistics.gov.uk/pdfdir/gdhi0508.pdf*
Notes:
1   Figures for GVA 2007 are at current basic prices on residence basis and are provisional.
2   Figures from the ONS 'Family Spending Report 2008 edition'.

point. The latest data shows that the Welsh GVA per head is one quarter lower than the UK average, representing a widening of the gap by around 4 percentage points since 2006. London's performance is clearly well above that of the rest of the UK (and highly influential in terms of relative GVA data) and in 2009 it increased its lead. This notwithstanding, Scotland closed the gap slightly while East Midlands remained stable. The fact that the performance gap between London and the regions is increasing so much is symptomatic of the growing divide between rich and poor in the UK and reflects the current government's apparent lack of will to arrest growing disparities. Total GVA growth in Wales

**Table 4.2**
**Sub-regional accounts**

| | GVA per head 2006[1] | | Household disposable income per head 2006 | |
| --- | --- | --- | --- | --- |
| | £ | % of UK | £ | % of UK |
| *West Wales and the Valleys* | *12,071* | *64* | *11,986* | *87* |
| Isle of Anglesey | 10,560 | 56 | 12,252 | 89 |
| Gwynedd | 12,972 | 68 | 11,849 | 86 |
| Conwy and Denbighshire | 11,529 | 61 | 13,096 | 95 |
| South West Wales | 11,711 | 62 | 11,388 | 83 |
| Swansea | 15,255 | 81 | 12,418 | 90 |
| Bridgend and Neath Port Talbot | 12,402 | 65 | 12,321 | 89 |
| Central Valleys | 11,347 | 60 | 11,583 | 84 |
| Gwent Valleys | 10,987 | 58 | 11,742 | 85 |
| *East Wales* | *17,984* | *95* | *12,881* | *93* |
| Flintshire and Wrexham | 16,442 | 87 | 12,998 | 94 |
| Powys | 13,258 | 70 | 11,909 | 86 |
| Cardiff and the Vale of Glamorgan | 20,087 | 106 | 12,951 | 94 |
| Monmouthshire and Newport | 18,537 | 98 | 13,161 | 96 |
| *Wales* | *14,226* | *75* | *12,312* | *89* |

Source: ONS
Note:
1   Figures for GVA 2006 (sub-regional areas) are provisional.

was 5.1 per cent and the lowest of all UK regions, and 2 percentage points lower than London. Of course, these figures do not yet reflect the fractures that first appeared in the financial sector in 2007 and it will be very interesting to see how far those impacts go to reducing the current regional disparities, a feature worth watching using official data next year or the year after.

GVA per head figures for Wales are for 2006 but they nonetheless show where the greatest challenges reside. The Vale of Glamorgan, Monmouthshire and Newport have a track record of leading GVA performance in Wales, and these regions continue to do so. However, their performance relative to the UK average has declined over the year. The Vale was 15 per cent higher than the UK average according to the 2005 figures but one year later was only 6 per cent higher than the UK average, reflecting once again the difficulties of playing catch-up. This increasing differential was common to most of the Wales sub-regions with the exception of South West Wales (up 1 percentage point on the UK average), Flintshire and Wrexham up to 87 per cent UK average (from 85 per cent), and

Anglesey (up from a very low 53 per cent to a still low 56 per cent). The improving picture for Anglesey is unlikely to persist over the longer term given the planned decommissioning of the nuclear power station in 2010 and the implications for massive local power user Anglesey Aluminium, unless a new plant is agreed. The fortunes of Flintshire, Wrexham and Bridgend are also at risk, and more immediately, in common with other areas in the UK which feature automobile supply chains and aerospace activity. However, Swansea, the Gwent Valleys and Powys showed stability over the somewhat historical period measured.

Earnings are discussed in some depth in a subsequent section. However, here we comment on household disposable income per head (gross earnings less deductions at source including tax), which relate to 2006 (one year behind the GVA figures). From 2005, the gap widened between London and the South West, the East, East and West Midlands and Yorks and Humber. The rest maintained stability on this measure. In terms of regional rankings, Wales was third from the bottom just in front of the North East and Northern Ireland, showing no change from the previous year's data.

Nowhere in Wales does household disposable income satisfactorily approach the UK average, and 2005 figures show there was an 11 percentage point difference between the highest and lowest in Wales, which increased over the year to 13 percentage points as a result of Monmouthshire closing the gap slightly between it and the UK average (currently recording 96 per cent).

The Index of Production shows trends in industrial output (a measure of the strength of an economy), and the Welsh and UK Indices are graphed in Figure 4.1 for the period 1998 to 2008 quarter 3. The graph has a history of 'lumpy terrain' for both Wales and the UK, and their respective performances do not always chime. Brief convergences occurred in 2003, and 2007, and more lately Wales experienced an apparent de-coupling at the beginning of 2008, with its index rising to 107, explained by electricity and gas output up by 16.8 per cent in the latest four quarters compared to increases of 2.5 per cent in the UK over the same period. Note the downward trend that is now emerging for both UK and Wales, with three successive quarterly falls.

The British Chambers of Commerce (BCC) Quarterly Economic Survey (2008Q3) reported declining confidence with respect to sales and profitability for both services and manufacturing. The regional indices for Wales followed the same pattern. In November 2008, the Business Confidence Monitor Index produced by the Institute of Chartered Accountants in Wales found a new low level, echoing the sentiments of the Institute of Directors Business Opinion Survey. This opinion is reflected in the realities of job losses reported in later sections.

**Figure 4.1**
**Recent Trends in the Welsh and UK indices of production**

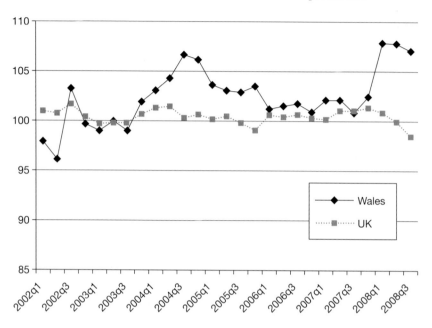

Table 4.3 shows that identifiable general government spending per head in Wales was £8,577 in 2007–8, up from £8,139 in 2006–7, and £7,666 in 2005–6. This is approximately 14 per cent higher than English levels of government spending per head but lower than Scotland and Northern Ireland. These distributions might indicate that Scotland and Northern Ireland are more accomplished at lobbying Westminster for favourable financial settlements, or that Wales is less of a drain.

Devolution should allow different spending priorities to emerge, and indeed Wales has developed a tendency to allocate relatively higher funding to enterprise and economic development than any other region. Meanwhile Scotland allocated a substantially higher per capita budget to transport than did any other region, while Wales's expenditure on agriculture has drifted well below Scotland and Northern Ireland. The latter regions both placed higher priority on housing and community amenities in this spending round, and Wales spent a notably low amount on science and technology. Government spending on general public services in Wales is twice as high as that of England.

Table 4.3
Identifiable general government expenditure on services by function: 2007–2008

| | £ per head | | | | Index (UK identifiable expenditure = 100) | | | |
|---|---|---|---|---|---|---|---|---|
| | England | Scotland | Wales | N. Ireland | England | Scotland | Wales | N. Ireland |
| General public services | 125 | 209 | 243 | 277 | 88 | 147 | 170 | 194 |
| International services | 4 | 4 | 4 | 4 | 101 | 95 | 95 | 95 |
| Defence | 2 | 1 | 1 | 0 | 108 | 72 | 66 | 9 |
| Public order and safety | 487 | 439 | 490 | 688 | 100 | 90 | 100 | 141 |
| Enterprise and economic development | 96 | 214 | 267 | 215 | 81 | 182 | 228 | 183 |
| Science and technology | 30 | 42 | 19 | 33 | 98 | 137 | 63 | 109 |
| Employment policies | 52 | 55 | 46 | 104 | 97 | 103 | 85 | 194 |
| Agriculture, fishes and forestry | 74 | 219 | 114 | 295 | 78 | 231 | 120 | 311 |
| Transport | 323 | 552 | 303 | 318 | 95 | 162 | 89 | 93 |
| Environment protection | 147 | 196 | 185 | 135 | 96 | 129 | 121 | 88 |
| Housing and community amenities | 184 | 387 | 193 | 439 | 88 | 186 | 92 | 210 |
| Health | 1,676 | 1,919 | 1,758 | 1,770 | 98 | 113 | 103 | 104 |
| Recreation, culture and religion | 119 | 203 | 220 | 226 | 89 | 151 | 164 | 168 |
| Education and training | 1,278 | 1,455 | 1,322 | 1,475 | 98 | 112 | 102 | 113 |
| Social protection | 2,938 | 3,284 | 3,413 | 3,810 | 97 | 109 | 113 | 126 |
| Total | 7,535 | 9,179 | 8,577 | 9,789 | 97 | 118 | 110 | 126 |

Source: HM Treasury Public Expenditure Statistical Analysis 2008
www.hm-treasury.gov.uk/pespub_pesa08.htm

## EMPLOYMENT

This section focuses on comparative employment indicators, illustrating changes in job totals in Wales against those experienced in UK regions. Some of the important and familiar issues in the Welsh labour market – such as relatively low participation rates – are revisited, and recent fortunes of inward investment explored. The major employment impacts in Wales resulting from the global economic downturn are also examined.

Table 4.4 shows *Annual Population Survey* data for employment by Government Office Regions. These figures are four-quarterly averages, seasonally adjusted, for the periods July 2006 to June 2007, and July 2007 to June 2008. Employment in the UK remained steady over the year, rising by 0.8 per cent to 28 million. Falls in employment levels were experienced in the West Midlands, the North West and the North East, while in Wales employment increased by 0.8 per cent to 1.28 million. The largest percentage increase in employment was again experienced in London (2.1 per cent).

Of continuing interest for Wales given the poor GVA performance outlined earlier is the *employment rate*. This is the number of people in employment of working age expressed as a percentage of all people of working age. Despite the employment rate in Wales showing an increase from 71.1 per cent to 71.5 per cent, over the year it remained well below the level for the UK (74.4 per cent). This means that compared to the UK as a whole, relatively fewer people in Wales are in or seeking work. Much of the improvement in the employment rate for Wales can be attributed to the increase in female participation from 67.7 per cent to 68.3 per cent. Historically, Wales has suffered from relatively low rates of participation for males in the employment market, with above average numbers of people classed as long-term sick, or having taking early retirement. Table 4.4 shows that over the period July 2007 to June 2008 only the North East of England had a lower male employment rate than Wales (73.4 per cent and 74.3 per cent respectively).

Table 4.5 highlights the employment rate for males in Welsh Unitary Authorities (UAs) over the period July 2007 to June 2008. The lowest rates here continue to be found in Neath Port Talbot (68.3 per cent), Ceredigion (69.2 per cent), Caerphilly (69.3 per cent), Torfaen (70.3 per cent) and Merthyr Tydfil (70.4 per cent). High rates of incapacity benefit claims are evident particularly in south Wales – in May 2008 there were 5,500 incapacity benefit claimants in Merthyr Tydfil, in an area with an estimated population of 55,600 (latest Mid Year Population estimate for 2007 based on the Census of Population [NOMIS]).

Table 4.4
Employment: Wales, United Kingdom and Regions, Labour Force Survey Employment (thousands and rate[1])

|  | July 2006–June 2007 | | | | | | July 2007–June 2008 | | | | | |
| --- | --- | --- | --- | --- | --- | --- | --- | --- | --- | --- | --- | --- |
|  | Male | Rate (%)* | Female | Rate (%)* | Total | Rate (%)* | Male | Rate (%)* | Female | Rate (%)* | Total | Rate (%)* |
| London | 1,976 | 76.4 | 1,524 | 62.8 | 3,500 | 69.8 | 2,021 | 77.4 | 1,552 | 63.4 | 3,573 | 70.6 |
| South East | 2,154 | 83.0 | 1,785 | 73.7 | 3,939 | 78.5 | 2,161 | 82.8 | 1,800 | 74 | 3,961 | 78.6 |
| East | 1,456 | 82.0 | 1,166 | 71.6 | 2,623 | 77.0 | 1,483 | 82.6 | 1,181 | 72.3 | 2,664 | 77.7 |
| South West | 1,299 | 81.4 | 1,086 | 74.6 | 2,385 | 78.2 | 1,311 | 81.5 | 1,099 | 75.2 | 2,410 | 78.5 |
| West Midlands | 1,326 | 77.7 | 1,044 | 67.1 | 2,369 | 72.7 | 1,310 | 76.6 | 1,052 | 67.7 | 2,362 | 72.4 |
| East Midlands | 1,134 | 80.1 | 922 | 71.9 | 2,055 | 76.2 | 1,137 | 79.4 | 927 | 72 | 2,064 | 75.9 |
| Yorkshire and The Humber | 1,291 | 77.5 | 1,041 | 68.4 | 2331 | 73.2 | 1,303 | 77.2 | 1,053 | 69 | 2,356 | 73.3 |
| North West | 1,652 | 75.5 | 1,393 | 68.9 | 3,045 | 72.3 | 1,660 | 75.4 | 1,382 | 68.5 | 3,042 | 72.1 |
| North East | 606 | 74.1 | 519 | 68.5 | 1,125 | 71.4 | 606 | 73.4 | 513 | 68 | 1,119 | 70.8 |
| Scotland | 1,284 | 78.5 | 1,140 | 73.2 | 2,425 | 75.9 | 1,312 | 79.7 | 1,135 | 72.8 | 2,447 | 76.3 |
| Northern Ireland | 416 | 75.0 | 335 | 64.2 | 750 | 69.8 | 420 | 75.1 | 344 | 65.4 | 764 | 70.4 |
| Wales | 687 | 74.2 | 581 | 67.7 | 1,268 | 71.1 | 692 | 74.3 | 586 | 68.3 | 1,278 | 71.5 |
| *United Kingdom* | *15,279* | *78.5* | *12,536* | *69.6* | *27,815* | *74.2* | *15,417* | *78.6* | *12,624* | *69.9* | *28,041* | *74.4* |

Note:
1  Denominator is all persons of working age.
Source: ONS *Annual Population Survey* [from NOMIS].

**Table 4.5**
**Male employment rate,[1] Wales Unitary Authority, July 2007–June 2008**

| | % | | % | | % |
|---|---|---|---|---|---|
| Anglesey | 72.5 | Denbighshire | 74.9 | Powys | 79.4 |
| Blaenau Gwent | 73.3 | Flintshire | 82.0 | Rhondda, Cynon, Taff | 72.9 |
| Bridgend | 73.8 | Gwynedd | 73.5 | Swansea | 73.9 |
| Caerphilly | 69.3 | Merthyr Tydfil | 70.4 | Torfaen | 70.3 |
| Cardiff | 73.6 | Monmouthshire | 79.4 | Vale of Glamorgan | 75.0 |
| Carmarthenshire | 75.3 | Neath Port Talbot | 68.3 | Wrexham | 80.7 |
| Ceredigion | 69.2 | Newport | 74.5 | | |
| Conwy | 75.4 | Pembrokeshire | 76.0 | | |

Note: [1] Denominator is male persons of working age.
Source: ONS *Annual Population Survey* [from NOMIS].

January 2008 saw consultation begin on the Welsh Assembly Government's strategy *Skills That Work For Wales* (STWFW). The strategy, which aims to address improving skills levels in line with business needs, included plans in its draft version to create a Wales Employment and Skills Board giving employers a greater say in the skills and qualifications system. Later, in April 2008, the Welsh Assembly Government unveiled new arrangements to deliver all of its business support finance through a single investment fund, replacing the many capital grants and business support programmes that were on offer. This bid to become more customer-focused will see the merger of tourism industry Section 4 grants, regional selective assistance, property development grants and Assembly investment. A dedicated phone number for business enquiries has been set up, along with a single application form.

There was optimistic news for inward investment in Wales at the start of 2008 with announcements of a number of major projects. Tata, the Indian conglomerate, unveiled a £60 million energy management technology investment in Port Talbot at its subsidiary company, Corus Strip Products UK. The announcement helped at the time to alleviate concerns for the site's future (which had arisen when Corus was acquired by Tata in April 2007). In March 2008 car manufacturer Toyota revealed plans for an £88 million investment at its Deeside plant in north Wales to produce a new 1.3 litre petrol engine. However, due to the economic global downturn this project was suspended in December as the company began a worldwide review of its investment decisions.

Further evidence of the effects of the slowdown of the UK economy were seen as the Quinn Group postponed investment plans to build a £67m production facility for insulation panels next to its existing radiator facility in Newport. The Irish company revealed in August 2008 that the plans were likely to be on hold until there were signs of an upturn in the UK construction sector. In October 2008 Ford Motor Company confirmed it was investing £70m in its Bridgend engine plant to produce a new generation of low $CO_2$, energy efficient petrol engines. The investment, which includes a £13.4m grant from the Welsh Assembly Government, was however accompanied by news that temporary staff lay-offs could be expected in the near future due to a significant reduction in the volume of engine orders.

Table 4.6 shows the employment breakdown by industry sector in Wales and Great Britain for September 2006 and September 2007. These data are taken from the ONS *Annual Business Inquiry* (ABI). There were a total of 26.6 million employee jobs in Great Britain in September 2007, an increase of 0.9 per cent from the previous September. Wales had a total of 1.19 million employees, a rise of just 0.2 per cent in the year. The increase in part-time work for males (5.5 per cent over the year) offset the decline in female part- and full-time jobs in Wales, while the number of male full-time jobs remained stable. Workers in part-time jobs naturally tend to earn lower incomes and with Wales having a greater proportion of employees only working part-time (33.0 per cent) compared to Great Britain (31.0 per cent), this is also a contributing factor to the relatively low levels of GVA per head described earlier.

The increasing reliance on the non-market sector in Wales is evident in Table 4.6 with public sector jobs increasing by 5,000 to 387,000 between 2006 and 2007. A total of 32.6 per cent of all employee jobs in Wales were in the non-market sector in 2007– a higher proportion than in Great Britain as a whole (26.9 per cent). Evidence from past recessions would indicate that this level of reliance on the public sector is likely to act as a buffer, protecting jobs in Wales in the next couple of years. Not only are the jobs in this sector relatively highly paid and geographically dispersed throughout the region but also their associated procurement activity is an important source of economic demand in difficult times. The banking, finance and insurance sector, which had been relatively fast-growing in Wales over the last few years compared to the UK, saw a slight decline in employment of 0.6 per cent (or 1,000 jobs) between 2006 and 2007. Growth in the UK financial sector was 3.1 per cent (or 69,000 jobs) over the year. Wales has a smaller employment share in banking, finance and insurance services (14.1 per cent of all employee jobs in 2007) than the UK (21.6 per cent).

Table 4.6 also shows that there was a fall in construction jobs in Wales in 2007 with the sector shedding 3,000 jobs – a reduction of 5.3 per cent. The

**Table 4.6**
**Employee jobs ('000s) in Great Britain and Wales, by industry, 2006 and 2007**

| | Great Britain | | | Wales | | |
|---|---|---|---|---|---|---|
| | **2006** | **2007** | **% change** | **2006** | **2007** | **% change** |
| Agriculture and fishing (SIC A,B) | 248 | 248 | 0.0 | 16 | 17 | 4.6 |
| Energy and water (C,E) | 157 | 173 | 10.0 | 7 | 7 | 2.0 |
| Manufacturing (D) | 2,868 | 2,821 | −1.7 | 159 | 161 | 0.9 |
| Construction (F) | 1,259 | 1,291 | 2.6 | 63 | 60 | −5.3 |
| Distribution, hotels and restaurants (G,H) | 6,186 | 6,200 | 0.2 | 275 | 276 | 0.5 |
| Transport and communications (I) | 1,559 | 1,558 | −0.1 | 51 | 51 | 1.0 |
| Banking, finance and insurance, etc. (J,K) | 5,588 | 5,758 | 3.1 | 168 | 167 | −0.6 |
| Public administration, education and health (L,M,N) | 7,094 | 7,163 | 1.0 | 382 | 387 | 1.4 |
| Other services (O,P,Q) | 1,392 | 1,387 | −0.4 | 65 | 61 | −5.1 |
| *Total* | *26,352* | *26,599* | *0.9* | *1,185* | *1,187* | *0.2* |
| Total male | 13,262 | 13,468 | 1.6 | 583 | 588 | 0.9 |
| Male part-time | 2,039 | 2,123 | 4.1 | 91 | 96 | 5.5 |
| Total female | 13,090 | 13,131 | 0.3 | 602 | 598 | −0.7 |
| Female part-time | 6,162 | 6,130 | −0.5 | 297 | 296 | −0.3 |

Source: ONS *Annual Business Inquiry* [from Welsh Assembly Government – *StatsWales*].

manufacturing sector meanwhile managed to halt its employment decline seen in recent years with the number of jobs increasing slightly by 0.9 per cent to 161,000 between 2006 and 2007. However, the economic downturn is producing a number of employment shocks to the Welsh economy. Manufacturing in the region was particularly hard pressed during 2008. The Cameo Sofa Company announced in February it was to move production from its Treforest factory to a lower cost base in Lithuania. Around 150 workers at the former Christie Tyler site were to lose their jobs. 3M revealed in April that it was to cut 185 jobs over the next year at its adhesive and tape production facility in Gorseinon. The decision was part of a move by the company aimed at reducing costs through consolidating its manufacturing base. Corus Packaging Plus announced plans to reduce its workforce in Trostre, Llanelli, by 300 due to overcapacity in the global tin market.

Around 460 workers were to remain employed at the site after these cuts and the previous shedding of 100 jobs in 2007.

Later in the year, Hoover revealed plans to cut 337 jobs at its Merthyr washing machine factory, where it has operated since 1948, due to difficulties in making competitively priced products at the site. An announcement was made in December that 250 jobs were at risk at the Miskin facility of automotive company Bosch following a decline in customer orders. The company started a ninety-day period of consultation with its plant council. The transport costs of imported raw materials were reportedly a major factor in the decision by cosmetics company L'Oreal to transfer work abroad from its Talbot Green, Llantrisant site. Around 200 jobs were expected to be lost, leaving only sixty staff at the location to help supply the UK market. Cosmetics maker Budelpack Cosi, went into administration threatening 389 jobs in Maesteg, and 200 staff at the Llantrisant site of Sun Juice faced redundancy following restructuring.

There was some positive news in the Welsh manufacturing sector. In February, Siemens Medical Solutions announced it was transferring work from its Los Angeles facility to Llanberis in north Wales, in a move creating 192 jobs, and helping to safeguard those of the existing 327 employees. Medical and diagnostic testing equipment are manufactured at the facility. US conglomerate Doncasters Group unveiled plans in April to expand its Blaenavon (Torfaen) facility with a £16m investment creating 125 aerospace jobs. The company manufactures products for gas turbine engine makers. Table 4.7 illustrates a selection of some of the larger scale jobs losses and gains in Wales in 2008.

In the services sector, call centre contractor Financial Services Data Management, a debt advice firm, announced in January plans to expand its call centre workforce by 200, moving to a new office location in Swansea. Increases in debt levels due to the onset of the global credit crunch were reportedly a determining factor in the decision. Next Generation Data revealed that it was to build a £200m green data centre at the site of the former LG Semicon plant in Newport, creating around 100 skilled jobs.

Ventura announced the closure of its Cardiff base in June with the loss of 600 jobs. The company, the UK's largest call centre outsourcer, had taken over the former Serco site in 2004. The move was seen as evidence of the effects of the credit crunch impacting along the financial services sector supply chain. Motor insurers Admiral unveiled plans to expand into Newport in the autumn of 2008, creating an initial ninety jobs at Langstone Business Park. This employment figure was expected to rise to around 450 over the next three years. In July Admiral also revealed it was to create a further 100 jobs in Cardiff by the end of the year.

**Table 4.7**
**Selected job losses and gains in Wales during 2008**

**Companies shedding >100 jobs**

| Company | Location | Sector |
| --- | --- | --- |
| 3M | Gorseinon | *Adhesive and tape manufacturer* |
| Barclays | Cardiff | *Banking* |
| Budelpack COSi | Maesteg | *Cosmetics manufacturer* |
| Cameo Sofa Company | Treforest | *Furniture manufacturer* |
| Corus (Distribution) | Shotton (N.Wales) and S.Wales | *Steelmaker – distribution* |
| Corus Packaging Plus | Trostre | *Tinplate works* |
| David McClean | Deeside | *Housing company* |
| Draka | Llanelli | *Copper wire factory* |
| Everwhite Plastics | Aberdare | *uPVC building products* |
| HBOS | Cardiff | *Banking* |
| HM Revenue & Customs | Wales-wide | *Public sector* |
| Hoover | Merthyr | *Washing machine factory* |
| International Greetings | Hengoed/Pentre | *Gift-wrap supplier* |
| L'Oreal | Llantrisant | *Cosmetics company* |
| Paramount Foods | Deeside | *Food supplier* |
| Stadco Powys | Welshpool | *Automotive supplies* |
| Sunjuice | Llantrisant | *Drink supplier* |
| Ventura | Cardiff | *Contact centre* |
| Woolworths | Wales-wide | *Retail* |

**Companies creating >100 jobs**

| Company | Location | Sector |
| --- | --- | --- |
| Admiral | Newport/Cardiff | *Insurance* |
| Capita Symonds | Bridgend/Merthyr Tydfil/ RCT | *Engineering* |
| Doncasters Group | Blaenavon | *Aerospace* |
| Financial Services Data Management | Swansea | *Debt advice* |
| McKesson | Bangor | *IT* |
| Next Generation Data | Newport | *Data services* |
| RCT Homes | RCT | *Housing Community Mutual* |
| Siemens Medical Solutions | Llanberis, N.Wales | *Medical equipment mnfr* |
| Waitrose | Cardiff | *Retail* |

In August HBOS announced it was to close its mortgage service centre in Cardiff with the loss of 150 jobs as part of a streamlining of its mortgage business. Around a half of the workers affected were reportedly found alternative roles within the group. In September, the bank revealed it was cutting a further 118 jobs at two further sites in the Capital – Cardiff Gate Retail Park and Cardiff Bay. These losses were attributed to a downturn in the company's credit card and loans business.

There were no new data available from ONS to update the figures for research and development activity, performed within UK businesses, from those that appeared in the last edition of the economic profile of *Contemporary Wales*. However, there were a number of noteworthy examples of collaborative research projects bringing together business and academic establishments in Wales in 2008. These include the Corus Centre of Excellence, launched at Cardiff University's School of Engineering as part of a £1.2m partnership agreement to aid training provision and research in the steel industry in Wales, and IBM setting up a research centre at Technium Pembrokeshire for environmental sciences and renewable energy, as part of a collaboration with Swansea University.

Facing a UK-wide recession with massive uncertainty over future job prospects, there is little evidence that Wales will be able to do much to resist the bleak times ahead, certainly outside of the non-market (public) sector. Many Welsh manufacturing companies have been unable to benefit competitively from the weakened position of the pound at the start of 2009 – being hit by the rising costs of imported raw materials and/or facing a reduction in demand from export markets as the fallout from the credit crisis impacts across the global economy. Furthermore, a high proportion of Welsh manufacturers are foreign owned and their prospects may depend on wider group sales and performance than on that of their Welsh operations. Although Wales has a relatively low concentration of jobs in the banking, finance and insurance sectors compared to the UK as a whole, a shakeout of jobs in the City and other UK financial centres is likely to have repercussions for the back-room type operations of the sort prevalent in Wales (such as call centres of banks). A decline in public finances in the coming years will also mean a lessening in the ability of the public sector to continue to contribute to employment growth in the region. During 2008 the UK Government announced that the second smaller phase of the £16 billion defence package destined for the Vale of Glamorgan – the logistics and personnel training side – had been dropped due to concerns around its affordability. The Metrix Consortium, the supplier behind the larger training academy, was to go ahead as planned with the initial phase at St Athan.

## UNEMPLOYMENT

This section presents comparative unemployment indicators, of particular importance given the rapid increase in the levels of those out of work in the UK during 2008 following the onset of the credit crunch.

Previous editions of the economic profile in *Contemporary Wales* have traced how Wales had succeeded in closing the unemployment gap with the rest of the UK. Table 4.8 shows regional claimant count unemployment rates, calculated by expressing the total number of unemployment related benefit claimants in an area as a percentage of workforce jobs plus the claimant count. From an annual average unemployment rate of 4.5 per cent in the UK in 1998, there was a sustained fall in claimant count rates down to 2.7 per cent in 2004. After rising to 2.9 per cent in the UK in 2006, the unemployment rate fell again in 2007 to an average of 2.7 per cent. Generally this pattern has been mirrored in each of the UK regions. The differential between the UK and Wales jobless percentages gradually diminished from 1998 so that by 2007, when the average annual unemployment rate in Wales was 2.8 per cent, it was down to its lowest level in the decade at 0.1 of a percentage point.

However, the economic slowdown is both a cause and an effect of falls in consumer spending in the face of higher levels of household debt and concerns over job security. This has had serious repercussions for the regional job market with Table 4.9 revealing an increase in the number of claimants in all of the UK regions in the year to November 2008. In the North West of England the number of claimants increased by 35,400 over the year to 137,600, and in Yorkshire and the Humber they were up 30,300 to 103,800. The highest proportionate increases were experienced in the South West and South East of England (58.2 per cent and 47.1 per cent respectively), and Northern Ireland (50.2 per cent), highlighting the across-the-board nature of the job impact. In Wales there was a rise of 16,400 claimants to 53,900 representing an increase of 43.7 per cent over the year.

By gender, Table 4.9 shows that male unemployment in the UK increased by 213,200 to 783,000 and female unemployment increased by 57,300 to 273,200. The proportion of females in the total number unemployed decreased in the UK (to 25.9 per cent of the total) and in Wales (to 23.7 per cent).

Table 4.10 highlights the relative duration of unemployment in the regions of the UK for November 2008. Duration of unemployment is a useful indicator to consider as it can help identify persistent pockets of long-term unemployment due to structural changes in the local economy, such as Wales experienced with the decline of its traditional industries. In November 2008, the proportion of

Table 4.8
**Annual average unemployment rates, Wales, United Kingdom and regions.**
**All persons, claimant count seasonally adjusted 1998–2007**

|  | 1998 | 1999 | 2000 | 2001 | 2002 | 2003 | 2004 | 2005 | 2006 | 2007 |
|---|---|---|---|---|---|---|---|---|---|---|
| South East | 2.6 | 2.3 | 1.8 | 1.5 | 1.6 | 1.7 | 1.6 | 1.6 | 1.8 | 1.6 |
| East | 3.2 | 2.9 | 2.4 | 2.0 | 2.1 | 2.1 | 2.0 | 2.1 | 2.3 | 2.1 |
| London | 5.1 | 4.4 | 3.7 | 3.3 | 3.5 | 3.6 | 3.5 | 3.4 | 3.4 | 3.0 |
| South West | 3.4 | 3.0 | 2.5 | 2.0 | 1.9 | 1.9 | 1.6 | 1.6 | 1.8 | 1.6 |
| West Midlands | 4.5 | 4.4 | 4.0 | 3.7 | 3.5 | 3.5 | 3.3 | 3.4 | 3.9 | 3.7 |
| East Midlands | 3.9 | 3.6 | 3.3 | 3.1 | 2.9 | 2.8 | 2.5 | 2.5 | 2.8 | 2.6 |
| Yorkshire and the Humber | 5.4 | 5.0 | 4.3 | 3.9 | 3.6 | 3.3 | 2.8 | 2.9 | 3.3 | 3.0 |
| North West | 5.0 | 4.6 | 4.1 | 3.7 | 3.5 | 3.3 | 2.9 | 2.9 | 3.3 | 3.1 |
| North East | 7.0 | 7.0 | 6.2 | 5.6 | 5.1 | 4.5 | 4.0 | 3.9 | 4.1 | 4.0 |
| Scotland | 5.3 | 5.0 | 4.5 | 3.9 | 3.8 | 3.7 | 3.4 | 3.2 | 3.3 | 2.8 |
| N.Ireland | 7.3 | 6.3 | 5.3 | 4.9 | 4.4 | 4.2 | 3.6 | 3.3 | 3.2 | 2.8 |
| *Wales* | *5.4* | *5.0* | *4.4* | *3.9* | *3.5* | *3.3* | *3.0* | *3.0* | *3.1* | *2.8* |
| *United Kingdom* | *4.5* | *4.1* | *3.6* | *3.1* | *3.1* | *3.0* | *2.7* | *2.7* | *2.9* | *2.7* |

Source: *Labour Market Trends* (Claimant Count), ONS.

**Table 4.9**
**Unemployment Wales, United Kingdom and regions, claimants, thousands,**
**not seasonally adjusted, November 2007 and November 2008**

| | November 2007 | | | November 2008 | | |
|---|---|---|---|---|---|---|
| | Male | Female | Total | Male | Female | Total |
| South East | 45.8 | 18.6 | 64.5 | 68.8 | 26.0 | 94.8 |
| East | 38.3 | 16.3 | 54.6 | 54.7 | 20.6 | 75.3 |
| London | 91.6 | 41.1 | 132.7 | 103.7 | 47.3 | 151.0 |
| South West | 26.8 | 10.8 | 37.6 | 43.7 | 15.8 | 59.5 |
| West Midlands | 68.7 | 25.2 | 93.9 | 90.7 | 30.7 | 121.5 |
| East Midlands | 37.6 | 15.0 | 52.6 | 53.8 | 19.0 | 72.7 |
| Yorkshire and the Humber | 54.3 | 19.2 | 73.5 | 79.0 | 24.9 | 103.8 |
| North West | 76.2 | 26.0 | 102.2 | 104.9 | 32.7 | 137.6 |
| North East | 34.5 | 11.3 | 45.8 | 47.3 | 14.5 | 61.8 |
| Scotland | 51.3 | 17.2 | 68.5 | 68.7 | 21.8 | 90.5 |
| Northern Ireland | 17.1 | 5.4 | 22.4 | 26.5 | 7.2 | 33.7 |
| Wales | 27.8 | 9.8 | 37.5 | 41.2 | 12.8 | 53.9 |
| United Kingdom | 569.8 | 215.9 | 785.8 | 783.0 | 273.2 | 1,056.1 |

Source: ONS [from NOMIS]. (NB columns may not add due to rounding)

claimants who had been out of work for more than one year in Wales was 9.0 per cent, down 4 percentage points from November 2007. This was below the all-UK percentage of 10.2 per cent (which had fallen 6.7 percentage points over the year). In all regions of the UK the amounts of long-term unemployed had decreased year on year from November 2007.

Table 4.11 shows the sub-regional level unemployment rates in Wales for November 2008. These rates are calculated by dividing the number of unemployment-related benefit claimants by the local resident population of working age, rather than the local workforce population. Using this denominator prevents distortions from commuting patterns influencing the values. The local authorities with the highest unemployment rates in Wales were Blaenau Gwent, up 1.6 percentage points over the year to 5.8 per cent, Merthyr Tydfil (up 1.4 percentage points to 4.8 per cent) and Caerphilly (also up 1.4 percentage points, to 4.0 per cent).

The Welsh Assembly Government has continued to be been active in addressing the problem of sub-regions with relatively high unemployment. In May 2008,

**Table 4.10**
**Male unemployment by duration: Wales, United Kingdom and regions,**
**November 2008**

|  | Unemployed for over 52 and up to 104 weeks | Unemployed for over 104 weeks | Percentage claiming over 1 year |
|---|---|---|---|
| South East | 4,215 | 1,170 | 7.8 |
| East | 3,875 | 985 | 8.9 |
| London | 10,360 | 3,200 | 13.1 |
| South West | 2,065 | 700 | 6.3 |
| West Midlands | 7,960 | 3,740 | 12.9 |
| East Midlands | 3,850 | 1,030 | 9.1 |
| Yorkshire and the Humber | 5,815 | 955 | 8.6 |
| North West | 8,375 | 2,520 | 10.4 |
| North East | 3,900 | 965 | 10.3 |
| Scotland | 5,040 | 1,395 | 9.4 |
| Northern Ireland | 3,065 | 610 | 14.0 |
| *Wales* | *2,610* | *1,070* | *9.0* |
| *United Kingdom* | *61,130* | *18,335* | *10.2* |

Source: ONS [from NOMIS].

it launched *Jobmatch*, a £38m regeneration scheme to help people back into work in the Heads of the Valleys. After an initial pilot of the scheme in Blaenau Gwent, where 1,300 people were aided, the scheme was to be rolled out to Caerphilly, Torfaen, Merthyr Tydfil and Rhondda Cynon Taff with the aim of helping 10,000 people into work by 2012. In June 2008, the Assembly Government and the Department for Work and Pensions announced the extension of the joint initiative *Want2Work* with the aim of helping 5,000 of the unemployed in Wales to get back into employment. A further £32m of funding for the project was secured through the European Social Fund and match-funding.

In the rural areas of Wales the rate of unemployment in Gwynedd increased from 2.0 per cent to 2.8 per cent and in Ceredigion from 1.3 per cent to 1.5 per cent. In Cardiff the rate rose from 2.1 per cent to 2.9 per cent, Swansea saw a climb from 2.0 per cent to 2.8 per cent, Wrexham 1.8 per cent to 2.8 per cent, and in Newport an increase from 2.5 per cent to 3.6 per cent. By gender, the male unemployment rate in Blaenau Gwent increased by 2.5 percentage points year on

**Table 4.11**
**Unemployment by unitary authority and Wales, unadjusted,**
**resident base, November 2008**

|  | Male | | Female | | All | |
|---|---|---|---|---|---|---|
|  | Number | Rate | Number | Rate | Number | Rate |
| Anglesey | 973 | 4.6 | 319 | 1.7 | 1,292 | 3.2 |
| Blaenau Gwent | 1,825 | 8.4 | 591 | 2.9 | 2,416 | 5.8 |
| Bridgend | 1,955 | 4.6 | 634 | 1.6 | 2,589 | 3.2 |
| Caerphilly | 3,142 | 5.8 | 999 | 2.0 | 4,141 | 4.0 |
| Cardiff | 4,703 | 4.4 | 1,483 | 1.4 | 6,186 | 2.9 |
| Carmarthenshire | 1,939 | 3.6 | 554 | 1.1 | 2,493 | 2.4 |
| Ceredigion | 541 | 2.1 | 181 | 0.8 | 722 | 1.5 |
| Conwy | 1,488 | 4.5 | 400 | 1.4 | 1,888 | 3.0 |
| Denbighshire | 1,343 | 4.6 | 370 | 1.4 | 1,713 | 3.1 |
| Flintshire | 1,651 | 3.4 | 568 | 1.3 | 2,219 | 2.4 |
| Gwynedd | 1,502 | 4.1 | 428 | 1.3 | 1,930 | 2.8 |
| Merthyr Tydfil | 1,246 | 7.1 | 364 | 2.2 | 1,610 | 4.8 |
| Monmouthshire | 674 | 2.5 | 252 | 1.0 | 926 | 1.8 |
| Neath Port Talbot | 1,923 | 4.5 | 620 | 1.6 | 2,543 | 3.1 |
| Newport | 2,342 | 5.3 | 693 | 1.7 | 3,035 | 3.6 |
| Pembrokeshire | 1,076 | 3.1 | 389 | 1.2 | 1,465 | 2.2 |
| Powys | 1,074 | 2.7 | 400 | 1.1 | 1,474 | 2.0 |
| Rhondda, Cynon, Taff | 3,885 | 5.2 | 1,160 | 1.7 | 5,045 | 3.5 |
| Swansea | 3,025 | 4.1 | 904 | 1.4 | 3,929 | 2.8 |
| Torfaen | 1,503 | 5.3 | 432 | 1.7 | 1,935 | 3.5 |
| Vale of Glamorgan | 1,624 | 4.3 | 522 | 1.5 | 2,146 | 2.9 |
| Wrexham | 1,733 | 4.0 | 516 | 1.3 | 2,249 | 2.8 |
| Wales | 41,167 | 4.4 | 12,779 | 1.5 | 53,946 | 3.0 |

Source: ONS [from NOMIS].

year to 8.4 per cent, and for females there was an increase of 0.6 of a percentage point in Caerphilly to 2.0 per cent.

The figures examined in this section so far have not taken into account those people who were economically inactive, that is those who are neither in employment nor unemployed, such as persons with a long-term sickness. The economic inactivity rate (working age) is the number of people who are economically inactive aged 16 to 59/64 expressed as a percentage of all working age people. Table 4.12 highlights economic inactivity rates for regions and then Welsh UAs taken from the *Annual Population Survey*. These figures give an indication of the extent of 'hidden' unemployment existing within the areas, and are four quarterly averages. In the reference period July 2007 to June 2008, Table 4.12 shows that Wales (24.2 per cent) had a higher rate of inactivity than the UK as a

**Table 4.12**
**Economic inactivity rates United Kingdom, regions and Wales unitary**
**authorities, combined males and females, July 2007–June 2008**

| Government office region | Rate | Unitary authority | Rate |
|---|---|---|---|
| South East | 17.9 | Anglesey | 23.6 |
| East | 18.8 | Blaenau Gwent | 29.1 |
| London | 24.5 | Bridgend | 22.3 |
| South West | 18.4 | Caerphilly | 29.3 |
| West Midlands | 22.6 | Cardiff | 24.7 |
| East Midlands | 19.7 | Carmarthenshire | 24.0 |
| Yorkshire and The Humber | 22.3 | Ceredigion | 30.0 |
| North West | 23.3 | Conwy | 22.4 |
| North East | 24.1 | Denbighshire | 24.2 |
| Scotland | 20.0 | Flintshire | 19.0 |
| Northern Ireland | 26.7 | Gwynedd | 23.7 |
| | | Merthyr Tydfil | 25.2 |
| *Wales* | *24.2* | Monmouthshire | 19.8 |
| | | Neath Port Talbot | 30.2 |
| *United Kingdom* | *21.4* | Newport | 23.7 |
| | | Pembrokeshire | 24.5 |
| | | Powys | 20.5 |
| | | Rhondda, Cynon, Taff | 24.3 |
| | | Swansea | 26.1 |
| | | Torfaen | 26.6 |
| | | Vale of Glamorgan | 20.9 |
| | | Wrexham | 18.9 |

Source: ONS *Annual Population Survey* quarterly: four quarter averages [NOMIS].

whole (21.4 per cent), with only London (24.5 per cent) and Northern Ireland (26.7 per cent) having higher rates. At a Welsh sub-regional level the highest rates of inactivity were found in Neath Port Talbot (30.2 per cent), Ceredigion (30.0 per cent), and Caerphilly (29.3 per cent).

The problems of economic inactivity in the over-50s in Wales were outlined in research for Prime Cymru, the Prince of Wales' initiative for mature enterprise. The report *Improving Employment Prospects for the Over-50s*, written by former chief economist of Barclays Bank, Christopher Isherwood, makes the case for more flexible working arrangements to help those with care responsibilities; better disabled facilities in the workplace; and increased skill levels to help overcome discrimination.

At the end of 2008 the nation was faced with massive economic uncertainty. The first months of 2009 saw Wales experience stark increases in the levels of unemployment that were very likely to spiral upwards as the year progressed.

## EARNINGS

This section focuses on comparative earnings indicators, examining discrepancies in average wage rates between Wales and the UK for different occupations and industries, as well as looking at Welsh sub-regional earning levels. These data are taken from the *Annual Survey of Hours and Earnings* (ASHE) published by the ONS.

A particular challenge to the Welsh economy in recent years has been to arrest the decline in incomes relative to the UK average. The previous earnings profile in *Contemporary Wales* showed average (median) gross weekly earnings in the UK at £456.7 having increased by 2.9 per cent in the year to April 2007. Gross weekly earnings for full-time women had increased by 2.8 per cent, compared to a 2.9 per cent rise for men. In Wales, earnings had increased by only 1.2 per cent to £404.7 per week in the year to April 2007.

Table 4.13 shows the occupational breakdown of earnings for Wales and the UK for April 2008. The ASHE for 2008 shows that average gross weekly earnings in the UK were £478.6, up 4.6 per cent on 2007. Gross weekly earnings for full-time men rose to £521.2 (+4.6 per cent) and for women to £412.0 (+4.4 per cent). In Wales, average gross weekly earnings rose by 4.1 per cent to £421.0, with male earnings gaining by 5.4 per cent to £464.9 and females by 3.8 per cent to £369.0. This has resulted in a widening of the gender pay gap in the region.

In recent years, earnings for occupations at the top end of the remuneration scale in Wales have been well below the levels found in the UK as a whole – with this contributing detrimentally to the overall earnings levels in Wales. With average weekly earnings for *all occupations* in Wales at £421 in April 2008 they remained at around 88 per cent of the UK level (£478.6). As in previous years, Wales performed relatively well in the professional occupations category with earnings increasing to £661.7 per week, or 97 per cent of the UK average. In the high earning category of managers and senior officials, average weekly earnings in Wales of £574.9 stood at just 83 per cent of the UK average. This represented an improvement of 5 percentage points from the 78 per cent of the previous April, but was still a long way from parity.

Relative earnings in process, plant and machine operative occupations decreased slightly in Wales by 1.0 percentage point to 95 per cent of the UK average in 2008. There were relative improvements for Wales in the administrative and secretarial occupations (with earnings in Wales 94 per cent of the UK level, up 1.3 percentage points on 2007), skilled trades (also 94 per cent, up 0.9 percentage points), sales and customer services (96.2 per cent, up 2.6 percentage points), and elementary occupations (97.2 per cent, up 1.8 percentage points).

**Table 4.13**
**Average (median) weekly earnings: UK and Wales, £s, all industries and services.**
**Full time males and females adult rates, April 2008**

| | United Kingdom | | | Wales | | |
|---|---|---|---|---|---|---|
| | **All** | **Male** | **Female** | **All** | **Male** | **Female** |
| *All* | *478.6* | *521.2* | *412.0* | *421.0* | *464.9* | *369.0* |
| Managers and senior officials | 693.0 | 766.6 | 574.9 | 574.9 | 628.3 | 478.4 |
| Professional occupations | 680.8 | 724.4 | 633.9 | 661.7 | 670.7 | 636.0 |
| Associate professional and technical | 539.7 | 574.9 | 502.1 | 514.3 | 542.2 | 481.5 |
| Administrative and secretarial | 359.0 | 397.4 | 351.5 | 337.5 | 369.5 | 330.7 |
| Skilled trades occupations | 451.4 | 460.0 | 308.1 | 424.3 | 439.0 | 277.2 |
| Personal service occupations | 316.0 | 353.1 | 305.0 | 291.9 | 330.3 | 285.2 |
| Sales & customer service | 286.5 | 302.7 | 274.5 | 275.5 | 304.0 | 261.0 |
| Process, plant and machine operatives | 414.6 | 429.2 | 302.1 | 394.4 | 410.6 | 268.5 |
| Elementary occupations | 317.9 | 341.7 | 262.5 | 308.9 | 333.0 | 265.7 |

Source: *Annual Survey of Hours and Earnings* (ASHE) 2008 ONS.

Gender differences in earnings are also highlighted in Table 4.13. Male earnings in Wales were lower than the UK average for every occupation except sales and customer services (100.4 per cent of the UK), falling well short in the higher paid managerial and senior occupations (at £628.3 per week only 82.0 per cent of the UK average of £766.6). Average pay for females in professional occupations remained slightly higher in Wales at £636.0 per week than for the UK female average (£633.9), but given the relatively few women employed in this category they can have little impression on overall averages. At the lower end of the earnings scale average pay for females in elementary occupations in Wales were also higher than the UK average (101.2 per cent of the UK).

A concern for Wales is the relatively high employment share in low skilled, and therefore lower paid, jobs. This contributes to poor aggregate earnings performance and partly explains the differentials in the GVA per head figures for Wales and UK. Table 4.14 indicates employment shares in each occupation category using data from the *Annual Population Survey* (four-quarter average July

**Table 4.14**
**Average gross weekly earnings and employment breakdown by occupation,**
**United Kingdom and Wales**

| Occupation | UK | | Wales | |
|---|---|---|---|---|
| | Average gross weekly earnings £ | % of all employ-ment | Average gross weekly earnings £ | % of all employ-ment |
| Managers and senior officials | 693.0 | 15.0 | 574.9 | 12.8 |
| Professional occupations | 680.8 | 12.9 | 661.7 | 11.4 |
| Associate professional and technical | 539.7 | 14.2 | 514.3 | 13.4 |
| Administrative and secretarial | 359.0 | 12.0 | 337.5 | 11.7 |
| Skilled trades occupations | 451.4 | 11.1 | 424.3 | 12.9 |
| Personal service occupations | 316.0 | 8.1 | 291.9 | 8.9 |
| Sales and customer services | 286.5 | 7.7 | 275.5 | 8.2 |
| Process plant and machine operatives | 414.6 | 7.3 | 394.4 | 8.8 |
| Elementary occupations | 317.9 | 11.5 | 308.9 | 11.9 |
| All occupations | 478.6 | 100.0 | 421.0 | 100.0 |

Sources:
Earnings – *Annual Survey of Hours and Earnings* (ASHE) 2008. ONS
Employment – *Annual Population Survey* (APS) – quarterly: four quarter averages: July 2007 to June 2008
ONS Crown Copyright Reserved [from Nomis].

2007 to June 2008). Here Wales is seen to have a lower proportion of employment concentrated in the occupations with the highest average weekly earnings than the UK as a whole. Only a 12.8 per cent share of employment in Wales is in the manager and senior official category, whereas for the UK it stands at 15 per cent. Similarly, the UK as a whole has proportionally more employment in professional occupations and associate professional and technical occupations than Wales.

Earnings by industry groupings for males and females in the UK and Wales are outlined in Table 4.15. Differences between wages remain at their smallest in manufacturing. In this industry earnings in Wales were 96.8 per cent of the UK as a whole in 2008, an improvement of 2.3 percentage points from the 94.5 per cent observed in the previous year. For males the level of Welsh manufacturing earnings was 98.0 per cent of the UK level. However, in the service industries, where much of the growth in Welsh employment has been centred over the last

Table 4.15
Average (median) gross weekly pay (£) by broad industry groupings, full-time employees,[1]
United Kingdom and Wales, 2008

| | Males | | | Females | | | All | | |
|---|---|---|---|---|---|---|---|---|---|
| | UK | Wales | % UK | UK | Wales | % UK | UK | Wales | % UK |
| All industries and services | 521.2 | 464.9 | 89.2 | 412.0 | 369.0 | 89.6 | 478.7 | 421.0 | 87.9 |
| All index of production industries | 523.0 | x | x | 376.9 | x | x | 494.8 | x | x |
| All manufacturing | 514.0 | 503.6 | 98.0 | 373.5 | 339.2 | 90.8 | 487.2 | 471.5 | 96.8 |
| All service industries | 521.9 | 444.2 | 85.1 | 416.4 | 373.5 | 89.7 | 471.5 | 408.0 | 86.5 |

Note:
1 Employees on adult rates whose pay for the survey pay-period was not affected by absence
Note: 'x' denotes no figure available
Source: *Annual Survey of Hours and Earnings* (ASHE) 2008.

decade, female earnings in Wales were just 89.7 per cent of the UK, and male 85.1 per cent.

Table 4.16 shows average (median) gross weekly earnings by local authority for 2008. This table is included with some concerns because data become statistically less reliable for small areas, with ONS advising against making year on year comparisons with earnings data at local authority level. Table 4.16 shows that higher average weekly earnings occur in Neath Port Talbot, The Vale of Glamorgan, Flintshire, Cardiff, Newport and Monmouthshire. At the other end of the scale the lowest earnings are observed for Ceredigion, Blaenau Gwent, Powys and Torfaen. By gender the highest female full-time average earnings were found in Newport, 7 per cent higher than the Wales average for females at £395.6 per week. While male earnings in Blaenau Gwent were relatively high at £494.1

**Table 4.16**
**Average (median) gross weekly earnings £s, wales and unitary authorities, all, male and female full-time employees on adult rates, 2008, workplace based**

|  | All FT | Male FT | Female FT |
|---|---|---|---|
| Blaenau Gwent | 370.1 | 494.1 | 330.1 |
| Bridgend | 430.2 | 503.3 | 375.1 |
| Caerphilly | 403.9 | 460.5 | 359.6 |
| Cardiff | 451.8 | 493.0 | 385.8 |
| Carmarthenshire | 418.7 | 450.0 | 359.5 |
| Ceredigion | 362.6 | 363.7 | 356.3 |
| Conwy | 417.4 | 428.4 | 378.3 |
| Denbighshire | 421.6 | 437.2 | 389.4 |
| Flintshire | 463.9 | 500.0 | 379.5 |
| Gwynedd | 389.8 | 435.3 | 336.1 |
| Isle of Anglesey | 430.6 | 474.5 | 362.2 |
| Merthyr Tydfil | 385.2 | 385.4 | 377.4 |
| Monmouthshire | 442.2 | 475.8 | 367.2 |
| Neath and Port Talbot | 491.9 | 534.8 | 394.0 |
| Newport | 449.5 | 472.4 | 395.6 |
| Pembrokeshire | 411.2 | 419.3 | 387.0 |
| Powys | 370.8 | 406.0 | 332.7 |
| Rhondda Cynon Taff | 409.0 | 425.1 | 369.3 |
| Swansea | 373.8 | 402.9 | 351.4 |
| Torfaen | 371.8 | 441.2 | 316.1 |
| The Vale of Glamorgan | 483.5 | 532.2 | 332.0 |
| Wrexham | 400.5 | 470.8 | 338.2 |
| *Wales* | *421.0* | *464.9* | *369.0* |

Employees on adult rates whose pay for the survey pay-period was not affected by absence
Source: *Annual Survey of Hours and Earnings* (ASHE) 2008.

per week, average wages for females in the authority were among the lowest in Wales at £330.1, or 89 per cent of the all-Wales average. This seems to suggest that female earnings were unusually influential in the area.

## HOUSING MARKETS

The 'credit crunch', originating in the United States, spilling over to the UK from October 2007 onwards (when Northern Rock's vulnerable business model was exposed) has since become an entrenched feature of 2008 and now 2009. While we now see the crunch in terms of its devastating impact on world-wide confidence and are all braced for a recession that has not been equalled since the 1930s, many house owners have already been suffering the effects of a stalled housing market – which also works back round to the construction sector and through to consumer spending on household goods and thence to the economy as a whole. There are a number of complex housing effects caused by and resulting from the UK's current economic status. Those who cannot afford their mortgage payments will be in default and face repossession. The Council of Mortgage Lenders (CML) estimates that repossession could reach 75,000 homes in 2009, a figure that was last recorded in the recession of 1991. This may come about because individuals have lost their jobs, or they were on fixed deals and facing significantly higher living costs (including other domestic borrowing). Potential purchasers who have been waiting for the market to bottom out are finding it difficult to read whether that point has been reached and/or may lack the much higher deposits that are currently a requirement of mortgage providers. The point is being increasingly well made that the problem with credit is not its cost but its availability. Further up the chain those who might benefit from up-sizing cannot do so because the market is sluggish below them. However, there are some winners. For example, those on variable rate or tracker mortgages will be enjoying a windfall, and their spending will be an important boost to the economy, but only if it compensates for the much diminished spending power of savers.

House prices in Wales rose by 7.3 per cent (HBOS) in 2005 and 10.3 per cent in 2006. In 2007, Wales experienced an annual house price growth of 8.7 per cent compared to 9.4 per cent for the UK (all buyers, all houses, non-seasonally adjusted). However, comparing December 2008 Q3 figures with the same quarter in December 2007 shows a fall in UK house prices of 12.4 per cent. The tipping point when prices turned negative occurred in April 2008. In the latest reported quarter (Q3 2008) house prices in the UK fell by 5.2 per cent since Q2, though slightly less so than the previous quarter (−5.1 per cent), which Halifax commentators take to be the appearance of stabilization. The effect of these much-subdued market prices is to return the value of the average house in the UK to £175,143 or the level of Q1 2006.

Table 4.17 provides seasonally adjusted house prices for the UK regions for the third quarter of 2008, and the annual change. As with better times the regions experience different fortunes during downturns. The greatest volatility has been experienced in Northern Ireland with a drop of 22.6 per cent on Q3 2007. Wales and Greater London experienced declines of 16.6 per cent and 16.5 per cent over the year to Q3 followed closely by Yorkshire and the Humber (−14.2 per cent) and so on, with the least drop felt by Scotland (−6.0 per cent). All regions have experienced a doubling (at the very least) of house prices over the last ten years, and the higher the gains the higher the falls.

In 2006, the average (standardized) house was worth just under £160,000, or 55 per cent of the value of the average Greater London house. By 2007 this proportion had dropped back to a little more than 51.5 per cent. Again, in 2006 the Welsh house price/earnings ratio was 6.6 compared to 7.0 in the UK, suggesting then that houses were actually slightly more affordable in Wales than the UK.

**Table 4.17**
**Average house prices,[1] third quarter 2008, United Kingdom and regions**

| Regions of the UK | £ | Annual % change |
|---|---|---|
| South East | 233,086 | −12.2 |
| East Anglia | 169,788 | −13.3 |
| South West | 185,691 | −12.9 |
| West Midlands | 162,861 | −9.5 |
| East Midlands | 147,559 | −13.1 |
| Yorkshire and Humberside | 128,591 | −14.2 |
| North West | 137,487 | −10.5 |
| North | 138,063 | −9.3 |
| Greater London | 269,723 | −16.5 |
| Scotland | 134,380 | −6.0 |
| Northern Ireland | 172,762 | −22.6 |
| *Wales* | *139,267* | *−16.6* |
| *United Kingdom* | *175,143* | *−12.4* |

Note:
1   Figures are for standardised average house prices.
Source: HBOS House Price Index.

In 2007, houses became relatively more affordable in Wales (7.2) than the UK average (7.6) whilst houses had become less affordable in the round over the year. By June 2008 the UK house price/earnings ratio dropped below 5.00 (falling to 4.44 in December), from 5.68 at the beginning of the year. Housing is then becoming more affordable, in one sense as prices drop while effectively not being affordable in the absence of the necessary credit, as lenders seek to recover profitability. 2009 is likely to be very difficult on this front.

Table 4.18 repeats average annual house prices to the third quarter of 2008 for the Welsh UAs. There is never much change to the UA rankings with Monmouthshire, the Vale of Glamorgan, Powys, and Pembrokeshire having the highest average house prices. Blaenau Gwent and Merthyr Tydfil have the lowest average

**Table 4.18**
**Average house prices,[1] third quarter 2008, Welsh unitary authorities**

| Welsh Unitary Authorities | £ | % change 2007–8 |
|---|---|---|
| Blaenau Gwent | 113,014 | 3.0 |
| Bridgend | 142,147 | −4.4 |
| Caerphilly | 136,115 | −6.4 |
| Cardiff | 161,356 | −7.1 |
| Carmarthenshire | 152,880 | −11.4 |
| Ceredigion | 179,776 | 1.0 |
| Conwy | 149,408 | −17.1 |
| Denbighshire | 150,839 | −3.4 |
| Flintshire | 172,457 | −4.6 |
| Gwynedd | 163,131 | 6.2 |
| Isle of Anglesey | 174,912 | −7.4 |
| Merthyr Tydfil | 115,179 | −6.9 |
| Monmouthshire | 212,603 | −10.8 |
| Neath Port Talbot | 134,359 | −1.1 |
| Newport | 158,407 | −1.3 |
| Pembrokeshire | 185,219 | 2.6 |
| Powys | 183,773 | −0.2 |
| Rhondda, Cynon, Taff | 126,379 | −5.1 |
| Swansea | 152,333 | −7.5 |
| The Vale of Glamorgan | 191,156 | −3.5 |
| Torfaen | 140,962 | −2.3 |
| Wrexham | 170,103 | −10.1 |

Note:
1   House price data for Wales given are arithmetic average prices of houses on which an offer of mortgage has been granted. Prices are not standardised.
Source: HBOS House Price Index

house prices, but the gap between the highest and lowest values is currently narrower than it was a year ago.

While a very muted housing market was expected for 2008, no one anticipated the degree of pessimism that is permeating the UK.

## REGIONAL COMPETITIVENESS

Table 4.19 repeats the GVA indicators shown in Table 4.1 together with household disposable income, income support and investment data by region in order to assess Wales's general level of competitiveness. In 2006, gross disposable household income in Wales was 10.8 per cent below the UK average, an improvement of only 1.2 percentage points on the year. The latest figures show Wales to have slipped back slightly to an 11 percentage point difference. GVA per head in Wales slumbers at the bottom (75 per cent of UK compared to 77 per cent the previous year) and is substantially below the next lowest (Northern Ireland and North East). It is noteworthy that Northern Ireland maintained its position against the UK average over the year while the North East's position, like Wales's, deteriorated.

In terms of proportions of income support claimants in the total population, Northern Ireland is the highest by far, as indeed it was in the previous review. Wales is lower than London, the North East and the North West, on this measure. The fact that Wales is middling on this while the worst in terms of GVA per head shows we still need to improve economic participation in order to gain ground.

Over successive reviews in *Contemporary Wales* we have commented on the ups and downs in the value of foreign manufacturing investment. Over those years, however, Wales maintained its share of attracted investment which was a steady 7 per cent of the UK total number of projects. The latest figures for 2006/2007 show that Wales's share of the total number of projects dropped slightly to 6 per cent. Foreign Direct Investment (FDI) is an important source of employment, creating over 13,000 jobs in the latest year recorded and, including safeguarded jobs, accounted for over 32,000 in total in Wales – which is 9 per cent of the UK's sum of FDI associated jobs. London and the South East of England dominate the picture in terms of relative share of projects, which also tend to be relatively more capital intensive.

## OVERVIEW

With even the emerging economies (who are not embattled by 'toxic' debt, such as China and India) feeling the knock-on effects of a falling away of demand from

Table 4.19
Regional competitiveness indicators

| Region | Gross disposable household income per head (UK=100) 2006 | Gross value added (workplace basis) per head (UK=100) 2007 | Proportion of income support claimants (in population over 16) May 2007 | Regional Inward Investment 2001/2002 to 2006/2007 totals* | | | |
|---|---|---|---|---|---|---|---|
| | | | | No. of projects | No. of new jobs | No. of safeguarded jobs | Total no. of associated jobs |
| London | 123 | 152 | 7.6 | 1,492 | 23,868 | 6,766 | 30,634 |
| South East | 112 | 113 | 4.0 | 1,014 | 24,464 | 14,143 | 38,607 |
| East of England | 106 | 103 | 4.4 | 404 | 8,555 | 11,175 | 19,730 |
| South West | 99 | 91 | 4.8 | 258 | 8,377 | 16,210 | 24,587 |
| West Midlands | 91 | 86 | 6.2 | 466 | 20,945 | 37,222 | 58,167 |
| East Midlands | 93 | 89 | 5.0 | 331 | 8,283 | 11,100 | 19,383 |
| Yorkshire and the Humber | 91 | 85 | 5.9 | 262 | 11,538 | 8,259 | 19,797 |
| North West | 92 | 87 | 7.5 | 460 | 23,192 | 14,285 | 37,477 |
| North East | 86 | 79 | 7.5 | 364 | 19,386 | 16,970 | 36,356 |
| England | 102 | 103 | 5.9 | 5,051 | 148,608 | 136,130 | 284,738 |
| Scotland | 95 | 96 | 7.1 | 399 | 20,863 | 11,833 | 32,696 |
| Northern Ireland | 87 | 81 | 9.4 | 178 | 13,297 | 19,618 | 32,915 |
| *Wales* | *89* | *75* | *7.3* | *362* | *21,123* | *17,329* | *38,452* |

Note:
* Totals do not include figures for inward investments classified as 'UK Wide' (11 projects)
Source: DTI *Regional Competitiveness and State of the Regions* May 2008/GVA figures – ONS
Inward Investment figures – Published figures from the UKTI Database

the West, it will be hard to know where to look for daylight. At the beginning of 2009 the UK faces the prospect of zero interest rates and 'quantitative easing' as successive government bailouts fail to generate confidence. Subdued spending in anticipation of the next price drop will cause a downward spiral, and could lead to a period of economic stagnation and contraction similar to that which occurred in Japan and lasted a decade.

Naturally people will be asking whether Wales's economic structure predisposes it to differences in how it may fare during the downturn. It has been noted that Wales has a smaller employment share in banking, finance and insurance services (14.1 per cent of all employee jobs in 2007) than the UK (21.6 per cent), and this may afford a level of protection. However, a shakeout in the city will also reverberate around the bank call-centres of Wales. Many Welsh manufacturing companies may have identified the potential trading advantage of a weak pound and then found it difficult to benefit, faced with rising costs of imported raw materials and reductions in demand from export markets. Foreign-owned manufacturers in Wales will depend on wider group sales and performance, outside the control of their Welsh operations. The experience of previous economic downturns would point to the high proportion of public sector jobs in Wales as being of assistance in safeguarding employment, but there are ever-growing pressures on public finances and demands for budget cutbacks on the horizon.

The fact that the data for 2008 are already registering the downward trend in Welsh economic activity demonstrates the nature of the current global turmoil and is a reminder of just how fragile Wales is.

## NOTES

1    The Nomenclature of Territorial Units for Statistics (NUTS), a geocode standard for referencing the administrative divisions of countries for statistical purposes developed by the European Union.
2    Tel: 0300 060 3000.

## REFERENCES

Bryan, J. and Roche, N. (2008). 'The Welsh economy: the state of the nation in 2007', *Contemporary Wales*, 21, 218–48.
Minford, P. (2008). 'Notes on the banking crisis and the economic outlook', *Welsh Economic Review*, Vol. 20, Welsh Economy Research Unit, Cardiff Business School.

Prime Cymru (2008). 'Improving employment prospects for the over-50s, Carmarthen-shire, Wales', *www.prime-cymru.co.uk/downloads/PRIME_Smallwood_report_2008_executive_summary.pdf.*

Welsh Assembly Government (2008). 'Skills that work for Wales: a skills and employment strategy and action plan', Cardiff, Wales, *http://new.wales.gov.uk/topics/educationand skills/policy_strategy_and_planning/skillsthatforwales/?lang=en.*

# 5. INSTITUTING CONSTITUTIONS: WELSH CONSTITUTIONAL DYNAMICS AND THE DEVELOPMENT OF THE NATIONAL ASSEMBLY FOR WALES 2005–2007

## Diana Silvia Stirbu

### ABSTRACT

*This article explores some distinctive constitutional dynamics in the institutional development of the National Assembly for Wales between June 2005 and May 2007, a period of intense institutional change when the Assembly readjusted its internal architecture, operation and procedures to respond to the new legislative frame-work and specific requirements of the Government of Wales Act 2006. Using 'snapshot ethnographies' and benefiting from a wide access to politicians, officials and internal operational documents, this article uses the core assumptions of new institutionalism to highlight the important constitutional implications of institutional adaptation. In exploring the less formal aspects of the institution's operation set against rapid institutional change, the article offers insights into the Assembly's internal development during this timeframe. On a more theoretical level, it offers some timely theoretical contextualization of Welsh devolution through an institutionalist perspective.*

## INTRODUCTION

The New Labour government's constitutional reform package, within which devolution to Scotland, Wales and Northern Ireland featured prominently, spurred some interesting institutional dynamics in British politics. At a UK level, for example, the House of Lords set up the Constitution Committee in 2001 to examine the constitutional implications of Public Bills and to look at broader constitutional issues (House of Lords, 2008). Similarly, Whitehall established a Department of Constitutional Affairs in 2003, whereas in Wales, the Welsh

Assembly Government appointed the Richard Commission in 2002 to look at the powers and electoral arrangements of the National Assembly for Wales. These developments are set against a backdrop of increased interest in institutional design and constitutional matters at EU level, triggered mainly by the rise of European Union institutions post Maastricht Treaty (Pollack, 1996; Bulmer, 1998; Eriksen et al., 2004), the fall of the communist regimes in the late 1980s in Eastern Europe, and the subsequent rise of new democracies in the former communist block (Lijphart and Weisman, 1996; Elster et al., 1998; Dimitrova, 2002; Gonenc, 2002; Shvetsova, 2002).

This article explores the essential fluidity of devolution by focusing on the institutional development of the National Assembly for Wales (henceforth 'Assembly') between June 2005 and May 2007 – more precisely, from the publication of the *Better Governance for Wales White Paper* ('White Paper'), through the passing of the Government of Wales Act 2006 ('the Act') by the UK Parliament, until the final confirmation of the revised Assembly Standing Orders ('standing orders') and, subsequently, the third Assembly elections in May 2007. This particular timeframe, referred to here as the *separation*, is characterized by a rapid pace of institutional change and adaptation with significant constitutional importance – the Assembly had to completely readjust its internal architecture, operation and procedures in order to be able to respond to the requirements of the, then, expected Act.[1]

Embracing new institutionalism's theoretical assumptions, which emphasize institutions' central role in shaping political life (March and Olsen, 1989; Powel and DiMaggio, 1991; Putnam, 1993), this article explores how institutional norms, rules, values and behaviours have shaped institutional change within the Assembly. More specifically, this article examines the evolution of the main *loci* of power and influence within the Assembly, and the struggle of privileged groups to secure or enhance their positions of power and influence over resources during the institutional schism caused by the dismantling of the corporate body. Furthermore, it looks at individual actors' behaviour within a distinctively sensitive institutional climate, and at some institutional responses to different internal pressures for change.

The article highlights the important contributions that institutional adaptations add to recasting of new constitutional frameworks. Within the British constitutional context, this is particularly relevant since, as Johnson (2004, p. 13) argues, the survival of the British constitution, in its informal and uncodified form, is down to 'a long history of institutional adaptation and of skill in the accommodation of the existing political order to new demands expressed in society'. The fluid nature of Welsh devolution to date and the Assembly's rapid pace of institutional change provide the appropriate context for testing institutionalist approaches, which depart from the traditional formal-legalistic takes on the study of constitutions and political institutions, and focus instead on the more informal features of institutional life (rules, norms, behaviours, cultures, conventions and precedents).

This institutionalist account of the Assembly's development is novel. Its relevance comes from the fact that recent developments in Wales (the coalition negotiations following the third Assembly elections, the operation of coalition government, the formal separation of the executive and legislature, the enhanced legislative competencies and the establishment of *All Wales Convention* in 2007) – have all impacted on the constitutional configuration and operation of the Welsh polity. This invites analysis of the roles that institutions play within the political process, and of the relationship between political actors and the institutional contexts in which they operate.

## BACKGROUND

Administrative preparations for the third Assembly began with the establishment, in January 2005, of the Separation Main Programme Board, an Assembly Parliamentary Service (APS)/ Welsh Assembly Government (WAG) joint project dealing with various aspects of separation (resources, finance, procedures and legislation) in relation to the White Paper, and the subsequent Government of Wales Bill/Act. Consequently, the Assembly set up the Shadow Commission in May 2006, with the view to planning aspects of the future Assembly Commission's operation, as set out in clause 27 of the Government of Wales Bill ('the Bill'), then in the final stages of its passage through the House of Lords. This marked a significant step towards creating a modern parliamentary structure, with a parliamentary commission in charge of overseeing the administration of the institution, as opposed to the corporate body settlement which saw the civil service administering parliamentary business. At the same time, the Assembly set up its own advisory committee (the Standing Orders Committee – 'SOC') to recommend changes to the Standing Orders (Assembly Plenary, 17 May 2006) in order to meet the requirements of the new Act. This research focuses on the interactions between these structures, offering insight into their evolution during the separation process.

Academic interest in Welsh devolution has gradually moved from descriptive and historical accounts of devolution (Osmond, 1998; Morgan and Mungham, 2000), to the monitoring of its development (Constitution Unit, 1999–2005; Jones and Osmond, 2002; Osmond and Jones, 2003) and to a sophisticated discussion over its impact on various aspects of political life: policy process (Greer, 2004), electoral results, politics, electoral arrangements and public perceptions towards devolution (Wyn Jones, 2001; Wyn Jones and Scully, 2005, 2006; Scully et al., 2006; McAllister, 2003; McAllister and Cole, 2007), civic society engagement (Royles, 2007), the role of women politicians in constitutional change in Wales (Chaney et al., 2007; McAllister and Stirbu, 2007b), Assembly's legislative powers (Trench, 2005; Lambert and Navarro, 2007), and to debate over the future of devolution (Jeffery, 2005; McAllister, 2008; Trench, 2008). Scholars such as Rawlings (2003, 2005), Chaney et al. (2001), Chaney et al. (2007), Wyn Jones (2001), Royles (2007), McAllister (1999, 2000, 2003, 2008) and McAllister and Stirbu (2007a, 2007b) have stimulated a more robust institutional analysis of the Assembly that now forms the basis for further exploration into institutional design and constitutional recasting in Wales.


## METHODOLOGY

This article draws upon research on institutional developments within the National Assembly for Wales undertaken between 2005 and 2007. Employing mainly ethnographic methods, this research used participant and non-participant observation alongside twenty-four semi-structured elite interviews (between 2006 and 2008) with politicians, and government and parliamentary officials in order to get an insider's perspective and to understand the Assembly's internal restructuring process. The observational work focused on political and administrative aspects of the separation, which included the preparations made by the institution with the view to meeting the requirements of the 2006 Act, and the writing of the new Standing Orders. These snapshot ethnographies were conducted within the Assembly, the author taking part, for several months (June 2006, and between November 2006 and April 2007), in the day-to-day operations of the APS. They were focused mainly on capturing and understanding how the formal and informal institutional features evolved and changed during the timeframe selected. Particular attention was paid to the more informal (soft) aspects of institutional change – the behaviour of political actors, overall institutional climate, tensions and their sources, institutional resistance to change, power struggles among various actors. The research benefited from a high degree of access both to Assembly's day-to-day activities, and to official and operational documents. However, given the sensitivity of some of the information, important ethical and confidential issues are considered throughout. Hence the identity of the interviewees, some of the sources of information and the exact dates of some of the interviews are protected. In addition, given the relatively small size of the APS (the main research locus) and of the government unit involved in the separation project, for reasons of confidentiality references to government and parliamentary officials will be made in the most general of terms (that is 'Official, year').

## WELSH CONSTITUTIONAL DYNAMICS IN CONTEXT

The process of devolution in the UK has prompted significant territorial constitutional movements in Scotland and Wales in particular. Prior to 1997, the Scottish Constitutional Convention brought together political parties and civic society in a democratic and participatory exercise that ultimately shaped the devolutionary model for Scotland (see *Scotland's Parliament: Scotland's Right,* 1995). More recently, under the leadership of SNP First Minister, Alex Salmond, Scotland launched *Choosing Scotland's Future* – a national conversation aimed at instigating an inclusive public debate on matters related to Scotland's constitutional future, more precisely on Scotland's independence (Scottish Executive, 2007).

Wales lacked any serious or thorough constitutional deliberation prior to 1997 (McAllister, 2004, 2008), but has already seen two constitutional Acts passed through the UK Parliament (see Government of Wales Act 1998 and 2006), and an important inquiry on the powers and electoral arrangements of the National Assembly for Wales (Richard Commission, 2002–4). In addition, Wales's demo-cratically elected body has witnessed a decade marked by continuous internal reconfiguration and operational re-adjustments. Following the results of the 2007 elections and the subsequent coalition government negotiations, Plaid Cymru and Labour committed to establishing an *All Wales Convention* in readiness for a referendum on primary powers (as set out in Part IV of the 2006 Act), which might prompt another wave of structural and operational changes.

## UNPACKING POLITICAL INSTITUTIONS

The underlying assumption behind institutionalist perspectives in political science is that political institutions matter; that the organization of the polity is essential in the study of political life (March and Olsen, 1989; Powell and DiMaggio, 1991; Goodin, 1996; Peters, 2005). New institutionalism in particular sought to counter-act the shortcomings of behaviourist and rational choice approaches in political science, by using an eclectic range of theory and methods, and by proposing that the basic units of analysis should be 'rules, routines, norms, and identities of an "institution", rather than micro-rational individuals or macro-social forces' (March and Olsen, 2006, p. 16). In defining political institutions, the new institutionalism considers them as collections of interrelated norms, rules, routines, and structures of meaning and behaviour (March and Olsen, 1989, 2006), which represent elements of both stability and change in the institutional life. Institutional dynamics cannot be understood unless the role of the institutions in the process of change is clearly identified and explained (Goodin, 1996). This is particularly relevant in the context of the constitutional process in Wales; thus, in order to properly understand it, it is crucial to understand the role of the political institutions involved in the process – the Assembly being at the very heart of this process. Furthermore, in the face of change, institutional rules are sustained through identities, which give institutions a relative enduring nature (March and Olsen, 1989). However, the structures of resources and capabilities, as well as the institutional rules, norms and conventions form effective regulatory machinery, helping institutions in the process of incremental change and adaptation. Regulation, Pitkin (1967) argues, is shaped by constructive interpretation and forms the base for institutional legitimacy. This focus on the internal institutional regulatory system will help explain some of the dynamics within the Assembly during the separation (e.g. power struggles, resistance to change, tensions).

In addition, new institutionalism departs from utilitarian and reductionist views on politics that see political action as the result of self-interested actors, claiming instead that political behaviour is shaped and limited by institutional rules, norms and procedures (Putnam, 1993; March and Olsen, 2006). Moreover, the reallocation of institutional resources causes alliance formation, competition and often conflicts within and outside the organization (March and Olsen, 2006). These are most visible at critical junctures, when important changes are taking place. Furthermore, emphasizing the dynamic nature of political institutions, Thelen (2006) sees them as 'places of constant struggle'; institutions are established and evolve in climates of fluid interests and alliances, coalition and conflicts (cited in March and Olsen, 2006). Within the new institutionalist paradigm, describing how politics works, how conflicts emerge, how actors behave within the confines of political institutions, is essential in explaining and understanding political life (Eulau and March, in March and Olsen, 2006).

Devolution in Wales lends itself well to an institutionalist perspective, given the role the Assembly played in Welsh political life after 1997, and its continuous restructuring and internal adaptation. More significantly, the Assembly is a relatively young political institution that, arguably, developed new structures of behaviour and meaning, and a distinctive institutional culture (McAllister and Stirbu, 2007b). The analysis that follows focuses on structures of norms and rules, meaning and resources that constitute the Assembly's building blocks, and emphasizes the constitutional relevance of its re-adjustment process.

## FROM A 'VIRTUAL' TO A 'REAL' LEGISLATURE: INSTITUTIONAL DYNAMICS IN THE NATIONAL ASSEMBLY BETWEEN 2005 AND 2007

As noted, the timeframe for this research covers the period immediately after the publication of the *Better Governance for Wales White Paper*, when the Assembly started administrative and (later) political processes towards dismantling the corporate body. However, the Assembly had been undergoing significant institutional changes long before 2005. After its first review of procedures, the Assembly re-modelled itself to fit a more traditional parliamentary structure (see the *Assembly Review of Procedures*, 2002), functioning *de facto* as a 'virtual parliament', whilst remaining constrained by its *de jure* the corporate body status (Rawlings, 2003; Osmond, 2005). Moreover, as earlier studies (McAllister and Stirbu, 2007b) suggest – and the evidence from interviews also reveals, the Richard Commission Report (2004) also triggered a series of operational changes, inviting a more thorough approach to the scrutiny process, the organization of business, and the focus and agenda of committees' work.

## NORMS, RULES, PROCEDURES AND THE CONSTRAINTS OF THE CORPORATE BODY

Proponents of historical institutionalism argue that early choices in institutional life will dictate the future evolution of the institution (Krasner, 1988; Pierson, 2000). Hence, the model put in place by the 1998 Act was bound to shape the subsequent evolution of the Assembly. Literature on Welsh devolution highlights tensions and operational difficulties created by the endemic conflict within the Assembly's corporate structure (executive/legislature struggle), whilst appreciating the merits of the corporate model (inclusiveness was one of them), critics have argued that it impaired the thoroughness of the scrutiny process, for instance (Rawlings, 2003; Richard Commission, 2004; McAllister and Stirbu, 2007a).

This tension deepened even further towards the end of the Assembly's second term. Although both government and parliamentary sides had agreed upon the goals of separation, the separation process was often hindered by various institutional constraints. Dividing the Assembly's resources, for instance, caused serious 'frictions', as one official put it, even over matters that seem at first trivial (access to WAG and Assembly buildings in Cathays Park and Cardiff Bay, the fifth floor in the Bay (where ministers' offices were located), the shuttle bus that connected the offices in Cardiff Bay (parliamentary side) and Cathays Park (government side)), but which constituted thorny issues at the time (Interview with Official, 2008). Given the complexity of the corporate body arrangement, other, non-physical assets (e.g. the information and communication technologies systems, the security and access of personnel) developed into integrated corporate services that were very difficult to separate. There is a very deep and symbolic value in this battle for resources. As one official admits, the stakes were higher for the parliamentary side – allegedly, the smaller and weaker side – which was breaking up from the resourceful corporate body dominated in terms of numbers, power and resources by the Welsh Assembly Government (Interview with Official, 2008). Hence it was essential that the new parliamentary institution secured adequate resources and negotiated its power base carefully.

Similarly, on the procedural side, Jenny Randerson AM, the Chair of the SOC admits that fully grasping the implications of separation represented the 'earliest sticking point', which accounted for tensions during the early stages of the negotiations (Interview, 20 March 2007). As means of illustration, the Business Minister strongly insisted that the Assembly's Standing Orders should not impose obligations on the government since this would be a separate organization with its own rules and norms. However, the strong line taken by the government side unsettled the opposition committee members, who were initially reluctant to give up any means of control over the government (such as formal requirements for the First Minister to announce any changes in the cabinet, or the allocation of plenary time for government and opposition parties). Retrospectively, most of these tensions were regarded as futile battles over 'silly things' (Jenny Randerson AM, March 2007). Several officials agree that once the general principles of the separation were fully understood, and once people started thinking outside the corporate model box (i.e. the Government has a level of agreement [a mandate] to pass its agenda through the Assembly and the opposition has rights to challenge and scrutinize), the negotiations became less confrontational.

These illustrations reveal the complexities behind the process of administrative and political separation, which involved not only bargaining for – and the division of – physical assets, but also a certain process of unlearning and forgetting habits and behaviours acquired during the corporate body days. They are also indicative of the constraints imposed by the complex set of formal rules and procedures associated with the corporate body. The idiosyncrasies associated with the Assembly's unusual status are quite clear; on the one side, the endemic conflict between executive and legislative arms acted as a permanent institutional irritant and trigger for change, whilst the constraining and complex framework was often a barrier for change.

## INSTITUTIONAL CONTEXT: TENSE POLITICAL CLIMATE

If the corporate body represented a systemic flaw that triggered a series of changes and shaped the evolution of the institution to a great extent, the rather tense political climate during the separation process is also significant to the present discussion. First, the party-political arithmetic of the Assembly was particularly finely balanced in the second part of 2006. One official noted:

> The [minority] government was often beaten on the floor of the Assembly, the business statement almost never got through and government motions were passed through the Assembly, [yet] amended beyond all recognition (2008).

Not surprisingly, during the negotiations for the Standing Orders, the government's agenda was clear – in the view of the same official, the goal was to make things easier for the government and to get the business through (Interview with official, 2008). Jenny Randerson AM also emphasized the conflicting agendas of the negotiating parties:

> We seemed to have this fundamental divide between government – and that's including government back-benchers – who wanted to cut anyone other than government out of all the action [. . .] So we had had that versus the opposition, wanting to ensure that with separation, we would have massive safeguards, by increasing the role of the Assembly in certain ways. (Interview, 20 March 2007)

This is indicative of how institutional contexts, influenced here by the political arithmetic at a certain moment in time, can influence the agenda and the behaviour of the main political actors involved. Secondly, evidence from observational research points to tensions arising from the often overlapping of roles of the structures of power operating in the Assembly, the clash of personalities and conflicting visions about the Assembly's future. The main institutional structures involved in separation were, at administrative level, the government officials on the one side, and the parliamentary (APS) officials on the other side. At political level, the Welsh Assembly Government (through the Business Minister), the Shadow Commission and the Standing Orders Committee were, perhaps, the principal actors in positions of power. Notably, there is no mention of the House Committee [HC] here, although the committee had already undertaken some work towards administrative separation (see the HC Annual Report for 2006). However, with the establishment of the Shadow Commission, the committee agreed that the 'matters relating to after the Assembly Commission had been formed should be considered by the Shadow Commission' (see HC Minutes for 18 May 2006). Hence the role of the HC in the future planning of the Assembly was significantly reduced.

The establishment of the Shadow Commission revealed a clash of personalities and conflicting visions surrounding the future of the Assembly, between individuals in privileged positions, in particular between the Presiding Officer (PO) and the Deputy Presiding Officer (DPO). Each had his own power base. The PO chaired the Shadow Commission, which was to become an extremely influential body in planning for the Assembly's future, whereas the DPO chaired the House Committee, which became almost powerless in the process of separation. On many occasions, the DPO, who was not included in the SOC membership either, publicly expressed his discontent at how the Assembly and those in positions of power were dealing with issues of separation, and how he felt sidelined in the third Assembly planning process (see 17 May and 15 November Plenary debates, 2006). This allegedly accounted for unprecedented tensions between the two most senior members of the Assembly as a legislature, who 'had completely fallen out and were not prepared to work with each other' (Interview with official, 2008). The Presiding Officer denied a personality clash with the DPO, claiming that they just had 'a different view of what the Assembly should be about' (Lord Dafydd Elis-Thomas, cited in the *Western Mail*, 29 September, 2006). This is relevant in the context of planning for the Assembly's future, since the 'winning' vision would most likely mark the Assembly's subsequent development to great extent.

The evidence from both participant observation and from interviews with officials reveals that this political turmoil impacted on the overall organizational climate as well (particularly on the parliamentary side). One official was of the view that these tensions could have been avoided had the Bill been more prescriptive and included provisions about the establishment of the Shadow Commission (Interview with official, 2006). This alludes to the fact that a statutory framework for the operation of the Shadow Commission might have endowed it with more legitimacy. Another official highlighted how powerful change driven by legislation makes organizations less resistant in the face of change (Interview with official, 2008). These illustrations are symptomatic of institutions as 'places of constant struggle' and reflect the fluidity of interests, the formation of conflicts and coalitions at critical moments of change.

## INSTITUTIONAL CHANGE: BECOMING A MODERN PARLIAMENTARY BODY

Against this backdrop of complex institutional settings and a tense political climate, the writing of the Assembly's new Standing Orders and the recasting of its internal operation and organizational structure were subject to intense bargaining between individual and collective actors. As expected in any case of major reform, planning for the Assembly's future, was surrounded by some controversy and critique too. External perceptions were that there was insufficient consultation on the drafting of new Standing Orders (Lambert, 2006); from the inside, some aspects of the Shadow Commission's work spurred tensions and suspicions. The first indication of a significant change, not merely of a process of institutional adaptation to a new legislative framework, came when the Shadow Commission publicized the specifications for the new (rebranded) position of a Chief Executive/Clerk of the Assembly. Many, including the former Clerk himself, perceived this as a fairly decisive signal that the Shadow Commission wanted 'someone with a different skill set' from the existing post holder (Paul Silk, former Clerk of the Assembly, cited in the *Western Mail*, 2 September, 2006). The imminent departure of the Clerk (Paul Silk did not apply for the new position that was then advertised), and the departure of other senior officials from the APS (in less than twelve months, the APS lost five of their most senior people), left the organization somehow at the discretion of the political actors, thus fuelling the staff's fears of political interference in the administration of the institution. As one official pointed out, 'if you want to disarm an organisation you create fear among the senior management' (2008).

Drawing attention to a certain 'stickiness' in politics, Pierson (2000, p. 490) claims that 'institutional arrangements in politics are typically hard to change'. This is down to systems of 'nested rules' (i.e. statutory frameworks, organizational culture, and members' identification with institutional norms and values) that become entrenched in the institutional life (Goodin, 1996). At an individual level, change brings along fear of the unknown, which becomes an important factor in causing resistance to change. In terms of organizational behaviour, most of the Assembly staff were faced with a set of unknown variables: their future career prospects (since, with separation, APS staff were to lose their privileged and secure civil service status), the new direction and values of the institution (the re-branding of the top official position was an indication that the new architects of the Assembly wanted a more dynamic, managerial style in the organization), and fears of political interference. In terms of the future career prospects of the parliamentary officials, some important safety nets were put in place (that is, staff had twelve months in which they could opt to return to the civil service in the WAG and, future APS pension rights were to be similar to the civil service ones). However, more problematic were the loss of senior and experienced staff and the questioning of the institutional identity, since the Shadow Commission's work included reviews, and internal 'health-checks' – some carried out by external consultants (see the Shadow Commission Minutes, June 2006). In the view of one official, there were doubts with regards to the Shadow Commission's ability to fully grasp the reality of the APS in order to make adequate decisions for the future (2008). This type of suspicion and resistance was partly caused by the idea that change came from outside, and that the outside environment was questioning internal rules and values. Not surprisingly, this brought along a re-enforcement of the organization's identity and values. Some officials mentioned their identification and loyalty to 'an organisation that promoted strong and traditional parliamentary values and culture' (2008), whilst other officials expressed concerns with regards to the losses on the parliamentary side during the separation process (in terms of resources, culture and identity). These illustrations evoke new institutionalist concerns over the importance of members' loyalty and identification with the institution, which, in March and Olsen's (1989) view, sustain the organization through moments of critical change, thus ensuring the relatively enduring nature of institutions.

In terms of drafting the Assembly's new set of operational procedures, the work of the Standing Orders Committee reveals interesting features in support of institutionalist claims that at times of change, privileged groups will use their position of power to re-enforce their status (Goodin, 1996) The committee had to work under constant pressure (there was the imperative to reach consensus – and the timescale was extremely tight), which meant that striking a deal on a particular Order was not always easy. Several officials commented that the negotiations were 'nasty' at times, or 'extremely fiery'. One of the criticisms addressed to the SOC at the time was the lack of transparency of its operations (most committee meetings were held in private) and the lack of open and thorough consultation. Jocelyn Davies AM, an opposition member in the committee, later admitted:

I did not want those meetings to be informal [. . .] but after I'd stormed out of a meeting I was very glad they were informal because they were not pleasant. They were confrontational [. . .] and very often I could see the staff that were supporting us were very frustrated as well. (Interview, 22 July 2008)

The writing of the new Standing Orders represented a major constitutional recasting for the Assembly. Although the committee did not have the luxury of a complete blank-slate, as one official notes – 'it was part blank sheet, part holding on to things from the previous Assembly that Members like, and part cherry picking from other institutions, mainly from Scotland and Westminster' (Interview with official, 2008) – the new Standing Orders devised operating procedures that departed from the status quo (e.g. the committee system, the conduct of business), and novel processes for which there was hardly any precedent (the Legislative Competence Order procedure).

It is beyond the scope of this article to make a substantive analysis of Standing Orders. Rather, the present discussion offers some insight into the process that shaped the Assembly's new internal 'operating skeleton'. As mentioned, this process was characterised by conflict, tension and harsh bargaining between various power structures. The negotiations for the Standing Orders in particular were characterized by a certain imbalance of power and influence. For, although at stake was the future operation of a parliamentary institution, as some officials perceived, the government side (i.e. WAG officials and the Business Minister) was, allegedly, 'the most powerful player' (Interview, official, 2007). Another official makes an important remark when noting that 'for the WAG, separation was business as usual' whereas for the APS, as a much smaller organization and much more political, the significance was greater and the climate was different (Interview, 2008). Commenting on the imbalanced access to support and legal advice during the negotiations, Jocelyn Davies AM claimed:

> there was no comparison. I think the difference was enormous. And she [The Business Minister] got lawyers and it was in the government's interest to get all her points through. I think that the legal support that we had . . . I don't mean to criticise . . . but it did feel as if we didn't have options to put in front of us in the same way as the Business Minister. (Interview July, 2008)

Nevertheless, from the parliamentary support perspective, this could be symptomatic of the institutional constraints placed on parliamentary staff (including here, the provision of legal advice), whose duty to impartiality prevented them from offering political advice and support for opposition parties for instance. This reflects inherent tensions that arise at moments of change, when privileged groups (in this case the Business Minister) use resources (legal services) in their favour (to get government's points through) in order to secure their position of power (i.e. no vote on the business statement in Plenary, where, previously, the minority government was often beaten).

## CONCLUSIONS

This article has examined the recent institutional recasting of the National Assembly for Wales – a political institution whose initial design contradicted all normal constitutional practices, and whose subsequent development reflected the vibrant process of constitutional adaptation in Wales. This insight into the internal development of the Assembly has reinforced some important themes of new institutionalist perspectives. The Assembly's initial design influenced its subsequent development, the corporate body status acting as a permanent institutional irritant throughout its life, causing operational tensions (for example in the scrutiny process, see Richard Commission, 2004; McAllister and Stirbu, 2007), as well as tensions related to institutional change (especially in relation to the balance of resources and expertise available to the two *de facto* arms of the Assembly). Furthermore, the reconfiguration of the Assembly since 1999 reveals some important general dynamics that political institutions might experience during the process of change. Their building blocks (structures, meaning, behaviour and norms) are subject to political bargaining, tensions and conflict on the one side, and constrain and shape the behaviour of political actors on the other. When outsiders, or even insiders in positions of power, question the institutional identity and values, the organization often resists change and questions the legitimacy of those that are shaping change. This research has also underlined the importance of institutional settings or contexts in the process of change, offering illustrations of how systemic barriers (such as the corporate body), or the overall organizational climate shape individual actors' agendas and behaviours.

Through an examination of the internal institutional dynamics during the Assembly's separation process, the implications of institutional adaptation on the broader constitutional process can be gauged. The link between constitutions (regarded here in the broad Aristotelian sense as 'the arrangement of the offices in a state') and political institutions is relatively straightforward. Constitutional settlements exist within, and shape political institutions – the National Assembly itself was established by a constitutional Act (Government of Wales Act, 1998), which shaped its internal architecture and provided a framework for its operation. Moreover, political institutions ensure that constitutional principles and provisions are put into practice. Furthermore, political institutions are both major actors on the constitutional arena (triggering debates or internally adapting to change) and arenas of constitutional debate. The Assembly's evolution to date suggests that it has shaped the Wales' constitutional landscape to a great extent, by moving towards a more traditional parliamentary structure and pushing its operation framework to its limits during the so-called 'virtual parliament' stage of devolution (Osmond, 2005). In addition, the Assembly's shortcomings triggered the first serious post-devolution constitutional debates in Wales (via the Richard Commission, 2002–4) (see McAllister and Stirbu, 2008).

This article has added a new perspective on the development of the National Assembly and on the wider constitutional landscape. The separation, which saw the dismantling of the corporate body, and established a 'new' political institution more in line with other modern parliamentary institutions, was a landmark event in the Assembly's short life to date. This insight into the separation process reveals political actors' behaviour in complex institutional settings and, how institutional norms and values limit and shape political behaviour. This re-affirms the importance of institutions in the political arena, confirming the main principles of new institutionalism.

## ACKNOWLEDGEMENT

I would like to thank Professor Laura McAllister for her very helpful comments and guidance, and to the anonymous reviewers for their very constructive comments.

## NOTES

[1]  One of the most important provisions of the White Paper was the commitment to formally end the corporate body legal status of the National Assembly – this process was subsequently known as the *separation project* and included preparations for the formal administrative, political and procedural split of the corporate body.

## REFERENCES

Bulmer, S. J. (1998). 'New institutionalism and the governance of the Single European Market', *Journal of European Public Policy*, 5, 3, 365–86.
Chaney, P., Hall, T. and Pithouse, A. (2001). *New Governance – New Democracy? Post-Devolution Wales*, Cardiff: University of Wales Press.

Chaney, P., Mackay, F. and McAllister, L. (2007). *Women, Politics and Constitutional Change. The First Years of the National Assembly for Wales*, Cardiff: Cardiff University Press.

Constitution Unit (1999–2008). *Devolution Monitoring Reports 1999–2005 and 2006–2008.*

Dimitrova, A. (2002). 'Enlargement, institution-building and the EU's administrative capacity requirement', *West European Politics*, 25, 4, 171–90.

Elster, J., Offe, C. and Preus, U. K. (1998). *Institutional Design in Post-Communist Societies. Rebuilding the Ship at Sea*, Cambridge: Cambridge University Press.

Eriksen, E. O., Fossum, J. E. and Menendez, A. J. (eds) (2004). *Developing a Constitution for Europe*, London: Routledge.

Flinders, M. (2004). 'Distributed public governance in Britain', *Public Administration*, 82, 4, 883–909.

Gonenc, L. (2002). *Prospects for Constitutionalism in Post-communist Countries*, The Hague: Martinus Nijhoff Publishers.

Goodin, R. E. (1996). 'Institutions and their design', in R. E. Goodin (ed.), *The Theory of Institutional Design*, Cambridge: Cambridge University Press.

Greer, S. L. (2004). *Territorial Politics and Health Policy: UK Health Policy in Comparative Perspective*, Manchester: Manchester University Press.

HMSO (1998). *Government of Wales Act*, London: HMSO.

HMSO (2006). *Government of Wales Act*, London: HMSO.

Jeffery, C. (2005). 'Richard's radical recipe', in Osmond. J. (ed.), *Welsh Politics Come of Age*, Cardiff: Institute of Welsh Affairs.

Johnson, J. (2001). 'Path contingency in post-communist transformations', *Comparative Politics*, 33, 3, 253–74.

Johnson, N. (2004). *Reshaping the British Constitution*, Basingstoke: Palgrave Macmillan.

Jones, J. B. and Osmond, J. (eds) (2002). *Building a Civic Culture. Institutional Change, Policy Development and Political Dynamics in the National Assembly for Wales*, Cardiff: Institute of Welsh Affairs and Welsh Governance Centre.

Krasner, S. (1988). 'Sovereignty: An Institutional Perspective', *Comparative Political Studies*, 21, 1, 66–94.

Lambert, D. (2006) Speech during Session 2 (Devolution Act 2: Towards a New Constitutional Settlement?) of the Wales Governance Centre Conference, 7–8 July 2006, *www.cardiff.ac.uk/euros/research/researchcentres/welshgovernance/events/conference2006.html* (accessed September 2008).

Lambert, D. and Navarro, M. (2007). 'Holding the reins', *Agenda*, winter, 16–19.

Lane, J. E., (1996). *Constitutions and Political Theory*, Manchester: Manchester University Press.

Lijphart, A. and Waisman, C. H. (1996). *Institutional Design in New Democracies: Eastern Europe and Latin America*, Boulder, CO: Westview Press.

March, J. G. and Olsen, J. P. (1989). *Rediscovering Institutions: The Organizational Basis of Politics*, New York: Free Press.

March, J. G. and Olsen, J. P. (2006). 'Elaborating the "new institutionalism"', in Rhodes et al. (eds), *The Oxford Handbook of Political Institutions*, Oxford: Oxford University Press.

McAllister, L. (1999). 'The road to Cardiff Bay: the process of establishing the National Assembly for Wales', *Parliamentary Affairs*, 53, 4, 635–48.

McAllister, L. (2000). 'The new politics in Wales: rhetoric or reality?', *Parliamentary Affairs*, 53, 3, 591–604.

McAllister, L. (2003). 'Steady state or second order? The 2003 Elections to the National Assembly for Wales', *The Political Quarterly*, 75, 1, 73–82.

McAllister, L. (2004). 'The Richard Commission – Wales's alternative constitutional convention?', *Contemporary Wales*, 17, 128–39.

McAllister, L. (2005). 'The value of independent commissions: an insider's perspective on the Richard Commission', *Parliamentary Affairs*, 58,1, 38–52.

McAllister, L. (2008). 'Igniting change', *Agenda*, Winter, 16–18.

McAllister, L. and Cole, M. (2007). 'Pioneering new politics or rearranging the deckchairs? The 2007 National Assembly for Wales Election and Results', *The Political Quarterly*, 78, 4, 536–46.

McAllister, L. and Stirbu, D. S. (2007a). 'Developing devolution's scrutiny potential: a comparative evaluation of the National Assembly for Wales's Subject Committees', *Policy and Politics*, 35, 2, 289–309.

McAllister, L. and Stirbu, D. S. (2007b). 'Opportunities for gender innovations in a new political space', *The International Journal of Interdisciplinary Social Sciences*, 1, CG Publisher.

McAllister, L. and Stirbu, D. S. (2008). 'Influence, impact and legacy: assessing the Richard Commission's contribution to Wales' evolving constitution', *Representation*, 44, 3, 209–24.

Morgan, K. and Mungham, G. (2000). *Redesigning Democracy. The Making of the Welsh Assembly*, Bridgend: Seren.

National Assembly for Wales (2001). *Assembly Review of Procedures*, Cardiff: NAfW.

National Assembly for Wales (2007). *Standing Orders of the National Assembly for Wales*, Cardiff: NAfW.

Osmond, J. (ed.) (1998). *The National Assembly Agenda. A Handbook for the First Four Years*, Cardiff: Institute of Welsh Affairs.

Osmond, J. (2005). 'Virtual parliament', *Agenda*, Summer, 25–8.

Osmond, J. and Jones, J. B. (2003). *Birth of Welsh Democracy. The First Term of the National Assembly for Wales*, Cardiff: Institute of Welsh Affairs and Welsh Governance Centre.

Peters, B. G. (2005). *Institutional Theory in Political Science: The "New" Institutionalism*, London: Pinter.

Pierson, P. (2000) 'The limits of design: explaining institutional origins and change', *Governance: An International Journal of Policy and Administration*, 13, 4. 475–99.

Pitkin, H. (1967). *The Concept of Representation*, Berkeley, CA: University of California Press.

Pollack, M. A. (1996). 'The new institutionalism and EC governance: the promise and limits of institutional analysis', *Governance*, 9, 4, 429–58.

Powell, W. W. and DiMaggio, P. (1991). *The New Institutionalism in Organisational Analysis,* Chicago, IL: University of Chicago Press.

Putnam, R. (1993). *Making Democracy Work. Civic Traditions in Modern Italy*, Princeton, NJ: Princeton University Press.

Rawlings, R. (2003). *Delineating Wales. Constitutional, Legal and Administrative Aspects of National Devolution*, Cardiff: University of Wales Press.

Rawlings, R. (2005). 'Hastening slowly: the next phase of Welsh devolution', *Public Law*, 824–52.

Rhodes, R. A. W., Binder, S. A. and Rockman, B. A. (eds) (2006). *The Oxford Handbook of Political Institutions*, Oxford: Oxford University Press.

Richard Commission (2004). *The Report of the Richard Commission on the Powers and Electoral Arrangements of the National Assembly for Wales*, London: The Stationery Office.

Royles, E. (2007). *Revitalising Democracy: Devolution and Civil Society in Wales*, Cardiff: University of Wales Press.

Scottish Executive (2007). *Choosing Scotland's Future: A National Conversation: Independence and Responsibility in the Modern World*, Edinburgh: Scottish Executive.

Scully, R., Wyn Jones, R. and Trystan, D. (2006). 'Turnout, participation and legitimacy in post-devolution Wales', *British Journal of Political Science*, 34, 3, 519–37.

Shvetsova, O. (2002) 'Institutions and coalition building in post-communist transitions', in A. Reynolds (ed.), *Architecture of Democracy. Constitutional Design, Conflict Management and Democracy*, Oxford: Oxford University Press.

Thelen, K. (2006). 'Institutions and social change', in I. Shapiro and S. Skowronek (eds), *Crafting and Operating Institutions*, New York: New York University Press.

Trench, A. (2005). 'The Assembly's future as a legislative body', in Osmond, J. (ed.), *Welsh Politics Come of Age*, Cardiff: Institute of Welsh Affairs.

Trench, A. (2008). 'Murphy's Law', *Agenda,* Spring, 16–17.

Wales Office (2005). *Better Governance for Wales,* White Paper, London: HMSO.

Wyn Jones, R. (2001). 'On process, events and unintended consequences: national identity and the politics of Welsh devolution', *Scottish Affairs*, 37, 34–57.

Wyn Jones, R. and Scully, R. (2005). 'What do people want?', in Osmond. J. (ed.), *Welsh Politics Come of Age*, Cardiff: Institute of Welsh Affairs.

Wyn Jones, R. and Scully, R. (2006). 'Devolution and electoral politics in Scotland and Wales', *Publius: The Journal of Federalism*, 36, 1, 115–34.

# 6. PLAID CYMRU AND THE CHALLENGES OF ADAPTING TO POST-DEVOLUTION WALES

*Anwen Elias*

## ABSTRACT

*This article examines how Plaid Cymru, the Welsh nationalist party, has adapted to post-devolution Wales, and the challenges it has faced in doing so. One aspect of party adaptation is focused upon, namely the adaptation of party goals. The main argument advanced is that the difficulties that Plaid Cymru has faced since 1999 – such as a declining electoral performance, internal divisions over programmatic priorities and party strategy, and leadership struggles – are not unique. Rather, they are difficulties that many political parties, regardless of their origin or ideological orientation, face when they attempt to adapt their goals to major changes in their operating environments. The article's findings provide preliminary insights into how minority nationalist parties more generally adapt as they evolve from being parties of protest to being parties in power.*

## INTRODUCTION

The creation of the National Assembly for Wales (NAW) in 1999 created a new institutional arena in Wales to which political parties of all persuasions had to adapt. There has been some scholarly work that has examined how statewide parties have sought to adapt their organizational and electoral strategies to post-devolution politics in Wales (Laffin et al., 2003; Fabre et al., 2005). Much less attention has been paid, however, to how Plaid Cymru, the Welsh nationalist party, has changed and evolved over the same period of time. A few authors have discussed Plaid Cymru's electoral performance in different Assembly elections (McAllister, 2001a; Wyn Jones and Scully, 2004b). However, there has been no in-depth systematic study of how Plaid Cymru sought to adapt to its new political status in Welsh politics post-1999.

That such an analysis is overdue is suggested by the contradictory nature of Plaid Cymru's electoral and political fortunes since 1999. On the one hand, Plaid Cymru has experienced a striking transformation in its electoral and political status. Prior to 1999, Plaid Cymru was a relatively marginal political force within Welsh politics. In the 1997 general election, the party polled 9.9 per cent of the Welsh vote, and came a distant second place behind the Labour Party's commanding 54.7 per cent share of the votes. In the first elections to the NAW, however, the party managed to poll just over 29 per cent of the vote and returned seventeen Assembly Members (AMs) (out of a total of sixty seats), making it the main opposition party within the NAW. The result was described by Plaid Cymru's leader at the time, Dafydd Wigley, as a 'quiet earthquake' which heralded a new era of Welsh politics dominated by a resurgent Welsh nationalist party (quoted in Wyn Jones and Trystan, 2000). Eight years later, Plaid Cymru seemed to have fulfilled this prediction when it entered into coalition government with the Welsh Labour Party after the 2007 NAW elections. This constituted the party's first experience of coalition government, and Plaid Cymru's position as a major political player in Welsh politics seemed to have been confirmed.

On the other hand, however, observers of Welsh politics will be very aware that Plaid Cymru has faced a number of difficulties since 1999. For one thing, the party has been unable to sustain the levels of electoral popularity witnessed in the first Assembly elections. The party's representation in the NAW fell from seventeen AMs to twelve AMs in 2003; a partial electoral recovery in 2007 saw this number increase to fifteen AMs. Since 1999, the party has also suffered from several leadership struggles and bitter internal debates over its programme, strategy and organizational structures. These observations do not sit easily with the idea that Plaid Cymru has 'come of age' in post-devolution Wales (McAllister, 2001a).

This article aims to explain this contradiction in Plaid Cymru's electoral and political fortunes in post-devolution Wales. In order to do so, it examines how Plaid Cymru has sought to adapt to devolution in Wales, and the challenges it has faced in doing so. The next section outlines a framework of analysis for evaluating party adaptation. It draws on a large literature on political party change, as well as on a more specific literature which has examined how 'new' or 'small' political parties (for example, Green parties and extreme right parties) have changed as they have grown in electoral and political significance, have secured institutional representation and have crossed the threshold of government and participated in coalitions. The article will focus in particular on how political parties adapt their goals in response to changes in their operating environment.[1] This literature gives rise to the following hypothesis that will be tested in the empirical section of the article: *all political parties, regardless of their origin or ideological orientation, face a common set of challenges when they try to adapt to a major change in their operating environment.* A series of more detailed propositions are formulated about the precise ways in which political parties are expected to adapt their goals in response to changes in their electoral and political status, or the institutional environment in which they are active. The challenges and dilemmas often associated with goal change are also identified.

The next section then analyses the ways in which Plaid Cymru has adapted its goals within the Welsh political arena since 1999, and the challenges it has faced in doing so.[2] After providing a brief summary of the party's political and electoral history prior to devolution, the article examines Plaid Cymru's behaviour in the first and second terms of the NAW in turn.[3] It is argued that Plaid Cymru's difficulties in responding to its new status as main party of opposition within the NAW are typical of the problems of adaptation any political party faces when its status changes very suddenly from being a marginal political force to being a central player in a political system. The contestation of party strategy and policy prioritization, party organization and leadership are certainly not unique to Plaid Cymru, but are part of the course for political parties attempting to make the difficult transition from protest to power. The shock of electoral decline in the 2003 NAW elections, followed by equally disappointing performances in European and general elections in June 2004 and May 2005 respectively, served as a catalyst for a far-reaching re-assessment of the party's role and ambitions in post-devolution Wales. It took Plaid Cymru until the end of the Assembly's second term to fully appreciate the challenges of being an aspiring party of regional government. This section concludes with a consideration of Plaid Cymru's first year in coalition government. The analysis highlights how the party dealt with the hard choices associated with deciding to enter public office (Strøm and Müller, 1999), and examines to what degree the party has already encountered the dilemmas that often accompany such a role. Finally, the article considers what this case study of Plaid Cymru can tell us more generally about how minority nationalist parties adapt as they evolve from being protest parties on the margins of a political system, to being parties in power.

## ASSESSING PARTY ADAPTATION: A FRAMEWORK

A substantial body of theoretical and empirical literature on political parties has argued that external shocks are produced as a result of important changes in a party's electoral fortunes or political status; failing to respond to such new situations risks the party's survival (Panebianco, 1988). In other words, significant electoral growth/decline, or securing/losing representation or office incumbency, may trigger new pressures that will force political parties to adapt to their new political and institutional environments.

Pedersen (1982) has linked these pressures to the different thresholds that political parties pass during their lifetime. He distinguishes between different stages in a political party's evolution, marked by the passing of different thresholds.[4] This model has been revised by Deschouwer (2008, pp. 3–4) to further specify the notion of 'relevance' in Pedersen's work,[5] and add a fifth threshold, namely the threshold of *governance* (when a party succeeds in entering government). Passing different thresholds will generate a new set of opportunities and constraints for a political party, and will modify the way a party prioritizes its goals. The notion of political parties as goal-pursuing entities is well established in the academic literature. Strøm (1990) distinguishes between three types of goals that political parties can pursue: votes, office incumbency and policy influence. Whilst vote-seeking parties aim to maximize their electoral support, office-seeking parties will prioritize the pursuit of public office and policy-seeking parties will aim to maximize their influence on public policy.

A party's goals are not static. Rather, they will change depending on the institutional setting a party finds itself in. It is helpful to think of these changes in institutional settings in terms of the different thresholds a political party passes, as outlined above. Passing different thresholds will prompt parties to re-think their goal prioritization. Thus, for example, a vote-seeking party that acquires sufficient electoral support to pass the threshold of representation may switch its attention to enhancing its policy influence, and/or occupying public office. A party that is elected to government will have achieved its office-seeking goal, and is likely to concentrate on shaping the government's policy output. It is also possible, of course, that a party will pass back over different thresholds, for example by not being re-selected as a coalition partner or by failing to maintain the electoral support necessary to retain representation in a legislative arena. Such failures will similarly prompt parties to re-assess their prioritization of goals, and adopt new strategies befitting of their new political, electoral and institutional status.

Moreover, whilst some political parties may choose to pursue all three goals simultaneously, it is more likely that they will prioritize one goal over another (Strøm, 1990; Appleton and Ward, 1997). For example, a party needs to get at least some degree of electoral success before attempting to gain office and to influence policy outcomes (Strøm and Müller, 1999; Elias and Tronconi, 2006). In particular, for 'niche' parties that raise novel concerns and limit themselves to a restricted set of issues (Meguid, 2005, pp. 347–8), vote maximization often means having to moderate your ideas in order to appeal to a broader electoral constituency. Securing votes may also mean a party having to broaden its policy repertoire beyond its 'core business' in order to compete with other political parties on a whole range of issues (Harmel, 1985; Müller-Rommel and Pridham, 1991; Poguntke, 2002; Müller-Rommel, 2002; Heinisch, 2003). Only when a certain level of electoral success has been achieved will parties be 'relevant' players in the party system, in the sense that they can force other political parties to respond to the issues they raise or affect the range of possible coalition agreements (Sartori, 1976; Deschouwer, 2008). It is at that stage that a party may switch its attention to achieving public office and policy influence. Some political parties may choose to exercise policy influence through participating in legislative bargaining with governing parties. However, a more effective way of influencing policy-making is by being in public office; maximizing policy influence may therefore depend on occupying public office (Strøm and Müller, 1999, p. 6).

However, whilst political parties choose to pursue one or more of the goals outlined above, doing so will not always be straightforward. On the contrary, political parties that pursue different goals face several difficult trade-offs (Strøm, 1990; Strøm and Müller, 1999). Firstly, for parties that want to maximize their vote share, moderating and broadening their political programmes may make strategic sense, but such a move may not go down well with core supporters who feel the party to be diluting fundamental party principles. This dilemma is likely to be particularly acute for niche parties attempting to make the transition from being single-issue parties to catch-all parties with a broad programmatic repertoire. This tension will be exacerbated in the case of parties who have to compromise on key party commitments once in government, or in order to secure policy influence through legislative bargaining. The experience of several Green parties in government is illustrative of such a dilemma. Many Green parties that were required to compromise on their policy agenda once in coalition government were punished in subsequent elections by their core electorate for having abandoned what were deemed to be fundamental Green values for the short-term gains of being in public office (Mair, 2001; Rihoux and Rüdig, 2006). Engaging in legislative bargaining or being in government with established political parties may also be difficult for core supporters to accept, especially if the party has a strong anti-system opposition to the political establishment (Heinisch, 2003, p. 102). A party that is deemed by its supporters to have become too mainstream may face competition from new political groups claiming to represent the original core values of the party. Such a risk is accentuated when in government, as parties find themselves forced to accept key policy compromises, or even justify policies that run counter to their own ideological predispositions (Mair, 2001, p. 111). In short, becoming 'established' could well lead to the undermining of the party's initial electoral appeal (Smith, 1989).

Political parties that are electorally successful enough to be seen as a threat to established political parties often have to face the prospect that their partisan rivals will adapt their strategies to deliberately fend off this new electoral threat. Established political parties can either ignore the issues raised by a competitor, adopt a similar position in an attempt to draw voters away from their competitor, or take a divergent policy position in an attempt to encourage flight from a rival party (Downs, 2001; Downs, 1957; Kitschelt, 1994; Meguid, 2005, p. 348). The former strategy in particular has frequently been adopted by established political parties as a way of undermining niche party ownership of a particular issue. For example, Bale (2007) documents how many established centre-right parties in Western Europe have responded to the rise of far-right parties by adopting many of their themes, such as immigration. Initial electoral success, therefore, may lead to a competition for the party's political space. If established parties are successful in undermining the appeal of a competitor, then the latter may well find itself struggling to define a distinctive political agenda which is distinct from that of its established rival.

Vote maximization, office incumbency and the pursuit of policy influence can all, therefore, have a damaging effect on a political party's electoral popularity. Electoral decline as a result of the pursuit of any of these goals can act as a further external shock that can prompt a new wave of ideological change in political parties (Panebianco, 1988; Harmel and Janda, 1994; Adams et al., 2006). Whether such a change will be a return to the traditional ideological values of the party, or whether the party will stick to the path of ideological moderation, will depend on the dominant coalition within a party (that is, the power centre within the party organization) (Panebianco, 1988; Harmel and Janda, 1994; Harmel et al., 1995). A dominant leadership coalition that is intent on pursuing the path towards the political centre ground may be sufficiently powerful to resist calls from the party grass roots for a return to ideological purity (although electoral defeat may well prompt a re-evaluation of the strategy for accessing the political mainstream). Where such a dominant leadership coalition is absent, the party may be unable to resist demands from its members to return to the traditional ideological roots of the party.

There may be a further trade-off between *policy* and *office*. In legislative bargaining (that is, support of a minority government in parliament in exchange for policy concessions) and/or government office, parties may trade public office for policy influence, or vice versa. A good example of this dilemma was the experience of certain minority nationalist parties in Spain in the mid 1990s. When national elections failed to produce a clear governing majority in 1993 and 1996, the Catalan Convergencia i Unio (CiU) and the Basque Partido Nacionalista Vasco (PNV) supported national governments without entering directly into a governing coalition. Office incumbency was rejected since policy compromises and constraints in coalition would have been too unpopular with party supporters, and would thus have jeopardized the parties' electoral standings. Instead, the CiU and the PNV used their pivotal position to extract support for further autonomy for the Autonomous Communities (Calvet Crespo, 2003; Guerrero Salom, 2003). In such a situation, policy gains were clearly valued more than office positions. However, other parties may perceive a larger scope for policy influence via government incumbency, and will therefore be willing to accept the risks that come with occupying public office in order to maximize their impact on political decision-making.

Finally, a party that consistently fails to meet its goals (whatever these may be) is likely to face serious questions from its members and supporters about its strategy/policy/organization. This, in turn, may produce splits in the party's leadership and the emergence of alternative alliances contesting the legitimacy of the dominant coalition within the party. Internal divisions are rarely considered to be advantageous for a political party, since 'being seen as divided undermines the degree of certainty that electors have about parties' trajectories' (Taggart, 1998, p. 373). Intra-party divisions may thus compromise a party's electoral standing if they are not resolved swiftly or dealt with carefully.

To summarize, this section has argued that all political parties, regardless of their origins or ideological preferences, will face a common set of opportunities and challenges as they pass different thresholds during their lifetime. In particular, crossing different thresholds will prompt political parties to rethink what goals they pursue. However, the pursuit of different goals can present new dilemmas for political parties; these dilemmas may well undermine a party's abilities to meet its objectives in the ways that have been outlined above. The next section tests these propositions as potential explanations for Plaid Cymru's problematic efforts to adapt to a new institutional, political and electoral environment in post-devolution Wales.

## PLAID CYMRU IN POST-DEVOLUTION WALES: AN EMPIRICAL ANALYSIS

### Background: the Limited Electoral and Political Impact of Plaid Cymru before 1999

Plaid Cymru was established in 1925, and for the first forty years of the party's existence, its goal was to get enough votes to secure representation at the statewide level. For most of this time, however, the party made very little impact on the British electoral scene; by the 1964 general election, the party's share of the vote only equated to 4.8 per cent of the Welsh vote. Among the contributing factors to Plaid Cymru's lack of electoral appeal were the party's chronic financial difficulties in its early years, which hampered the organization of effective electoral campaigns (Elias, 2006). The party's leaders and political programme were also 'too controversial to sway the hearts and minds of many Welsh people' (Morgan, 1998, p. 256).

The party finally succeeded in getting an MP elected to the House of Commons in 1966, with the party's President, Gwynfor Evans, being elected in the Carmarthen by-election on the 14 July of that year. A combination of fortuitous local factors – an unprepared and internally divided Labour Party, an unpopular Labour candidate, and a Plaid Cymru campaign tailored to the specific issues of concern to the community – enabled the party to cross the threshold of representation at the state level for the first time in its history (Evans, 2005, pp. 271–9).[6] This achievement enabled Plaid Cymru to complement its vote-seeking ambitions with the explicit goal of influencing policy-making on Welsh issues in the House of Commons (Elias, 2006). Evans's strategy was one of 'guerilla warfare', which meant bombarding the government with hundreds of questions regarding the state of Welsh politics, society and the economy (Evans, 2005, p. 289). Paradoxically, however, this strategy undermined, rather than enhanced, Plaid Cymru's ability to shape policy, since the governing Labour Party's hardening of its anti-Welsh sentiment constrained Plaid Cymru's ability to put Welsh issues on the agenda (Evans, 2005, p. 296). Plaid Cymru failed to hold on to its Carmarthenshire seat in the 1970 general election, despite the party's overall share of the Welsh vote increasing to 11.5 per cent (compared to 4.3 per cent in 1966). The loss of the party's first MP, and the perception among party members that Gwynfor Evans had failed to make advances on the issue of Welsh self-determination during his term in the House of Commons, prompted a period of internal debate over the party's goals. The result was a renewed focus on electoral strategy – including improving the party's political message and campaigning techniques – in order to boost the party's vote share (Elias, 2006).

Plaid Cymru crossed the threshold of representation at the state level for the second time in the 1974 general election, and has maintained a presence in the House of Commons ever since.[7] Policy influence once again became a priority for Plaid Cymru, alongside that of increasing the party's electoral standing in Wales. Interestingly, however, the party experienced the trade-offs that come with the pursuit of policy influence as suggested in the preceding section, and which would be experienced by the party again within the NAW (see below). For example, when the Labour government's plans for devolution for Scotland and Wales were published in 1975, Plaid Cymru's MPs were quick to declare their support for the proposals even though they fell short of the kind of self-government the party had demanded. Opposition to the same plans by the party's membership led to a move by the party executive to warn their own MPs that the party was 'not for sale' (Evans, 2005, p. 394). Attempts by Plaid's MPs to exchange legislative support for Labour's devolution plans for concessions on other key policy issues affecting Wales did little to unite a deeply divided party. These divisions were exacerbated as a result of the Welsh electorate's rejection of the devolution proposals in a referendum, and Plaid Cymru's heavy electoral losses in the general election a few months later.[8]

This electoral defeat sparked an internal crisis within Plaid Cymru, and led the party to re-brand itself gradually throughout the 1980s as a left-of-centre party committed to securing Welsh self-determination with the framework of a Europe of the Regions (Lynch, 1995; Elias, 2006, 2008; Wyn Jones, 2007). The result was that the cause of Welsh nationalism gained in credibility throughout the 1980s and 1990s. However, the party failed to translate this into substantial electoral gains at the state level over the same period, not least because of the constraints of the British first-past-the-post system in place for general elections (Wyn Jones, 2007, p. 260).[9] Even though the party performed better in local and European elections over the same period (McAllister, 2001b, p. 84; Elias, 2008, p. 48), Plaid Cymru's political clout in Westminster – the only arena where decisions about Wales's constitutional future could be taken – remained limited. The party's presence within the House of Commons undoubtedly added weight to calls from other quarters (particularly from a resurgent SNP) for a programme of constitutional reform and de-centralization within the UK. However, the emergence of devolution onto the political agenda by 1997 was arguably just as much the result of the Labour Party's eighteen years in opposition as a response to autonomist demands from the Scottish and (to a lesser extent) Welsh peripheries (Geekie and Levy, 1989; Mitchell, 1998). Up until 1999, therefore, Plaid Cymru remained a relatively minor electoral and political force within British politics.

**1999–2003: From vote maximization to the pursuit of policy influence**

The programme of devolution undertaken by the New Labour government in the late 1990s led to a major re-structuring of Plaid Cymru's operating environment, by creating a new Welsh political arena. For a party that had had to accept that elections to Westminster were 'the only game in town' for over eighty years,[10] the creation of devolved political institutions in Wales constituted a major external shock to which Plaid Cymru (as well as other political parties in Wales) had to adapt. The party responded by defining an ambitious programme for Wales that reflected the new responsibilities of the NAW.[11] In preparation for the first elections for the newly established NAW in May 1999, Plaid Cymru invested significant time, financial and human resources in the development of an extremely detailed manifesto that went far beyond the party's core business of constitutional reform, to address all of the issues that fell within the NAW's competences.[12] The manifesto spelt out in considerable detail how a Plaid Cymru government would act to ensure 'economic success, social justice, cultural vitality, democratic renewal and environmental stability' (Plaid Cymru, 1999). Such was the thoroughness of the manifesto, that one political commentator even suggested that, in the absence of any kind of coherent programme by the Welsh Labour Party, Plaid Cymru offered the only credible working programme for the Assembly's first term (Wyn Jones, 1999).

The result of the first elections to the NAW constituted a second external shock for Plaid Cymru. As noted earlier, the party surpassed even the most optimistic predictions to get seventeen AMs, making Plaid Cymru the main party of opposition within the NAW. Several factors have been offered to explain Plaid Cymru's electoral breakthrough in 1999. These include the internal leadership struggles of the Labour Party in the run up to the election, the professional electoral campaign mounted by Plaid Cymru, and a tendency among voters to associate devolution with Plaid Cymru as opposed to any other political party (Wyn Jones and Trystan, 2000; interviews 1 December 2003, 19 March 2003, 26 March 2008). The change in the electoral system to a partially proportional one[13] also made it easier for Plaid Cymru to turn this surge in support into representatives in the NAW. The impact of this electoral breakthrough on Plaid Cymru is difficult to understate: after eighty years in the electoral wilderness, Plaid Cymru polled its largest ever vote share, and more than quadrupled its number of elected representatives. To use Pedersen's (1982) terminology, these elections marked a turning point in the lifespan of Plaid Cymru.

As the discussion in the previous section would lead one to expect, passing the threshold of representation on the Welsh level in such a dramatic fashion prompted Plaid Cymru to reconsider its prioritization of goals. The party's priority became that of influencing policy-making within the NAW (interviews 16 February 2003; 19 March 2003). In contrast to the party's previous attempts to shape policy-making at the state level, Plaid Cymru's policy ambitions within the NAW were both broader in scope and had the potential to be substantially more successful. The scope of policy influence was defined as relating to the whole range of issues within the remit of the NAW rather than the core 'Plaid' issue of constitutional reform. Indeed, as will be argued below, the party would deliberately play down its long-term constitutional aspirations for Wales during the Assembly's first term, preferring to focus on the bread and butter issues of governing Wales. Moreover, that policy influence could be realistically expected reflected the organizational evolution of the party and the specific institutional context within which the party was operating. For one thing, as already noted, Plaid Cymru was potentially better prepared for policy-making within the NAW because of its comprehensive policy programme. Moreover, the architects of the NAW designed an institution that would promote a new inclusive style of consensus politics in Wales, as opposed to the confrontational nature of Westminster politics (Patchett, 2003, p. 3). Within this so-called 'corporate body', the conventional distinction between executive and legislative roles would be removed, with both the government and the opposition parties participating in the policy formulation process. The key for doing so lay with several subject committees, each one corresponding to the portfolios of the Assembly Executive (or Secretaries as they were called), and which would have both a policy development and legislative scrutiny function.[14] In principle, therefore, all political parties would have an opportunity to contribute constructively to the policy development process. Finally, the Labour Party's lack of a governing majority boosted Plaid Cymru's confidence in the prospects of shaping policy within the NAW (Interviews, 16 December 2003, 28 March 2008).

Plaid Cymru debated two possible strategies for achieving its policy goal: an oppositional strategy vis-à-vis the minority Labour government or a cooperative strategy which privileged consensus-seeking over confrontation. It was the latter that was adopted by the party, for the following reasons. First, there was a desire among Plaid Cymru AMs to enhance the Assembly's legitimacy in the eyes of a Welsh public divided on the virtues of devolution. Given the narrow margin of support for devolution expressed in the referendum in 1997, Plaid Cymru perceived a responsibility to work with the Labour Party to make devolution work, rather than seek to undermine it by assuming a more traditional oppositional role within the NAW. To this end, 'we [Plaid Cymru] tried to be a constructive opposition' (Interview, 24 April 2008) and endeavoured 'to be positive in our critique of the [Labour] government' (Interview, 29 March 2008). Secondly, there was a reluctance to criticize a devolved institutional settlement that represented a concession to the party's long-articulated demands for constitutional reform, even though it fell far short of Plaid Cymru's constitutional aspirations. Instead, the party adopted the position that 'some form of devolution was better than no devolution at all' (Interview, 29 March 2008). From this starting point, the priority for Plaid Cymru was to demonstrate to Welsh voters what could be achieved through devolution (Interview, 1 December 2003). This translated into a desire to shift the focus away from the party's long-term territorial ambitions for Wales, and onto more concrete proposals for addressing other non-territorial policy challenges.[15] By doing so, Plaid Cymru sought to cultivate the image of a responsible and credible potential party of government able to deliver across the whole gamut of policy areas within the remit of the NAW.

Plaid Cymru's success in meeting its policy goals was, however, frustrated for several reasons. The committee system proved itself to be a poor motor for consensus politics, not least because members of the Executive approached the committees as fora for debate and scrutiny, rather than for formulating and agreeing policy objectives and delivery mechanisms. There were some notable successes in shaping policy outcomes on subject committees that were chaired by Plaid Cymru AMs (interviews, 16 February 2004; 26 March 2008; 24 April 2008). Under Plaid Cymru's chairmanship of the Rural Affairs and Education committees, for example, a comprehensive review of Welsh language policy was conducted, leading to the publication of a national action plan aiming at the creation of a bilingual Wales, entitled *Iaith Pawb* ('Everyone's Language').[16] On the whole, however, there was a consensus among interviewees that the party had fallen far short of shaping policy within the NAW in a clear and decisive way. One Plaid Cymru AM expressed his disillusionment with a 'fraudulent' committee system which allowed Ministers to go through the motions of deliberation but under no formal requirement to feed these debates into actual policy proposals (Interview, 19 March 2003). The distinction between executive and legislative functions within the NAW was exacerbated after February 2000, when Rhodri Morgan replaced Alun Michael as leader of the Welsh Labour Party. This not only gave the Labour Party a more charismatic leadership, but the agreement of a 'partnership' with the Liberal Democrats produced a governing majority in the NAW for the first time and a clearer set of policy priorities than had hitherto been the case. This further limited the ability of Plaid Cymru to seek to shape the policy agenda through cooperation with the Labour Party (Interviews, 19 December 2003, 28 February 2008, 4 April 2008). As the first term of the NAW drew to a close, there was growing disappointment within Plaid Cymru's rank and file with devolution in practice, and their party's association with it (Dafis, 2003, p. 41).

Much of this disappointment with Plaid Cymru's achievements during the first term related to the lack of focus on 'traditional' Plaid issues such as the protection of the Welsh language, culture and the regeneration of rural Welsh communities. Such concerns led some members to participate in the formation of a new pressure group, *Cymuned* (Welsh for 'community') in 2001. The group campaigned on the issues of the housing crisis in rural Wales, and the social and cultural implications of rising migration into Welsh-speaking areas. Another faction, known as the Triban Coch ('the Red Flag') also became more vocal within the party. These members from the left-wing within Plaid Cymru called on the party to distinguish itself more clearly based on its socialist credentials, by prioritizing the reform of public services and welfare provisions ahead of 'nation building', in the sense of promoting a more encompassing socio-economic and cultural project for Wales. Together, these different groups served to highlight the growing discontent among Plaid Cymru's grass roots with the party's strategy and priorities within the NAW.

At the same time, Plaid Cymru also struggled to articulate a clear and convincing account of its long-term constitutional goals. The party was subject to repeated challenges from its partisan opponents to come clean on the true nature of its territorial aspirations for Wales. Plaid Cymru's ambiguous aim of securing 'full national status for Wales in Europe' was denounced as a ruse to distract attention from the party's true separatist aspirations. Such was the implication of Lembit Opik MP's ten-point 'IQ test' (independence question) for Plaid Cymru, consisting of a series of questions on how Wales would fit into the existing British and European institutional architecture if Plaid Cymru had its way (Western Mail, 2001). The party's failure to respond to such attacks with a robust defence of its long-term territorial goals was due in no small part to the growing awareness among key figures within Plaid Cymru of the inadequacy of the party's constitutional terminology (Elias, 2008, pp. 68–9). As a result of other parties' insistence on pursuing the constitutional question, however, Plaid Cymru's attempts to switch the focus of political debate onto detailed policy proposals were continually frustrated.

A further difficulty faced by Plaid Cymru during its first term in the NAW related to the response of other political parties to the electoral rise of Welsh nationalism. Statewide parties responded to the electoral breakthrough of Plaid Cymru by adapting their positions on issues traditionally 'owned' by the nationalists. In particular, statewide parties gave their programmes a more distinctive territorial slant, by proposing regional solutions for regional problems. Whereas Plaid Cymru had long fashioned itself as the only true 'party of Wales', able to defend Welsh interests within British and European politics (Elias, 2008, pp. 70–1), within post-devolution Wales statewide parties re-packaged their political programmes in order to give them more of a 'Welsh face'. Thus, for example, the Welsh Labour Party rebranded itself in February 2000 as 'the true party of Wales', a move clearly aimed at challenging Plaid Cymru's political appeal (Osmond, 2007). There were even voices within the Conservative Party in Wales suggesting that their party should develop a distinctly Welsh political agenda in response to devolution.[17] As a result of this issue re-alignment, Plaid Cymru struggled to retain a distinctive policy agenda and a clear 'nationalist' political space within the NAW (Wyn Jones and Scully, 2004b).

All of these factors – disappointment among party supporters with Plaid Cymru's performance in the NAW, internal debate over policy priorities, pressure to clarify its long-term constitutional goals, and the struggle to retain a distinctive nationalist political space – contributed to the party's failure to emulate its 1999 electoral performance in May 2003. These 'failures to come to terms with the success of 1999' (Interview, 24 April 2008) saw the party's share of the Welsh vote decline substantially, with the number of Plaid Cymru AMs falling from seventeen to twelve (Wyn Jones and Scully, 2004a). To this stock set of problems often faced by political parties who have struggled to adapt to a new political and institutional setting, other party- and context-specific factors can be added that compounded the party's electoral demise. Thus, for example, some senior party members cited the absence of a clear campaigning message and a sense of complacency ahead of the election as further causes of the party's poor perform-ance. One interviewee suggested that his party seemed to 'assume that we didn't have to do anything' in order to repeat its 1999 performance (Interview, 24 April 2008). Wyn Jones and Scully (2004b) also point to the role of the media and the broader international context in undermining Plaid Cymru's electoral appeal, as well as the better organized campaign mounted by a Labour Party keen to win back key seats lost to the nationalists in 1999. Together, all of these factors translated into an electoral result that was 'a blow to the solar plexus of Plaid Cymru' (Dafis, 2003, p. 41).

In keeping with the expectation that the shock of electoral defeat may well prompt a debate about the ideological and strategic direction of a political party, Plaid Cymru was forced to address difficult questions about its leadership, organization and political programme in the aftermath of the 2003 NAW elections. The next section examines the ways in which Plaid Cymru sought to respond to the dramatic change in electoral fortunes.

## 2003–7: Re-thinking policy and strategy within the NAW

> One danger in these circumstances is that [Plaid Cymru] reverts to a total concentration on its ultimate constitutional aim. (Dafis, 2003, p. 41)

As is often the case after political parties suffer an electoral defeat, Plaid Cymru's disappointing electoral performance prompted a period of intense debate within the party with regard to its political image, message and strategy. In what was effectively a struggle for the soul of Plaid Cymru, a debate was held on the fundamental purpose of the party: was it a pressure group for core Plaid issues (Welsh self-determination and the protection of the Welsh language) or an aspiring party of government within Wales? This debate crystallised during a bitterly fought leadership contest sparked by the resignation of the party's President and Leader of the Plaid group in the NAW, Ieuan Wyn Jones, after the 2003 elections.[18] The two candidates for the party Presidency[19] represented two contrasting visions of Plaid Cymru's political project (Taylor, 2003a, p. 62). On the one hand, Dafydd Iwan – a veteran Welsh-language activist and prominent cultural figure – focused on the issues in rural and agricultural communities in the Welsh-speaking heartlands of Wales, and advocated a more oppositional role within the NAW and vis-à-vis other political parties. His opponent, Cynog Dafis, argued that a renewed focus on long-term constitutional goals would distract the party from the more immediate policy challenges facing Wales (Dafis, 2003). Instead, Dafis proposed to pursue a more progressive socio-economic and environmental policy agenda that would enable Plaid Cymru to appeal to voters outside its traditional support base. This would see Plaid Cymru continue on the path towards government incumbency, rather than return to the days of campaigning on a traditional nationalist agenda. The election was eventually won by Dafydd Iwan.

Plaid Cymru also sought to clarify its political message, given the perceived failure to communicate a clear political narrative during the election campaign. A priority in this respect was the party's constitutional policy. As already noted, the party had come under pressure for some time to spell out its long-term aspirations for Wales. The shock of electoral defeat prompted the party's Annual Conference in September 2003 to re-examine the party's constitutional ambitions. A motion was approved to replace the goal of 'full national status within Europe' – the party's aim since the late 1980s – with 'independence in Europe' as the constitutional formulation most likely to advance the Welsh national interest. This decision was defended as a change of terminology rather than a significant change of policy (Elias, 2008). It was hoped that the decision would allow the party to 'free ourselves from some of our past defensiveness and step up our campaign significantly' (Thomas, 2003).

This change in Plaid Cymru's leadership, and the renewed concern with long-term constitutional goals, could be interpreted as the party shifting back towards the status of 'niche' party as defined by Meguid (2005), with a focus on campaigning for a narrow set of issues, in this case constitutional reform. However, such a move was strongly resisted by a dominant coalition made up of AMs and other senior figures within the party. Cynog Dafis warned the party against 'becoming obsessed' with independence, and stressed the need to develop a comprehensive policy programme in order to ensure a prosperous and vibrant Welsh nation (Taylor, 2004, p. 39). In a similar vein, the party's ex-President and Presiding Officer within the NAW, Dafydd Elis Thomas, argued that 'Plaid Cymru has not adjusted to devolution because you have this improbable allegiance of some people to something called Welsh independence' (Elis Thomas, 2004). Instead, he argued that Plaid Cymru's responsibility was to deal with the social, economic and environmental issues facing the country, and face up to the realities of coalition politics:

> I think what we should be doing is offering ourselves as a proper alternative government, or part of a government, to break the hegemony of Labour . . . That is an issue that we can tackle if you abjure having a nationalist programme because it's clear to any observer of the Welsh political scene that the vast majority of the Welsh electorate don't want nationalism. The majority of us want proper governance and by going for nationalist rather than a proper governance programme what we are doing is betraying our own voters. (ibid., 2004)

A series of subsequent electoral defeats for Plaid Cymru in European and general elections intensified the debate over Plaid Cymru's future role in Welsh politics.[20] A new lobbying group was formed within Plaid Cymru called Dewis (Welsh for 'choice') on 16 May 2005. The group defended the conviction that Plaid Cymru had a credible chance of gaining power within the NAW, and urged the party to embrace the politics of coalition and consider new political alliances in order to realize the goal of being the party of government within Wales (Thomas et al., 2005, pp. 61–2). Plaid Cymru's National Council immediately rejected the proposals by Dewis to consider future coalition possibilities within the NAW. At the same time, however, a key group of decision-makers within the party hierarchy embarked on a far-reaching programme of ideational and organizational change with a view to putting Plaid Cymru firmly back on the road towards government incumbency. A re-branding exercise was launched early in

2006 that saw the party change its name and adopt a new logo.[21] A six-month policy consultation process with the people of Wales was launched at the same time, in an attempt to formulate a more appealing political programme for the 2007 elections to the NAW. The party's goal was to formulate a 'brand of nationalism that is less of a risk for people to support' (Interview, 24 April 2008), a far cry from the narrow linguistic nationalism of previous generations of Plaid Cymru activists. A new campaigning unit was also established to oversee preparations for the third Assembly election, with new technologies being used to regularly poll Welsh voters, tap into trends in public opinion, and target specific sections of the electorate with a view to recuperating the party's vote share (Interview, 9 May 2008). In the run-up to the third round of NAW elections, Plaid Cymru's aim was to rebuild its electoral share as a prerequisite for establishing the party as a real contender for government office.

Plaid Cymru's strategy within the NAW during this second term was also adapted in light of the party's previous experience of constructive opposition. Contrary to the party's decision in 1999 not to seek to undermine the devolution settlement granted to Wales, the party was no longer ambivalent about its relationship to the devolved structures: 'it was not our responsibility to uphold the institution' (Interview, 24 April 2008). The fact that the incumbent Labour government did not have a governing majority within the NAW gave Plaid Cymru an incentive to cooperate with other opposition parties to threaten to defeat Labour on key issues, or to win policy concessions in return for enabling the government to pass bills.[22] Such success enabled Plaid Cymru to demonstrate to its supporters how policy influence could be exercised within the NAW, something that had been less easy to communicate during the first term.

By the 2007 election campaign, Plaid Cymru had learnt key lessons following the shock of electoral decline four years previously. Plaid's election campaigning had been substantially updated, encompassing a more effective targeting of key seats and use of voter identification software, a new party logo and much improved campaigning materials, and an election manifesto with more appealing policies (Scully and Elias, 2008). The party's efforts were rewarded with an advance in vote share and an increased number of seats in the NAW, from twelve to fifteen. The Labour Party, however, whilst retaining its position as the largest party in the NAW, fell far short of a governing majority. This result led to several weeks of confusion about which parties would take power. Protracted coalition negotiations saw a first proposal to form a 'rainbow' coalition between Plaid Cymru, the Conservatives and the Liberal Democrats be abandoned in favour of a final red-green coalition between Labour and Plaid Cymru. A detailed account of these discussions is provided by Osmond (2007). The next section examines debates within Plaid Cymru as it contemplated the prospect of government incumbency, and examines the party's record after just over a year in office. It is argued that the party faced the same difficult choices as any other political party which has to decide whether it will accept to join a coalition government. Moreover, the party has already faced many of the tensions that come with public office, tensions which are likely to become more acute as Plaid Cymru's term in office proceeds.

**Plaid Cymru in Coalition: Adapting to the Challenges of Governing**
Deciding to cross the threshold of representation is a 'hard decision' (Strøm and Müller, 1999). A party that decides to enter government hopes that doing so will be an effective way of influencing policy, but risks being blamed at the polls for what goes wrong (Deschouwer, 2008). It also hopes to benefit from the visibility that comes with public office, but also risks alienating militants opposed to compromises on key party values that have to be made to maintain a coalition government.

In the coalition debates that followed the 2007 election, Plaid Cymru was very aware of the potential pitfalls of entering into a coalition government. A minority supported the option of not participating in any coalition and remaining a party of opposition within the NAW; for these members, the policy compromises and constraints that are an inevitable part of coalition government were deemed to be too high a cost to pay for office incumbency (Interview, 9 May 2008). For the majority, however, the opportunities of government office were deemed to be too great to forego. However, overwhelming support for passing the threshold of government masked divided opinions on the advantages and disadvantages of different coalition options. Some expressed unease at the prospect of working alongside the Conservative Party; the ideological gulf between the two parties risked making such an alliance deeply unpopular among certain sections of Plaid Cymru's support base (Interview, 29 March 2008). Others raised a similar objection, but this time with regard to the Labour Party, historically Plaid Cymru's fiercest rival in the competition for Welsh votes. The eventual decision to agree to a Labour-Plaid Cymru government was based on the belief that this represented the best option for achieving Plaid Cymru's policy goals. The *One Wales* coalition agreement (Welsh Labour Party/Plaid Cymru, 2007) was widely seen to have gone a long way towards satisfying the latter's demands.[23] Particularly significant concessions for Plaid Cymru were the commitment to holding a referendum on further law-making powers for the NAW ahead of the next round of Assembly elections, and new legislation on the Welsh language.

Since occupying government office in Wales, however, Plaid Cymru has been forced to prioritize its agenda and focus on those issues that can realistically be achieved. This has required taking difficult decisions of the kind that face any political party in a coalition government. The provision of a Welsh-language daily newspaper is a case in point. Plans to launch such a newspaper under the title *Y Byd* ('The World') – were already in place prior to Plaid Cymru's accession to office. Moreover, on the insistence of Plaid Cymru, the coalition agreement with the Labour Party contained a commitment to 'expand the funding and support for Welsh-medium magazines and newspapers, including the establishment of a Welsh-language daily newspaper' (Welsh Labour Party/Plaid Cymru, 2007, p. 35). However, in February 2008, Plaid Cymru's Minister for Heritage, Rhodri Glyn Thomas, announced that whereas some money would be given over to supporting a Welsh-language publication, this was neither specifically allocated to support the launching of *Y Byd* nor would the money be sufficient to launch this project in its anticipated format. With the future of *Y Byd* in jeopardy as a result of this decision, Plaid Cymru members have publicly expressed their disillusionment with this 'betrayal' of a key party commitment to promote the Welsh language through the print media. More recently doubt has been cast on the prospects of holding a referendum on law-making powers for the NAW before 2011, another key concession to Plaid Cymru in the coalition agreement with the Labour Party. Lord Dafydd Elis Thomas, former Plaid Cymru leader and Presiding Officer in the NAW, has cautioned his party against rushing into an early referendum (Western Mail, 2008). His warning may have reflected his desire to hold off on a referendum until such time as a positive outcome could confidently be predicted. But failing to meet such a core Plaid Cymru objective would undoubtedly be a blow to Plaid Cymru's image as a party able to deliver on key nationalist promises (Interviews, 28 February 2008; 9 May 2008). Slow progress on other key Plaid Cymru policies in the coalition agreement, such as new legislation on the Welsh language, has provided further cause for concern among Plaid Cymru supporters and may aggravate feelings of disillusionment with the party's performance in government.

Falling short on policy delivery may also compromise Plaid Cymru's valence standing among voters. It is well established in the academic literature on voting behaviour that voters are also concerned with issues of delivery and competence when it comes to deciding which political party to vote for in an election (Stokes, 1992; Clarke et al., 2004; Pattie and Johnston, 2007). Governing parties who fail the valence test risk a decline in vote share in subsequent electoral contests. Appearing competent and credible in public office will be especially important for political parties in government for the first time, since there is a much greater pressure on them to prove themselves as parties that are able to rise to the challenges that such a position presents (Deschouwer, 2008). Parties that fail to meet expectations of professionalism in public office risk damaging their image in voters' eyes as well as their chances of being considered as a potential coalition partner in future governments (Heinisch, 2003, p. 102). It is not surprising, therefore, that in government, Plaid Cymru's ministers have focused on portraying an image of competence with a view to decontaminating the common view of the party as 'a collection of wild-eyed romantics and language zealots' (Wyn Jones and Scully, 2008). The swift and unexpected resignation of the Culture Minister, Rhodri Glyn Thomas, in July 2008 after several public 'gaffes' (BBC, 2008) reaffirmed the party's keenness to uphold this perception of competence in public office. Whether such moves will be sufficient to affirm Plaid Cymru's image as a competent party of government in the eyes of voters remains to be seen.

## CONCLUSION

This article has analysed the ways in which Plaid Cymru has sought to adapt to its new electoral and political status within post-devolution Wales. The findings summarized throughout this article demonstrate that many of the party's problems in adapting to post-devolution Wales are not unique. Rather, they are challenges that many political parties face when they are required to adapt to major changes in their operating environments. These challenges are particularly acute for small or new parties making the transition from being relatively marginal protest parties campaigning on a limited range of issues, to being major political players in a political system that strive to compete on a full range of issues beyond their 'niche'. For Plaid Cymru, this transition from protest to power began with the creation of a devolved political arena in Wales, and the party's electoral break-through in the first Assembly elections in 1999. Having established itself as a major political party in post-devolution Wales, the party's changing goals – from vote-seeking to policy- and (later on) office-seeking – have given rise to a host of new challenges. These include the difficult task of broadening the party's appeal whilst remaining faithful to core ideological principles, fending off partisan competition for the ownership of 'niche' issues, and reconciling the desire to influence policy with the constraints of being in coalition government. As has been the case for many green and extreme right parties, the difficulties associated with these trade-offs have undermined Plaid Cymru's electoral standing since 1999. As expected, however, electoral decline also served as a further 'external shock', prompting new efforts at adapting to the political dynamics of post-devolution Wales. Plaid Cymru's first experience as a party of government will be a further test of the party's ability to adapt to a new political context.

What do these findings suggest more generally about how minority nationalist parties adapt as they evolve from being parties of protest to being parties in power? This aspect of minority nationalist party politics has thus far received very little scholarly attention. This is surprising when one considers that in many places, minority nationalist parties have for many years been major political players in their respective regional political arenas, and have been parties of regional – and even national – government in some instances (Elias and Tronconi, 2006). Case studies of individual minority nationalist parties suggest that many have indeed faced the challenges of adaptation faced, not only by Plaid Cymru, but also more generally by political parties in ever-changing political contexts.[24] However, this hypothesis requires further empirical study before it can be confirmed.

To conclude, the experiences of other small or new parties that have made a similar transition from protest to power are helpful in attempting to grasp the longer-term implications for Plaid Cymru from its attempts to transform itself from a party of protest to a party in power. It is possible to identify at least two fundamental dangers that face political parties making a similar transition, whatever their ideological preferences. First, the tension between remaining faithful to a party's founding ideological principles and broadening its political programme beyond its core business has, in many cases, led to party frag-mentation. Severe factional divisions, even a splitting up of the party, are a common feature of the transition effected by many green and extreme right parties from protest to power (Heinisch, 2003; Rihoux and Rüdig, 2006). Minority nationalist parties are not immune from this danger. To date, Plaid Cymru has succeeded in maintaining party unity. After the party's 2003 electoral decline, senior figures rejected calls from one academic for the party to split because 'presenting a united front on the national question, let alone on specific economic and social policies', was increasingly difficult to achieve (McAllister, 2003). However, party fragmentation remains a danger. One interviewee insisted that 'there will come a day when Plaid [Cymru] will split. Because it is an uneasy coalition at times ... between [being] a party of socialists and a party for the [Welsh] language' (Interview, 9 May 2008). Other minority nationalist parties have not been able to eschew party fragmentation. In the Basque Country, Eusko Alkartasuna split from the larger nationalist party, the Partido Nacionalista Vasco, in 1986 in protest at the latter's excessive ideological moderation (Ugarte, 2006). The Volksunie in Flanders experienced a number of scissions as the moderate nationalist party sought to define a new role for itself in a newly federalized Belgian political system (De Winter, 2006).

This last example points to a second danger facing small or new parties when a party succeeds in meeting its core policy goals. In such a situation, the challenge for a political party is that of defining a new role for itself when its political function has been exhausted. Failing to do so is likely to endanger a political party's survival. The Flemish Volksunie's terminal demise has been attributed to 'an overdose of success' in meeting its demands for a federal Belgian state (De Winter, 2006). Efforts to carve out a new political space may lead a party to radicalize its core demands, or abandon its 'niche' interests definitively in order to present itself as a conventional left- or right-wing party competing on traditional socio-economic issues. Both strategies are likely to involve a difficult and potentially divisive process of redefining political purpose and devising new strategies and policy objectives, with no guarantee of electoral success.

These observations are not intended as predictions of Plaid Cymru's fate over the coming years. However, they are a useful warning of the difficulties that many political parties face when they strive to adapt to major institutional and political changes in their operating environments. Plaid Cymru may well have to confront a paradox that faces the vast majority of political parties that struggle to make the transition from protest to power, regardless of their ideological persuasion: at the same time as Plaid Cymru has established itself as a major player in Welsh politics, the party also faces an increasing number of fundamental challenges to its survival. It remains to be seen how the party responds to these challenges, and what the future holds for the Welsh nationalist party.

## NOTES

[1]    Political parties will also change their strategies and organizational structures (Elias and Tronconi, 2006). However, these aspects of party adaptation are not considered here.

[2]    It should be noted that the impact of devolution on Plaid Cymru is not limited to the NAW; devolution has also had implications for the party's representation and organization at different territorial levels. For example, within the House of Commons, the mandate and function of Plaid Cymru representatives has changed as the scope of Welsh issues being discussed in this arena post-devolution has also changed. The party has also had to develop new organizational structures that are appropriate for multi-level political representation, such as mechanisms for coordinating party activity at different territorial levels (Elias, 2006). However, due to constraints of space, this article will only consider Plaid Cymru within the NAW.

3    This analysis draws extensively on two rounds of interviews conducted by the author with key individuals within Plaid Cymru. These included past and present party leaders, chief executives, members of the party's executive committee and elected representatives within the NAW and the House of Commons. A first wave of interviews was conducted between November 2003 and March 2004 (ten interviews); a second wave of interviews was conducted between March and May 2008 (seven interviews). In order to preserve the anonymity of interviewees, in the text interviews have been referred to with only the date on which they were conducted.

4    These are the threshold of *declaration* (announcing the intention to become a political party), the threshold of *authorization* (meeting the necessary requirements to compete in elections), the threshold of *representation* (winning seats) and the threshold of *relevance* (Pedersen, 1982).

5    Deschouwer (2008: 3) draws on Sartori's (1976) discussion of 'relevance' as having two manifestations: blackmail potential and coalition potential. A political party has blackmail potential when it forces other political parties to respond to it but is not prepared to enter government or is not accepted by other political parties as an acceptable governing partner. In contrast, a political party can be said to have coalition potential when it is seen – both by itself and by other parties – as a possible governing party.

6    The party received an impressive 39.0 per cent of the votes cast, compared to only 16.1 per cent received in the same constituency in the general election held a few months previously.

7    There were two Plaid Cymru MPs in the House of Commons between 1974 and 1987. This number increased to three after the 1987 general election, and to four in the 1992 general election. The failure of Plaid Cymru to retain the constituency of Ceredigion in the 2005 general election reduced the number of Plaid Cymru MPs to three (Thrasher and Rallings, 2007).

8    A referendum was held on 1 March 1979 on devolution to Scotland and Wales. The proposals were rejected by an overwhelming 79.74 per cent of the electorate, on a turnout of 58.8 per cent. In the 1979 general election, Plaid Cymru polled 8.1 per cent of the Welsh vote (compared to 10.8 per cent in 1974) but returned its two MPs to the House of Commons (see Thrasher and Rallings, 2007).

9    In the 1983 General Election, the party polled 7.8 per cent of the Welsh vote. By 1997, the party's performance was only slightly better, with a vote share in Wales of 9.9 per cent.

10   Whilst Plaid Cymru also participated in local elections and, since 1979, in European elections, these were deemed to be of less consequence than elections to Westminster. The party thus developed and organized itself around the need to win representation at Westminster (Elias, 2006; for the dominance of Westminster elections more generally in British politics, see Judge, 1993).

11   These were defined in the 1998 Government for Wales Act as being the policy areas previously the responsibility of the Secretary of State for Wales. These were as follows: education, the environment, leisure, culture, the Welsh language, health, transport and tourism, agriculture, town planning, economic development, industry, local government, housing and social services (Osmond, 1998).

12   In expectation of devolution, in 1994 Plaid Cymru created the post of Director of Policy, responsible for coordinating the policy-development process. Previously, this task had

been carried out by individual policy spokespeople working within the loose coordinating framework of the National Executive Committee. The party also professionalized its election campaigning, by experimenting with innovative techniques such as telephone campaigning. The party spent close to £250,000 on the Assembly elections (compared to £40,000 during the 1997 general election); this was largely funded by two sizeable bequests received by the party just before the election (McAllister, 2001a: 111).

[13] Of the NAW's sixty seats, forty represented individual constituencies and are elected using the same first-past-the-post system used in Westminster elections. The remaining twenty seats are selected from party lists using a proportional 'alternative member system', and represented five larger regional constituencies within Wales.

[14] For a detailed account of the institutional architecture of the NAW, see Patchett (2003).

[15] The fact that Plaid Cymru's goal of 'full national status within the European Union' was increasingly at odds with developments in European integration, provided another incentive for the party to shift attention away from its constitutional ambitions and onto more concrete policy challenges within Wales. For a more detailed discussion of Plaid Cymru's constitutional goals, see Elias (2008: chapter 3).

[16] For a summary of the aims of this policy, see Williams (2005: 4–5).

[17] See, for example, Melding (2003).

[18] Ieuan Wyn Jones took over from the Dafydd Wigley as Plaid Cymru's President after the latter's resignation from the post in May 2000 for reasons of ill health. Lacking Wigley's charisma, Jones became the scapegoat for the frustration of party members at the lack of policy achievements during the Assembly's first term. After the election defeat, Jones resigned after rumours emerged that a group of Plaid Cymru AMs were plotting to challenge his leadership of the party (BBC, 2003). Jones was nevertheless re-elected as leader of the Plaid Cymru group in the NAW after fending off competition from two other candidates, Helen Mary Jones and Rhodri Glyn Thomas.

[19] Prior to this election, Plaid Cymru's President had also been an AM, and therefore became by default the leader of the Plaid Cymru group in the NAW. However, as neither of the two candidates in this Presidency election were AMs, it was decided to hold a second election for party leader in the NAW. This resulted in the re-election of Ieuan Wyn Jones to this role in August 2003. For a detailed account of these developments, see Taylor (2003a: 62; 2003b: 64–5).

[20] In the June 2004 European elections, Plaid Cymru's share of the vote declined from 29.6 per cent in 1999 to 17.4 per cent (with the loss of one of the party's two MEPs). In the 2005 general election, even though the party's performance nationally was not disastrous – the party's vote was down by only 1.7 per cent – the party failed to win its target seat in Ynys Môn (which had been lost to Labour in 2001) and lost the Ceredigion seat to the Liberal Democrats by 219 votes (a seat which the party had held since 1992).

[21] Since 1933, Plaid Cymru's logo was three green peaks, representing Plaid Cymru's key values: self-government, cultural prosperity and economic prosperity. More recently, a red dragon was added onto the three peaks. The new logo is based on a yellow poppy, and the party will no longer use the word 'Cymru', Welsh for Wales, referring to itself simply as 'Plaid' (although its full name remains 'Plaid Cymru – The Party of Wales').

22   For example, opposition parties in the NAW threatened to block the budgetary package proposed by the Labour government in December 2006 if no concessions were made to demands for greater funding in specific policy areas. In the event, Plaid Cymru broke ranks to negotiate more spending on education with the government, in return for abstention in the plenary vote on the budgetary package. This enabled Labour to pass its budget in spite of continued opposition from the Conservatives and Liberal Democrats.

23   The deal saw Plaid Cymru's Ieuan Wyn Jones assume the posts of Deputy First Minister and Minister for the Economy and Transport, Rhodri Glyn Jones become Minister for Heritage, Elin Jones be appointed Minister for Rural Affairs, and Jocelyn Davies as Deputy Minister for Housing.

24   See, for example, the case studies included in De Winter et al. (2006). Whilst the case studies do not address the issues of party adaptation explicitly, they provide evidence of many of the challenges and difficulties that in this article (and more generally in the party politics literature) have been attributed to the passing of different thresholds and/or responding to external shocks.

## ACKNOWLEDGEMENT

The research for this paper was conducted with financial assistance from the Saunders Lewis Memorial Scholarship.

## REFERENCES

Acha Ugarte, B. (2006). 'Eusko Alkartasuna: a party in search of a third space', in L. De Winter, M. Gómez-Reino and P. Lynch (eds), *Autonomist Parties in Europe: Identity Politics and the Revival of the Territorial Cleavage – Volume I*, Barcelona: ICPS.

Adams, J., Clark, M., Ezrow, L. and Glasgow, G. (2006). 'Are niche parties fundamentally different from mainstream parties? The causes and the electoral consequences of western European parties' policy shifts, 1976–1998', *American Journal of Political Science*, 50, 3, 513–29.

Appleton, A. M. and Ward, D. S. (1997). 'Party response to environmental change: a model of organizational innovation', *Party Politics*, 3, 3, 341–62.

Bale, T. (2007). 'Cinderella and her ugly sisters: the mainstream and extreme right in Europe's bipolarising party systems', *West European Politics*, 26, 3, 67–90.

BBC (2003). 'High noon for Plaid Cymru', 4 July 2003, *http://news.bbc.co.uk/1/hi/wales/3045414.stm* (accessed 8 November 2008).

BBC (2008). 'Gaffes stub out minister's career', 18 July 2008, *http://news.bbc.co.uk/1/hi/wales/south_east/7515008.stm* (accessed 8 November 2008).

Calvet Crespo, J. (2003). 'Gobiernos minoritarios, pactos parlamentarios y producción legislative en España', *Política y Sociedad,* 40, 2, 89–103.

Clarke, H. D., Sanders, D., Stewart, M. C. and Whitely, P. (2004). *Political Choice in Britain*, Oxford: Oxford University Press.

Dafis, C. (2003). 'Nation-building', *Agenda*, Winter 2003/2004, 41–3.

De Winter, L. (2006). 'In memoriam the Volksunie 1954–2001: death by overdose of success', in L. De Winter, M. Gómez-Reino and P. Lynch (eds), *Autonomist Parties in Europe: Identity Politics and the Revival of the Territorial Cleavage – Volume II*, Barcelona: ICPS.

Deschouwer, K. (2008). *New Parties in Government*, London: Routledge.

Downs, A. (1957). *An Economic Theory of Democracy*, New York: Harper & Row.

Downs, W. (2001). 'Pariahs in their midst: Belgian and Norwegian parties react to extremist threats', *West European Politics*, 24, 3, 23–42.

Elias, A. (2006). 'The long and difficult road to political representation: the case of Plaid Cymru', paper presented at the conference *From Protest to Power: Minority Nationalist Parties and the Challenges of Political Representation*, Aberystwyth University, 26–28 October 2006.

Elias, A. (2008). *Minority Nationalist Parties and European Integration: A Comparative Study*, London: Routledge.

Elias, A. and Tronconi, F. (2006). 'Minority nationalist parties and the challenges of political representation: a framework of analysis', paper presented at the conference *From Protest to Power: Minority Nationalist Parties and the Challenges of Political Representation*, Aberystwyth University, 26–28 October 2006.

Elis Thomas, D. (2004) 'No room for nationalism', *Epolitix*, 16 September 2004, *www.dodonline.co.uk/engine.asp?lev1=4&lev2=38&menu=71&showPage=article& id=135&article_display=all* (accessed 10 November 2008).

Evans, R. (2005). *Rhag Pob Brad*. Talybont: Y Lolfa.

Fabre, E., Maddens, B., Swenden, W. and Pogorelis, R. (2005). 'Partis politiques nationaux en crise? Organisation des partis et decentralisation. Une comparaison de l'Espagne et du Royaume Uni', *Res Publica*, 47, 1, 36–57.

Geekie, J. and Levy, R. (1989). 'Devolution and the tartanisation of the Labour Party', *Parliamentary Affairs*, 42, 399–41.

Guerrero Salom, E. (2003). 'Apoyo(s) parlamentario(s) antes que gobierno(s) de coalición. El caso espanol: 1993–1996 y 1996–2000', *Política y Sociedad*, 40, 2, 77–88.

Harmel, R. (1985). 'On the study of new parties', *International Political Science Review*, 6: 4, 403–18.

Harmel, R. and Janda, K. (1994). 'An integrated theory of party goals and party change', *Journal of Theoretical Politics*, 6, 3, 259–87.

Harmel, R., Heo, U., Tan, A. and Janda, K. (1995). 'Performance, leadership, factions and party change: an empirical analysis', *West European Politics*, 18, 1, 1–33.

Heinisch, R. (2003). 'Success in opposition – failure in government: explaining the performance of right-wing populist parties in public office', *West European Politics*, 26, 3, 91–130.

Judge, D. (1993). *The Parliamentary State*, London: Sage.

Kitschelt, H. (1994). *The Transformation of European Social Democracy*, Cambridge: Cambridge University Press.

Laffin, M., Taylor, G. and Thomas, A. (2003). 'Devolution and party organisation: the case of the Wales Labour Party', paper presented at the *Annual Conference of the Political Studies Association*, April 2003, University of Leicester.

Lynch, P. (1995). 'From red to green: the political strategy of Plaid Cymru in the 1980s and 1990s', *Journal of Federal and Regional Studies*, 5, 2, 197–210.

McAllister, L. (2001a). 'The National Assembly elections: Plaid Cymru's coming of age', *Contemporary Wales*, 14, 109–14.

McAllister, L. (2001b). *Plaid Cymru: the emergence of a political party*, Bridgend: Poetry Wales Press.

McAllister, L. (2003). 'Splitting headache for Plaid Cymru; but it could work', *Western Mail*, 29 August 2003, p. 12.

Mair, P. (2001). 'The green challenge and political competition: how typical is the German experience', *German Politics,* 10, 2, 99–116.

Meguid, B. (2005). 'Competition between unequals: the role of mainstream party strategy in niche party success', *American Political Science Review*, 99, 3, 347–58.

Melding, D. (2003). *New Dawn or Sunset Boulevard – What Role for the Welsh Conservative Party?*, speech to the Institute of Welsh Politics, University of Aberystwyth, 27 October 2003.

Mitchell, J. (1998). 'The evolution of devolution: Labour's home rule strategy in opposition', *Government and Opposition*, 33, 4, 479–96.

Morgan, K. (1998). *Rebirth of a Nation: Wales 1880–1980*, Oxford: Clarendon Press.

Müller-Rommel, F. (2002). 'The lifespan and the political performance of Green Parties in Western Europe', *Environmental Politics*, 11, 1, 1–13.

Müller-Rommel, F. and Pridham, G. (1991). *Small Parties in Western Europe*, London: Sage.

Osmond, J. (1998). *National Assembly Agenda*, Cardiff: Institute of Welsh Affairs.

Osmond, J. (2007). *Crossing the Rubicon: Coalition Politics Welsh-Style*, Cardiff: Institute of Welsh Affairs.

Panebianco, A. (1988). *Political Parties: Organization and Power*, Cambridge: Cambridge University Press.

Patchett, K. (2003). 'The new constitutional architecture', in J. Osmond and J. Barry Jones (eds), *Birth of Welsh Democracy: The First Term of the National Assembly for Wales*, Cardiff: Institute of Welsh Affairs.

Pattie, C. and Johnston, R. (2007). 'Positional issues, valence issues and the economic geography of voting in British elections', *Journal of Economic Geography*, 8, 1, 105–26.

Pedersen, M. (1982). 'Towards a new typology of party life-spans and minor parties', *Scandinavian Political Studies*, 5, 1, 1–16.

Plaid Cymru (1999). *Plaid Cymru Manifesto 1999*, Cardiff: Plaid Cymru.

Poguntke, T. (2002). 'Green parties in national governments: from protest to acquiescence?', *Environmental Politics*, 11, 1, 133–45.

Rihoux, B. and Rüdig, W. (2006). 'Analyzing Greens in power: setting the agenda', *European Journal of Political Research*, 45, s1, 1–33.

Sartori, G. (1976). *Parties and Party Systems. A Framework for Analysis*, Cambridge: Cambridge University Press.

Scully, R. and Elias, A. (2008). 'The 2007 Welsh Assembly election', *Regional and Federal Studies*, 18, 1, 103–9.

Smith, G. (1989). 'A system perspective on party system change', *Journal of Theoretical Politics*, 1, 3, 349–63.

Stokes, D. (1992). 'Valence politics', in D. Kavanagh (ed.), *Electoral Politics*, Oxford: Clarendon Press.

Strøm, K. (1990). 'A behavioral theory of competitive political parties', *American Journal of Political Science*, 34, 2, 565–98.

Strøm, K. and Müller, W. (1999). 'Political parties and hard choices', in K. Strøm and W. Müller (eds), *How Political Parties in Western Europe Make Hard Decisions*, Cambridge: Cambridge University Press.

Taggart, P. (1998). 'A touchstone of dissent: Euroscepticism in contemporary West European party systems', *European Journal of Political Research*, 33, 363–88.

Taylor, G. (2003a). 'Political parties', in John Osmond (ed.), *Wales Unplugged. Monitoring the National Assembly for Wales, June–August 2003*, Cardiff: Institute of Welsh Affairs.

Taylor, G. (2003b). 'Political parties', in J. Osmond (ed.), *Wales is Waiting. Monitoring the National Assembly for Wales, September–December 2003*, Cardiff: Institute of Welsh Affairs.

Taylor, G. (2004). 'Political parties', in J. Osmond (ed.), *End of the Corporate Body. Monitoring the National Assembly for Wales, December 2003–March 2004*, Cardiff: Institute of Welsh Affairs.

Thomas, S. (2003). 'Routemap to Independence in Europe', document presented to the Plaid Cymru National Council, November 2003.

Thomas, H., Morgan, K. and Ceredig, M. (2005). 'Political parties and the general election 2005', in R. David (ed.), *Minority Government – by Selective Co-operation*, Cardiff: Institute of Welsh Affairs.

Thrasher, M. and Rallings, C. (2007). *British Electoral Facts 1832–2006*, Aldershot: Ashgate.

Welsh Labour Party/Plaid Cymru (2007). *One Wales. A Progressive Agenda for the Government of Wales*, http://news.bbc.co.uk/2/shared/bsp/hi/pdfs/27_06_07_onewales.pdf (accessed 28 June 2007).

Western Mail (2001). 'IQ test', 21 September 2001.

Western Mail (2008). 'Don't rush referendum, warns Dafydd El', 22 December 2008.

Williams, C. (2005). '*Iaith Pawb*: the doctrine of plenary inclusion', *Contemporary Wales*, 17, 1–27.

Wyn Jones, R. (1999). 'Polisiau a phleidiau', *Barn*, April 1999, p. 6.

Wyn Jones, R. (2007). *Rhoi Cymru'n Gyntaf: Syniadaeth Wleidyddol Plaid Cymru*, Cardiff: University of Wales Press.

Wyn Jones, R. and Trystan, D. (2000). 'A "quiet earthquake": the first national elections to the National Assembly for Wales', *CREST Working Paper*, No. 85, September 2000.

Wyn Jones, R. and Scully, R. (2004a). 'Minor tremor but several casualties: the 2003 Welsh election', *Journal of Elections, Public Opinion and Parties*, 14, 191–207.

Wyn Jones, R. and Scully, R. (2004b). 'Must Plaid lose?', *Agenda*, Haf 2004, 60–2.

Wyn Jones, R. and Scully, R. (2008). *Wales Devolution Monitoring Report: January 2008*, London: Constitution Unit.

# 7. THE LEARNING JOURNEY: STUDENTS' EXPERIENCES OF FURTHER EDUCATION IN WALES

*Martin Jephcote, Jane Salisbury and Gareth Rees*

## ABSTRACT

*This paper draws attention to the experiences of students in colleges of further education in contemporary Wales, tracing their 'learning journeys' over a two-year period from September 2005 to July 2007. Drawing from an in-depth qualitative study, data confirm that the learning journeys upon which students embarked had their own antecedents rooted in, for example, disparate experiences of schooling and employment and, that during their studies, many learners led and managed complex private lives. Thus, being a learner had to be accommodated within students' wider lives and circumstances and often involved overcoming significant barriers to engaging in formal learning. From the vast array of data collected, here a focus group and two learner vignettes are used to illustrate these matters.*

## INTRODUCTION

An analysis of official statistics over the last few decades or so, illustrates the patterns of participation in further education colleges across the UK (Raffe et al., 2001). In 2004/2005 there were some 90,000 enrolments by young people aged 19 or under involved in learning outside the school sector in Wales, with almost two-thirds of enrolments being at one of Wales's twenty-three further education (FE) institutions (Welsh Assembly Government, 2006). FE colleges in Wales, as elsewhere in the UK, are important spaces for learners of all abilities and ages to study a subject or course to gain knowledge and skills either for their intrinsic interest, or for a qualification. Students present themselves at an FE college for a variety of reasons and enrol on academic or vocational courses as either full time, part time, or on 'day release' from work. However, as our findings revealed, the boundaries between enrolment types is blurred in consideration of the fact that many so-called 'full-time' students worked in 'part-time' jobs, some in excess of thirty hours a week. The uniqueness of FE's role was described by Kennedy (1999, p. 3):

> It is further education which has invariably given second chances to those who were forced by necessity to make unfulfilling choices. It said 'try again' to those who had been labelled as failures and who had decided education was not for the likes of them. (Kennedy, 1999, p. 3)

The Welsh context also has specific characteristics and, following devolution in 1999, there has been the pursuit of a 'made in Wales' agenda (Davidson, 2004). Increasingly, FE is seen by policy makers as a means to overcome social inequality and to support economic growth and competition. Policy rhetoric highlights their importance in the 'learning age' and to the need for Wales to compete in the global economy. An emphasis on lifelong learning runs through key Assembly Government publications (WAG, 2001 and 2004). The *Learning and Labour Market Intelligence for Wales* national and regional reports (Welsh Assembly Government, 2006) provide information relevant to the learning agenda in Wales and illustrate well the complexity of Wales as a distinct economic region and the sub-regional disparities that exist. More recently, though post-dating our study, there has been the publication of Wales's response to the Leitch Review (2006), that is, the Webb Review (2007) of the mission and purpose of FE, but perhaps this has been somewhat overtaken by the Welsh Assembly Government's (2008) strategy document 'Skills that work for Wales'. Taken together, these documents further underline the positioning of FE as having to operate a 'deficit model' of provision (Jephcote et al., 2008a, p. 164), that is, having to fill gaps in learners' prior education and skills, its role often compensatory and ameliorative.

Whereas much attention has been given by policy makers to patterns of participation in further, adult and continuing education, this we assert, needs to better engage with growing recognition of the lived experience of learning through exploring the nature of 'learning careers' (Bloomer and Hodkinson, 2000), learning lives and 'learning trajectories' (Gorard et al., 1999). What these point to is not just the influences on participation but also to the nature of the engagement with learning opportunities and, importantly, how life outside college affects this. The concepts of learning careers and learning lives conveys the ways in which engagement can change over time, but individual trajectories suggest that they are constrained within the parameters of their social group. In what follows we hope to depict the complexity and often thwarted nature of an individual's 'learning journey'.

## SETTING THE SCENE

At both the macro political level and micro level of colleges, there is a strong concern with performativity, which, in turn, drives the ways in which colleges are managed, the curriculum organized and how learning and teaching is 'delivered'. As we and others have reported elsewhere, there is a real and pressing concern with recruitment, retention and results (Jephcote and Salisbury, 2007). At the same time, what came through from teachers' interview accounts, journals and more so from our close engagement with them over the last two years, was that for many of them a concern not just with measurable performance in the form of examination results, but also the acquisition of life skills, social competences and all that is involved with staying on, often against the odds (see Salisbury et al., 2008a). Many, but not all of the teachers in our study, did their best to attend to what was needed in order to maximize the performance potential of their students, but also went much further in recognizing the importance of students' wider lives, and how this impacted on their learning and engagement at college. A number of teachers stated how they could not ignore what was going on in their students' wider lives because this affected what went on in classrooms. Indeed, some, for example, told us that the week could not begin until these 'personal' issues had been listened to.

What these teachers were pointing to is the complexity of students' lives and, indeed, this was also evident from our interactions with them. Increasingly, we became aware that to be a 'full-time' student at a college of FE was only a part, in many cases only a small part, of the make up of a student's life and, moreover, we were struck by the ways in which many young people's lives were so complex. In obvious ways, this translated for some students into little real engagement with their college courses and many openly told us about how little time they spent on their studies. As they revealed to us, there was in fact much to occupy their lives, some of it to do with prevailing financial circumstances, some of it to do with relationships and some of it to do with being on inappropriate courses or not having the skills and attitudes to 'succeed'.

So, for us, as with many of the teachers in our study, we have become interested in the individual, with their individual stories and lives, captured in what we call the 'learning journey'. Thus, the focus here is 'listening' to learners and has provided us with an empirical framework within which to take up several analytic themes that have been prominent in the discourses on those in further and adult education in recent years. These themes will be summarized briefly as a conceptual background, and subsequently will be interrogated in the light of the learners' 'voices' that follow. They are important for a number of reasons. First, they remind us that students are flesh and blood people who should not only or primarily be regarded as 'learning units' which draw down money. Second, and related to the first point, individuals are just that. They come with different histories, they have differing aspirations and in different ways they exercise their free will, and it is evident that the collectivized approaches of mass education seem to be a poor fit for so many. Third, the point is not just to draw attention to the sometimes dire circumstances in which people struggle to be 'full-time' or 'part-time' students. There are important messages for FE teachers and college managers, and for those who comprise the policy communities that can make a difference. In short, for many of our learners, the learning journey is a perilous one and, whereas we can continue to use aggregated notions of learners and their backgrounds to produce aggregated responses, there is a need to be more mindful of what it is like to live in contemporary Wales and what it is like to be a student in contemporary FE.

## METHODS

The paper arises from the work of a research project funded by the Economic and Social Research Council (ESRC) through the Teaching and Learning Research Programme (TLRP), entitled '*Learning and Working in Further Education in Wales*'. The fieldwork was conducted in a two-year period up to July 2007. It explored the relationships between forty-five 'core' students' learning journeys and twenty-seven 'core' teachers' working lives in ten pro-gramme areas, on seven campuses in three colleges of further education in south Wales. Both the students and teachers were interviewed at the start and end of this period. In between, they completed up to seven periodic Learning Journals, in which they usually responded in writing, to a set of questions. In effect, these journals were structured diaries, with questions designed to capture the changing nature of the learning journey. Thus, the nature of the questions was determined as time went on, and focused on emergent themes. In addition, there was extensive ethnographic observation of the learning settings in which the selected teachers worked with the selected students. Eight focus groups also took place in the colleges at the start and end of the project, that is, sixteen in total, involving over 100 students. The purpose of these was to gauge the extent to which the issues and themes identified by the 'core' students were more generally applicable as well as providing another source of data. As the project developed data were subjected to thematic analysis relating to the research question, in this case: to determine the ways in which learner identities are shaped by the social settings in which they are formed; and, to analyse the nature of social interaction in learning settings in FE and the influence of the wider economic, social and cultural environment on this interaction.

From an early stage, the study provided a rich source of qualitative and ethnographic data about learning (and teaching) in further education and enabled us both to identify new themes and build on the analytical insights provided by previous research, as illustrated in the following.

## EMERGENT ANALYTIC THEMES

Essentially, we were interested in learners' biographies and identities, and in the ways that these were revealed through students' own narrative accounts. Early into our fieldwork, from listening to students it became apparent that our own findings were, on the one hand, congruent with what others had found, and on the other, gave new and often more in-depth insights into students' lives. We found the notion of identity to be dynamic, in a temporal sense, changing over time, as the metaphors of learning career, learning trajectory and learning journey denote. Identity is also dynamic because it is a multiple construct formed out of personal history, biography, and place, linked to roles and situations compounded with disposition to learn, motivation and aspiration.

We were struck by the complex and what we termed the 'wider lives' of the students in our study, that is, in the ways that they resolved the tensions of being a student and dealing with life at home, with friends, in part-time work and so on. So, as Atkins (2008) also noted, we found a tension in balancing the demands of social lives and learning. While it is axiomatic to say that learners' life-worlds are complex, it is valuable to be reminded not only of the very large set of influences that are interrelated in the way they affect learners' lives but also how the complex and intricate interplay and interrelatedness can work. An appreciation of the denseness of this complexity shows up the limitations of the notions of 'barriers' to participation and learning that were developed extensively, and conceptualized to include, for example, situational and dispositional barriers (McGivney, 1990).

In rather obvious ways, most students said that they were in further education to improve their qualifications and to increase their chances of getting a job or of getting better jobs. It was common for students to believe in the transformative capacity of further education, that is, to not just lead to better jobs and to higher earnings, but also to change their lives. However, only time will tell if the envisioned futures described by students will be realized. As we found in our research, Ball et al. (1999) for example has identified the sorts of fantasy futures some students construct, and Atkins (2008) to the preoccupation with celebrity lifestyle, particularly among younger learners and the gap between these and their occupational aspirations. Some not only were unaware of the ways to explore and fulfil their career pathways (Bathmaker, 2001), but in some cases we also found something of a gap between student rhetoric about their hopes for the future and their reluctance to undertake study inside and outside of the college day. At the same time, FE was being promoted in policy documents as a means to transform lives and to increase earnings by obtaining the skills needed by a globally competitive economy. Envisioned futures were in part, therefore, driven by what Goodlad and Thompson (2007, p. 2) called 'policy dream weavers', in turn, 'caught' by students and turned into 'dream careers'.

Indeed, in many ways, the idealised learner constructed in policy contrasts with the rich and varied individuals uncovered by in-depth research. It might be inevitable that governments place their emphasis on economic performance, and students do demonstrate, at least in part, an instrumental motivation to achieve the qualifications so widely promoted by policy makers (see Ecclestone, 2002). However, the importance of super-complexity in learners' lives is not sufficiently understood or reflected in national policies of lifelong learning linked to the Lisbon Strategy of 2000 (Brine, 2006), nor in the discourse of the responsible learner (Webb and Warren, 2007). Alternatively, where policy does take an interest in the harder to reach groups, they are often characterized as a problem. For example, they are viewed as being located at the margins; but little is known about their lives and motivations (Quinn et al., 2008). Closely associated with policy, attention is paid in research to the interplay between the public policies and problems and the private lives and decisions, as private stories are written in conditions determined by structures. Individual narratives reveal how structural forces operate and also how aspects of structure may be influenced by learners (see James and Biesta, 2007). The decision not to progress on a course of study might well be a pragmatic one (Hodkinson, 1996).

In further education in the UK, attention to the quality of teaching in FE is a relatively recent matter (Harkin, 2005) while Coffield et al. (2004, p. 47) have referred to learning and teaching practice in further education lacking an 'explicit, coherent and agreed theory of pedagogy' and Salisbury et al. (2008b) reported that FE teachers did not readily draw on established bodies of knowledge of learning and teaching when discussing their own approaches to practice. Students also have a view of what works for them, for example, preferring to work in groups and engage in discussion, rather than being 'talked at'. Elsewhere (Jephcote et al., 2008a, 2008b) we have drawn attention to the complex interplay between learners, their outside college lives and interactions with teachers to suggest that learning is a highly negotiated activity.

The metaphors 'learning journey', 'learning career' (Bloomer and Hodkinson, 2000) and 'learning trajectory' (for example, Gorard, 2002) are constructs for seeing learning in context, acknowledging social and cultural influences and their impact on individual learner identity; they provide opportunities to explore the individual's relationship to their own learning (Goodlad and Thompson, 2007). However, 'career' misleadingly suggests a linear process while many learners' 'journeys' are fractured, precarious ones, to the extent that the notion of 'revolving doors' has become commonly used as a representation of the frequent and abrupt changes of direction that learners display. Perhaps then, too much is expected of some students, at least as indicated by formal measures and outcomes and not enough credit is given to other benefits, such as social gains, and the support provided by FE in what for many students is a critical stage of their transition. As Schuller (2003) has proposed, it might be time to recognize a triangle of wider benefits that embraces enhancement of human capital, social capital and personal identity.

The themes identified here can be discerned in the glimpses of learners' lives that are presented below. Choosing who should 'speak' for or be taken as 'representative' of learners in further education colleges in Wales is not without its own problems, especially given the size and diversity of the sector. We draw here on one focus group interview with part-time female access students to give voice to those who in fact are representative of the sector which in Wales, in which the vast majority are adults, on part-time courses (85 per cent) and, in higher age groups, are mostly female (62 per cent). Two vignettes of full-time male students illustrate the experiences of those on what are often referred to as more 'traditional' courses. In all cases pseudonyms have been used.

## SOURCE ONE: FOCUS GROUP INTERVIEW

This focus group meeting with seven students, which lasted for two hours, provided a rich survey of the realities of life as an adult, returning learner. Before discussing the interview we should note the context. The group members were on an Access to Nursing and Health Professions course. All the group members have applied to local universities. The area is still blighted by the disappearance of heavy industry and coal mining, and has had relatively little direct benefit from the economic development evident elsewhere. With high rates of economic inactivity, it is a focus of major regeneration efforts and a drive to raise the qualification and skill levels of the population.

The importance of these contextual factors came out clearly when the group was invited to look back over earlier experiences, including their education. There were numerous tales of constraints and disruptions in schooling arising from familial or structural influences. Sue Keane (31) had: 'been brought up in an environment where girls are not really looked upon to go far in education'. Di Nissons (38), out of education for twenty-two years, was twice divorced and had five children: 'my parents were divorced. . . . I grew up in domestic violence, I experienced domestic violence . . . and it's made me stronger and it's made me want to go out and prove to the world – that I can do it'. Carrie Morris (27), who described herself as 'always in trouble as a child', had been a teenage mother who was not allowed to resume her studies: 'I've just been determined right the way through that I'm going to finish this course no matter what.'

Almost without exception, like Carrie above, the students were vehement about their determination to achieve, and saw their opportunity to study in FE in a focused and purposeful way that contrasted strongly with the low levels of engagement and commitment exhibited by many younger students in our project. Becoming and being a student involved transitions and challenges. Sue described the course as a 'rollercoaster' and for several students the middle period was like being stuck in a 'dark tunnel'. For some learners a key challenge was coming to terms with the unfamiliar processes of assessment and the discouraging experience of referral grades on assignments. Molly Shears (20) expressed it like this:

> Next day boom, bang, wrong, referred and it's like – It seems to be a continuous thing. Every single lesson, every single thing you give in you've worked really hard, you've given in – referred. You do it again. . . . you think, oh I've put so much into it . . . then that's what really knocks your confidence.

By Christmas, Molly was very close to giving up, and her parents made clear that they would support her; however, the strength of her dream kept her on the course:

> But I want to see myself in ten years' time living in that penthouse suite in America, married to a doctor with four children running round me. I want to see that, I want to be there, and I know if I don't work that out I'm not going to get it.

One student spoke of her sense of a more profound threat, of a change in her identity and possible alienation from former friends:

I've met certain people that have, erm, been and gone through university and I've like noticed a change in them. And I'm really scared because I don't want to lose – You know, I don't want to lose my past, do you know what I mean? I know where I'm from and I'm really proud of that . . . But I know, I understand there will be a change. There's got to be hasn't there otherwise you don't progress . . . But do you also think that the people around you change as well towards you . . . because you're trying to progress and further yourself? Although you are not changing these people . . . have changed around you because they've still stood . . . whereas you have gone on to improve yourself.

Group members had many tales of finding that wider-life influences conspired to thwart or interrupt their studies, and feeling that dice are stacked against them. A main part of their effort and struggle was about money; everyone in the group reported financial hardship, whatever their circumstances. None of the women who were divorced received maintenance payments from their former partners. Several Access learners received £500, including coverage of travel costs. Nevertheless, a number of the group still needed to work part-time, evenings and weekends, and they described the stresses and pressures on them resulting from this. Molly had two part-time jobs, and Elly Amos (33), a single mother, worked two night shifts each week, while Carrie Morris was married and received no grant because of her husband's income.

Sue Keane (31) and Molly were full-time students on the Access course. Sue was ill and unable to work and was conscious of the effects on her children. For Shelley, the stress was that her employment consumed vital study time, making her frustrated:

I work as a part-time customer assistant . . . and I also work still on the NHS . . . But I don't get a grant because I still live at home with my parents and they take in their wages into account even though I'm 20 . . . I've got my own things to worry about and it's just not fair and I mean I do work. I work all weekends it's seven days a week constantly for me, it's not a day off. I don't get the option to have a day off!

These learners were juggling college attendance, the demands of study and course work, paid employment and family responsibilities, displaying immense determination and tenacity. Like Sue, above, they were not unaware of the costs, including the effects on others, including experiencing some alienation within the family, and other double-edged or negative effects of studying, for example having less time to devote to care and 'service' within the family. Molly said that she was: 'a bad mother at the moment because I don't get to spend time with my daughter. I haven't seen my mother for a fortnight 'cos I'm there every night on the laptop, you know.' Rennie Ellis summed up the single-mindedness required to stick with the course despite the difficulties: 'I'm forgetting myself most of the time, becoming hard to myself.' Sue spoke of a degree of family estrangement due to her changed circumstances: 'I've noticed I don't see a lot of my family, actually, yeah, they definitely think I am having a midlife crisis. They look at me weirdly.'

Unconditional support from wider family members was not universally available, some experienced little help, while some did report support from both their neighbours and relatives living nearby, with mothers, sisters or even 19-year-old daughters to collect their children from school and baby sit whilst they studied or did paid night or weekend shifts. In their turn, college teachers and systems responded by straining to provide the support that would retain the students on the course and to foster constructive and nurturing responses and group relationships. Almost all students admitted to feelings of self-doubt about their abilities as well as personal difficulties relating to wider outside lives and situations. Sue told of the importance of the group in giving her support after her home had been burgled: '. . . my fellow students as well, they've been absolutely marvellous, absolutely better than my family.'

In describing what they thought constituted effective learning and teaching methods there was strong support for the use of whole class discussion. They were equally emphatic about the value of informal discussion between themselves, something clearly seen to involve collaborating to translate, or decode, the subject-specific language ('jargon') into something comprehensible.

The group members had much to say about what they had gained from the course, and generally this involved increased self-awareness and self-belief. These are typical statements:

'a lot more faith in my own abilities' . . . 'a lot more confident in what I can do' . . . 'ready now to progress to the next level and looking forward to it whereas before I was dreading the thought of even applying to university'. . . 'improved key skills with maths and English and things and sort of proving to yourself that nothing's impossible' . . . 'You can do anything you want to do'.

Sue made clear that this increase in self-confidence is not inevitable and that the process of transition is complex: 'Mine's going down whereas, you know, others seems to go up . . . I was an auxiliary [nurse] . . . I felt really, you know, confident and competent in what I was doing . . . and I've come here and I feel a little bit out of water.' Two group members emphasized that their worlds had been enlarged; according to Elly Amos: . . . 'being a single mum, you know, there's not many – not much opportunity to meet other people that are in a different mindset to what they tend to label us as.' Molly Shears was now impatient to go further: 'I like the thought of meeting new people from different places, getting to know them. That's why university and college have always appealed to me . . .' Can't wait to meet new people, get in there, get stuck in.'

## SOURCE TWO: LEARNER VIGNETTES

As a means to draw together and make sense of the data, we have drawn from a variety of the sources such as journal entries, interviews and observation to compile learner vignettes to illustrate some of the constraints and difficulties in the students' wider outside college lives, alongside their on-campus experiences. Space does not allow the reproduction of the full accounts, but here we highlight those features more pertinent to the analytic themes.

*Howard: GNVQ Intermediate in Computing and BTEC National Certificate in Computing*
Howard was aged 18 at the start of the study and described himself as a 'very poor school attender' who was off school for most of his final year with irritable bowel syndrome, spending much of his time confined to the house. Howard had 'nerves' and admitted that he came to college because his neighbour was coming and it made it easier to come with a friend. He often arrived at college tired but keen. He completed assignments in his bedroom on a computer and he won the 2006 GNVQ Intermediate Computing student prize following a 'stack' of distinctions grades. Howard was irritated when classmates did not do the necessary coursework and felt held back from starting new assignments by other students who took up teachers' time on their late submissions, catch up work and re-drafting. Howard felt this was unfair.

Howard found things financially difficult, relying on his mum and dad for 'handouts'. He was very judgemental about mates who wasted their £30 Educational Maintenance Allowance money on alcohol. He worked for four months in a part-time agency cleaning job at a supermarket, working 4.30–8 a.m., but his early rising disturbed the household causing rows with his step father and also made him fall asleep in class! Howard had left home a few times when things were difficult but returned for his mum. Family life sounded fraught and Howard became quite emotional when talking about it.

Penny, his course tutor, championed his case, kept in touch with him via email and phone calls. She offered praise and affirmed him. In the micro lab Howard was a serious and industrious student, who felt significant and enjoyed the effort:

> and it's paying off with all of the Ds [distinctions] I'm getting and the way the lecturers look at me – they treat me differently compared to some of the people who are scraping passes – and Penny thinks it's brilliant that she gets the pleasure to teach people like me.

He liked what he called 'hands on learning and self researching' and loved doing witty IT presentations. In class he was strategic about his seating position: 'Being around friends can make me comfortable, being in the same class as friends is comfortable but when you sit with them that's a distraction'.

He was unsure about ideas for future employment, 'I don't know what jobs I can get with this qualification. Er – there was an article in the newspapers saying they're crying out for IT technicians and everything in Wales'. But Howard had concerns about the value of his IT qualifications in the labour market, 'the only fear I've got about doing all of this work is that one of my classmate's father has a degree in IT but works as a security guard in Tesco!' He hoped to continue computing studies at a local university but would like to go with mates, not alone. Close relationships with his teachers and peers along with tangible success, was Penny felt, compensation 'for a difficult home situation'. She described Howard as having 'blossomed from the nervous awkward student who joined the GNVQ course in September 2005'.

### Sam: BTEC National Certificate in 3D Design

Sam was aged 19 at the start of the study and reported a chequered school history. His school teachers would remember him as 'a rather difficult pupil . . . often in trouble . . . I just didn't want to be there . . . I was a bit of a rebel . . . I didn't take it all that serious'. That said, he obtained nine GCSEs grades B to D, remained at school for most of year 12 and did AS level Design and Technology, but was rebellious and left at 17 to work in Halfords for eighteen months. He surprised and delighted his parents when at 19 and 'having had enough of working in a dead end job' he secretly enrolled on the BTEC 3D Design Course and announced it over the phone to his dad.

College staff reported mixed efforts in year one: 'He didn't exactly kill himself and put the hours in!' Nevertheless, he achieved an overall merit and continued to a higher course with firm ideas for university in 2007. Convicted of actual bodily harm following an incident in a pub, two months in prison caused him to reflect on this as 'a real learning experience' and believed that it helped him sort himself out. Community service followed and he worked on the allotments of senior citizens, did some anger management training and met with a probation officer weekly. His parents were supportive and forgiving as the pub incident was related to a bad relationship with a girl who had 'put me under pressure to leave school, rather than go to college and get qualified'.

He worked at Halfords, just part-time at weekends. He tended to do course work in college, though he did lots of Internet searching and used Google Sketcher at home for his design work. In his Learning Journal entries he described enjoying:

'. . . planning projects and working things out by trial and error. I learn best that way. It works or it doesn't and the problem solving helps me find solutions. Tutors are on hand to suggest ideas and show us what might work and I like the individual one-to-one way in which they work with us'.

Course tutor Doug was delighted with Sam's progress and standard of design and practical work. As a result he was 2007 Student of the Year for his course and received a prize at the prestigious College Summer Exhibition and Prize Giving. His parents, especially his mum, were visibly emotional. He has accepted a place at the University of Glamorgan and his ultimate goal is civil engineering like his dad, whom he clearly admires.

He was motivated by ideas of material wealth and lifestyle, his dad's status and new Volvo: 'Obviously, like at home, I look at my life now and I just think I've got it really easy, like my parents and stuff, I get everything off my dad. But I want to be able to *give* that – where we live, and the money, the job, I want all of it.' Describing the influences on his dreams and goals he depicted his father: 'My dad's a project manager so he does different jobs all the time . . . He really enjoys it. There's not many people above him, he's worked really hard like that. So I want to – I kind of want to *be* like that.'

## CONCLUDING REMARKS

Significant circumstantial barriers to participating in formal learning did not deter several of the learners in this project, including some of those referred to above.

The interviews highlight the limitations and dangers of over-emphasizing the metaphor of 'barriers' to participation; several of these learners have not been deterred by traditional barriers such as time, cost, travel and lack of initial qualification (Gorard et al., 1999). However, explorations of individuals' narratives reveal the impact of the resulting conditions of difficulty and the attendant risks that learners strove to cope with. Our learners' lives and identities were about much more than being a learner – as the focus group and the different cases of Howard and Sam make clear. They were appreciative of the support provided by their teachers and their ethic of care, displayed in attending to students' wider lives and circumstances and deployed through teachers' emotional labour (Hochschild, 1983). This aspect of teachers' work was central to the positive aspects of accounts provided by learners here and elsewhere in our research (Salisbury et al., 2008).

With regard to learning outcomes, Schuller (2003) had noted that, compared to the attention given to motivation and participation, much less work has been done on the more complex questions of what happens as a result of learning, especially the wider benefits. The learners featured above were clear not only about skill acquisition and the achievement of formal learning outcomes but were emphatic about the wider benefits they had gained from their learning in terms of increased confidence and self-belief. Some, for example, parents of young children, were able recover a sense of adult identity, while others were able to develop an identity as a learner that had been denied to them earlier in life.

These individual private stories were played out in the structural contexts of policies and institutions. Policies, at a macro-level, are far removed from the often messy realities of learners' lives yet they are founded on conceptualizations of learners, for instance in the ever-increasing emphasis on skills agendas for 'lifelong learning' in the 'knowledge economy'. Brine (2006) has delineated ways in which, for example, European Commission policy documents categorize learners crudely, yet with unflinching consistency, continue to ignore and obscure vital features, such as class, ethnicity, gender and power relations. As Quinn et al. (2008) also noted, too often learners are problematized and pathologized. In this context it is necessary for policy formation to recognize and understand both the social and cultural conditions of learning experienced by adult learners and the complex realities of learning lives as they are lived. The need for this is emphasized by the fact that further education colleges, and present policy preoccupations, in Wales and the UK, are dominated by concerns about 14–19 learners and a degree of invisibility surrounds adult students in further education.

Coming to college was seen by both young and older learners as an important part of their lives. It was, of course, only a part of their lives, so that managing lives included managing learning and often, as an individual's situation became complex and demanding, it was 'learning' that was the casualty. Students adopted a range of coping strategies; many tried to contain their studies within the timeframe of the college day, others studied when their children were asleep or partners out of sight. Thus, at other times, they could attend to matters arising in their wider lives. In turn, teachers were acutely aware of, on the one-hand, the need to strive for academic results and, on the other, the need to cater for and accommodate the wider realities of their students' lives. In these ways learning was negotiated within classroom settings.

Ongoing analysis of our data confirms that the learning journeys that students embark on have their own antecedents rooted in disparate experiences of schooling and, that at relatively young ages, learners lead and manage complex private lives. This points to the almost self-evident fact that 'learning journeys' do not start or end at common points and, crucially, the nature of the 'journeys' are not only different but also impact on the 'destination'. Our conclusion does not offer a neat set of solutions. On the contrary, in recognition of the complex and individual nature of 'learning journeys' and the 'collision' of experiences that underpin learning calls for something of a complex response. Not least, although we have found the metaphor of a 'learning journey' helpful it is also problematic in the ways in which it might suggest a planned, linear and continuous route.

## ACKNOWLEDGEMENTS

1. The paper arises out of an ESRC funded research project – *Learning and Working in Further Education in Wales* which is part of the ESRC/TLRP extension to Wales programme.
2. We are of course grateful to the three participating colleges whose managers and teaching staff from across seven campuses have opened their doors to us and who along with students, agreed to participate in the research project and given us their permission to use interview, journal and observational data.
3. John Roberts, University of Wales Newport, was a member of the research team.

## REFERENCES

Atkins, L. (2008). 'Travelling hopefully: an exploration of the limited possibilities for Level 1 students in the English Further Education System', *Research in Post Compulsory Education*, 13, 2, 195–205.

Ball, S., Macrae, S., and Maguire, M. (1999). 'Young lives, diverse choices and imagined futures in an education and training market', *International Journal of Inclusive Education*, 3, 3, 195–224.

Bathmaker, A. M. (2001). 'It's a perfect education: lifelong learning and the experience of foundation-level GNVQ students', *Journal of Vocational education and Training*, 53, 1, 81–100.

Bloomer, M., and Hodkinson, P. (2000). 'Learning careers: continuity and change in young people's dispositions to learning', *British Educational Research Journal*, 26, 5, 583–97.

Brine, J. (2006). 'Lifelong learning and the knowledge economy: those that know and those that do not – the discourse of the European Union', *British Educational Research Journal*, 32, 5, 231–56.

Coffield, F. (2004). *Should We Be Using Learning Styles? What Research Has to Say to Practice*, London: Learning and Skills Research Centre.

Commission of the European Communities (2000). *Presidency Conclusions: Lisbon European Council*, 23 and 24 March 2000, Commission of the European Communities.

Chappell, C. (2003). *Reconstructing the Lifelong Learner: Pedagogy and Identity in Individual, Organisational and Social Changes*, London: Routledge/Falmer.

Davidson, J. (2004). 'Distinctive education policies in Wales', *Forum*, 46, 2.

Eccelstone, K. (2002). *Learning Autonomy in Post-16 Education: The Politics and Practice of Formative Assessment*, London: RoutledgeFalmer.

Flint, C. (2004). *Further Education and Adult Learning*, Leicester: NIACE.

Goodlad, C. and Thompson, V. (2007). 'Dream weavers and dream catchers: exploring the aspirations and imagined futures of students in transition from further education to higher education', a paper presented at the International conference on Researching Transitions in Lifelong Learning, University of Stirling, 22–4 June 2007, *www.sheffield.ac.uk/further/higher*.

Gorard, S., Fevre, R. and Rees, G. (1999). 'Patterns of participation in lifelong learning: do families make a difference?' *British Educational Research Journal*, 25, 4, 517–32.

Gorard, S. (2002). *Lifelong Learning Trajectories in Wales: Results of the NIACE Adult Learners' Survey 2002*, Cardiff: NIACE.

Harkin, J. (2005). 'Fragments stored against my ruin: the place of educational theory in the professional development of teachers in further education', *Journal of Vocational Education and Training*, 57, 2, 57–79.

Hodkinson, P. (1996). 'Careership: the individual, choices and markets in the transition to work', in J. Avis, M. Bloomer, G. Esland, D. Gleeson and P. Hodkinson, *Knowledge and Nationhood*, London: Cassell.

Hochschild, A. (1983). *The Managed Heart: Commercialisation of Human Feeling*, Berkeley, CA: University of California Press.

James, D. and Biesta, G. (eds) (2007). *Improving Learning Cultures in Further Education*, Abingdon: Routledge.

Jephcote, M. and Salisbury, J. (2007). 'The long shadow of incorporation: the further education sector in devolved Wales', *The Welsh Journal of Education*, 14, 1, 100–16.

Jephcote, M., Salisbury, J. and Rees, G. (2008a). 'Being a teacher in Further Education in changing times', *Research in Post-Compulsory Education*, 13, 2, 16–171.

Jephcote, M. and Salisbury, J. (2008b). 'The wider social context of learning: beyond the classroom door', *International Journal of Learning*, 15, 6, 281–8.

Kennedy, H. (1999). *Learning Works*, Coventry: Further Education Funding Council.

Leitch, S. (2006). *Prosperity for All in the Global Economy: World Class Skills*, Norwich: HMSO.

McGivney, V. (1990). *Education's for Other People. Access to Education for Non-Participant Adults*, Leicester: National Institute of Adult Continuing Education.

McGivney, V. (2003). *Adult Learning Pathways: Through Routes or Cul-de-sacs?* Leicester: NIACE.

Quinn, J., Lawy, R. and Diment, K. (2008). 'Dead end kids in dead end jobs? Reshaping debates in young people in jobs without training', *Research in Post Compulsory Education*, 13, 2, 185–94.

Raffe, D., Croxford, L. and Brannen, K. (2001). 'Participation in full-time education beyond 16: a "home-international" comparison', *Research Papers in Education*, 16, 1, 43–68.

Salisbury, J. and Jephcote, M. (2008a). 'Initial encounters of an FE kind', *Research in Post-Compulsory Education*, 13, 2, 149–63.

Salisbury, J., Jephcote, M., Rees, G. and Roberts, J. (2008b forthcoming). 'Emotional labour, ethics of care and work intensification in FE colleges, *Research Papers in Education*.

Sargant, N. and Aldridge, F. (2003). *Adult Learning and Social Division: A Persistent Pattern*, Leicester: NIACE.

Schuller, T. (2003). *The Benefits of Learning*, in N. Sargant, and F. Aldridge (eds), *Adult Learning and Social Division: A Persistent Pattern*, Leicester: NIACE.

Webb, A. (2007). *Promise and Performance: The Report of the Independent Review of the Mission and Purpose of Further Education in Wales in the Context of the Learning Country: Vision into Action*, Cardiff: Welsh Assembly Government.

Webb, S. and Warren, S. (2007). 'Public problems and private troubles: adult learners, "responsible learners" and the "new" FE', paper presented at BERA Conference, University of London Institute of Education, 6 September 2007.

Welsh Assembly Government (2001). *The Learning Country: A Paving Document. A Comprehensive Education and Lifelong-Learning Programme to 2010 in Wales*, Cardiff: Welsh Assembly Government.

Welsh Assembly Government (2006). *Learning and Labour Market Intelligence for Wales*, Cardiff: Welsh Assembly Government.

Welsh Assembly Government (2006). *The Learning Country2: Delivering the Promise*, Cardiff: Welsh Assembly Government, Department for Education Lifelong Learning and Skills.

Welsh Assembly Government (2007). *Wales: Moving Towards the Learning Country: Survey on Adult Participation in Learning in Wales 2007*, Cardiff: Welsh Assembly Government, Department for Children, Education Lifelong Learning and Skills.

Welsh Assembly Government (2008). *Skills that Work for Wales: A Skills and Employment Strategy*, Cardiff: Department for Children, Education, Lifelong Learning and Skills.

# 8. YOUNG PEOPLE'S VIEWS ON STATUTORY DRUG EDUCATION IN WALES

*Stuart Jones, Penny Byrne, Richard Williams, David Adamson and Morton Warner*

## ABSTRACT

*This paper explores young people's perceptions of statutory drug education in Wales. The research data presented in this paper are derived from a series of focus groups (n=32) conducted in 2001/2002 and 2005 with young people aged between 11–18 years. It also draws on data produced through semi-structured interviews conducted with substance misuse professionals. Despite some improvement between 2001/2002 and 2005, participants were generally critical of statutory drugs education. They argued that drug education (1) needed greater prioritization, (2) required more innovative, interactive and discursive modes of delivery (3) should be delivered by individuals with direct personal experience of substance misuse issues and (4) information should be balanced, accurate and objective. The research also identified problems in the consistency of provision (although this was a key area of improvement between 2001/2002 and 2005), and recorded areas of fundamental confusion and misunderstanding in the participants' knowledge of different substances. Although its impact and effectiveness remains to be seen, there is, however, evidence of an improving picture in drug education policy which now appears to be developing in ways that would be welcomed by the young people in this study.*

## INTRODUCTION

This article is based on results from two qualitative research projects examining young people's perceptions of statutory drug education in Wales. For both studies, drugs were defined as including misuse of prescribed substances, as well as alcohol and tobacco. The research revealed a population that frequently displayed some knowledge about different drugs and their effects, but whose knowledge was also subject to some fundamental gaps, misunderstandings and inaccuracies. The young people were also frequently highly critical about their experiences of drug education and expressed concerns about the content, delivery styles, teaching personnel, frequency and prioritization of drug education. However, the findings also suggest that recent developments in drug education policy and guidance, such as an emphasis on harm reduction and more interactive and innovative styles of delivery, would be welcomed by the young people in this study.

## ABOUT THE STUDIES

The findings presented in this article are drawn from two separate qualitative research projects conducted in Wales in 2001/2002 and 2005. Both studies employed a combination of semi-structured interviews with individuals from drug education and treatment services and focus groups with young people aged between 11–18 years held in schools and in community based settings. Although this article draws upon some of the interview data, its main concern is with young people's perceptions of drugs education recorded during the focus group discussions.

The use of focus groups enabled the research team to consult a relatively large number of young people whilst the discursive format allowed the participants considerable scope to define the agenda for discussion and to elaborate on the issues they felt were important. Additionally, it is likely that the group format meant that individuals were less likely to feel targeted, an important consideration given the sensitivity of the subject matter and the classroom venue for the majority of the focus groups.

At the beginning of each session, the researchers established a number of ground rules and emphasized that participants were not being asked about their own or others drug use and would be discouraged from doing so if they brought it up of their own volition. Discussion was generated from a series of prompts about participants' knowledge of drugs and their effects, perceptions of local availability of drugs and levels of peer group use, extent of drugs education received (including education received outside school) and their feelings towards it. A general discussion then took place about the group's preferred format for drug education.

In total, thirty-two focus groups were conducted with groups of between eight and fifteen young people and with groups which varied in composition according to age, gender and venue. In the 2001/2002 study, the groups were conducted in a variety of contrasting areas within a single unitary authority area in south Wales, whereas the 2005 study sought a broader perspective by selecting three contrasting unitary authority areas in Wales (a rural area, an industrial valleys area and a large city). In part, this wider perspective was selected as a means of validating the findings from the earlier 2001/2002 study against those of a broader sample of young people in Wales. Several focus groups were conducted in youth projects to try to reach those who might not have been attending school. This was partially in recognition of the correlation between increased likelihood of drug use and truancy (Johnston et al, 2000) and/or school exclusions (Powis et al, 1998; Fuller, 2005) and vulnerable young people generally (Becker and Roe, 2005). These venues were also identified in recognition of the particular and distinctive contribution of community-based organizations in devising and delivering drug education (White and Pitts 1998; Black et al, 2003), an issue which is explored further in later sections of this paper.

However, logistical difficulties meant that only a small proportion of the total number of focus groups were conducted in community-based settings, and even then did not necessarily enable the research team to talk to truanting, excluded or otherwise vulnerable young people. Consequently, the research dealt primarily with the views and opinions of 'ordinary' young people and their experiences of statutory drugs education delivered in a school setting. In keeping with this, the discussion here restricts itself to mapping the considerable commonalities of perception and experiences of drug education focus groups among focus group participants rather than exploring differences between different groups.

This latter task is best left to other research, more specifically focused on the detailed exploration of the intricate and nuanced differences which might exist between different social groupings. Our dataset is not particularly well suited to this task, as although (in terms of qualitative research) quite sizeable in its aggregate form, individual sample sizes are much smaller when disaggregated into different groupings. We would not, for example, feel confident in arguing that any difference between the focus groups conducted in what amounts to a handful of rural areas were representative of rural Wales. Equally, the sample is not structured in a way that would allow meaningful insights about differences in attitudes and perception according to differences in socio-economic backgrounds. Whilst considerable differences exist between the socio-economic profiles of the different areas in which the research was conducted, we cannot confer these differences upon the individual focus group participants. To do so would be a matter of ecological fallacy. It is also worth noting that whilst examining young people's likes and dislikes in terms of drug education, the authors do not claim that these perceptions are necessarily coincidental with what is effective in drug education. As is discussed below, assessing the effectiveness of drug education is an area of considerable methodological complexity and debate. It is, however, reasonable to assume that there is some relationship between the extent to which drug education packages are well received (or otherwise) by their target audiences and their effectiveness. It is in this context that we hope to make a practical contribution to the drug education debate.

## YOUNG PEOPLE, DRUG USE AND DRUG EDUCATION

Despite a variety of available data sources, it is impossible to provide an exact assessment of the extent and nature of illegal drug use among young people in the UK. However, at least two points can be established fairly easily. The first is that young people's use of illegal drugs is dominated by occasional use of cannabis, and that problematic use of hard drugs such as crack and heroin is a marginal activity. This is consistently the case, whether data are drawn from police arrest figures (Hough, 1996), drug seizures (Sutton and Maynard, 1992), or self-report surveys (Smith and Nutbeam, 1992; Coffield and Gofton 1994; Parker and Measham, 1995; Roberts et al., 1995; Wright and Pearl, 1995). The second is that the use of illegal drugs has risen considerably during the last thirty years, an increase which has been linked to the emergence of the 1990s dance culture (Gilvarry, 2000). Young people's consumption of illegal drugs has now reached a level where the 2002/2003 British Crime Survey estimated that nearly half (47 per cent) of all 16–24-year-olds had used an illegal drug in their lifetime (Condon and Smith, 2003).

One of the implications of such widespread consumption of illegal drugs is that it is increasingly problematic to conceptualize drug use as an activity engaged in by only a deviant and marginalized minority. Consequently, Parker and Measham (1995, 1998) developed the normalization thesis as a means of conceptualizing the way in which illegal drug use has drifted from the margins to the mainstream. The normalization thesis has been criticized for overplaying the significance of statistics relating to drug use (Shiner and Newburn, 1997), failing to account for geographical variations (Coffield and Gofton, 1994) and ignoring the heterogeneity of young people, their cultures and experiences (Shildrick, 2002). To these criticisms could be added the failure to account for temporal variations as different drugs and drug taking itself drift in and out of fashion. However, though critics have tended to disagree with the detail of the normalization thesis, its core premise that drug use is increasingly widespread in young people's lives holds up.

As our research deliberately did not ask participants about their own or others' attitudes towards or patterns of drug consumption, and also asked about legal drugs, we are unable to comment upon the veracity of the normalization thesis in this respect. However, it is possible to argue that there was evidence of normalization of illegal drug use in the sense that it formed part of an unquestioned backdrop of the participants' everyday lives. The drugs issue was not an abstract issue, but something which happened visibly within their community, peer groups and family networks. This is not to equate normalization with universal approval, however, as many participants felt it to be a negative facet of their social world. For example, one group of younger participants spoke of their parents not allowing them to play in the park because of the older boys who smoked cannabis there. Likewise, a group of sixth form students expressed irritation at the 'goths' who were felt to dominate parties with their 'bongs'. However, normalization in the sense of drug use as an unexceptional feature of young people's social worlds does not necessarily entail an accurate or comprehensive knowledge of the subject. As is explored elsewhere in this paper, one of the most striking findings of the research was participants' distorted understanding of the relative risks and prevalence of different forms of drug use. Such a finding serves to underscore the importance of effective education.

## THE IMPORTANCE OF DRUG EDUCATION

The widespread and apparently embedded nature of illegal drug use among young people in the UK means that the provision of accurate and effective education programmes is of importance. Historically, however, much drugs education appears to have been profoundly influenced by the moral panics that surround illegal drug use, has ignored the dangers of legal drugs and routinely used a combination of shock tactics and a strict abstinence message. Such approaches have been criticized for their poor and unreliable evidence base (Farrell and Strang, 1998) and their ineffective and even counterproductive impact on young people's behaviour (Buckley and White, 2007). As the results of this research further confirm, this type of approach is deeply unpopular with its target audience. More recently, there has been recognition of these shortcomings as policy makers have sought to implement more accurate and balanced drug education packages cast in the harm reduction rather than abstinence mould. The latest Welsh Assembly Government guidance, for example, explicitly advises schools against reliance upon 'fear arousing approaches' and 'single messages (e.g. 'just say no')' (NAW, 2002, p. 18).

Similarly, in England research conducted for the Department for Education and Skills (DfES) by Crompton (2003) made a number of recommendations, which included that drug, alcohol and tobacco education be needs driven and incorporate a harm reduction approach. These recommendations are reflected in the subsequent production of guidelines (DfES, 2003) focused upon the provision of relevant and appropriate, fact-based information delivered through more discursive, active and participatory learning models. For McWhirter and Roberts, these guidelines constitute 'a further step away from the 'just say no' approach in favour of drug education that concentrates on providing accurate information and engaging young people in a reasoned and sensible discussion about drugs' (2004, p. 3).

Our research, therefore, took place during a period of quite fundamental change in drug education as official guidance increasingly both urged and required educators to move away from single message shock tactics and towards a more balanced harm reduction-based model of education. Significantly, the revised WAG guidance which marked this development in Wales was released after the first phase of focus groups drew to a close. Our research should not, however, be interpreted as a straightforward 'before and after' comparison of two distinct and oppositional models of drug education. During the first phase of focus groups in 2001/2002, drug education was subject to considerable local variation both across Wales and within individual local authorities. Participants in these focus groups described a wide variation in both the amount of school-based drug education they received and the model of delivery. This variation included examples of education clearly based on harm reduction principles, as well as education based on the 'just say no' approach. The second phase of focus groups occurred shortly after the introduction of the All Wales School Liaison Core Programme (AWSLCP), which was launched in September 2004 with the aim of promoting greater standardization and professionalization of drug education in schools.

However, the development of effective drugs education continues to be hampered by an evidence deficit. This is related to the lack and poor quality of evaluative research which has been identified as a major concern by various analysts (White and Pitts, 1998; Allot et al., 1999; Lloyd et al., 2000; Parkin and McKeganey, 2000; McGrath et al., 2006). Such concerns are perhaps best exemplified by the experiences of those who have attempted to identify evidence of effectiveness through reviews of existing evaluation research. White and Pitts' (1998) review of drug education evaluations found that only one third of the fifty-five separate evaluations they examined met their criteria for being 'methodologically sound' (White and Pitt, 1998, p. 1479). Similarly, McGrath et al. (2006) felt compelled to reject more than 90 per cent of the evaluation reports they accessed in their review of grey literature. Buckley and White's (2007) review of the role of external contributors in drug education reported that only 42 of the 114 reports they reviewed were considered to be methodologically sound.

In a sense, this is scarcely surprising given the multitude of epistemological, methodological, practical and ethical difficulties which beset any attempts at determining effectiveness in drug education. Problems include, but are not limited to, the imprecise nature of drug use datasets and self report data collection methods, attributing causality, identifying appropriate timescales, determining appropriate criteria of effectiveness and attrition within evaluation samples. This is especially the case in the longer term longitudinal studies needed to assess effectiveness into the critical years of early adulthood (see White and Pitts, 1998).

## THE RESEARCH FINDINGS: YOUNG PEOPLE'S PERCEPTIONS OF DRUG EDUCATION

Each focus group began by asking participants to list the names of different drugs that they knew and from this a discussion was generated about the effects and relative dangers of different drugs. There is not the space here to describe these findings at length but it is worth noting that there was evidence of considerable confusion, misunderstanding and ignorance in participants' understanding of drug related issues. This was most apparent in their perceptions of the relative risks and dangers associated with different substances. Most significantly, the dangers associated with alcohol, volatile substances and, to a lesser extent, nicotine and Benzodiazepan-based prescription pills were routinely underestimated. There is tentative evidence to suggest that perceptions of relative harmfulness are influenced by legal status, levels of media attention which individual drugs had received and the emphasis of the drugs education packages they had previously been exposed to. For example, the first round of focus groups occurred in the wake of widespread media publicity of ecstasy related deaths and in an area where a drug education video had been developed for schools which specifically focused upon ecstasy. Many participants in these focus groups overestimated the dangers of ecstasy and significant numbers believed ecstasy to be more dangerous than heroin. This phenomenon is also commented upon by Manning (2002), who contrasts the high news media profile of ecstasy use with the more muted coverage of volatile substance abuse despite the latter's greater mortality levels.

## INCONSISTENCY OF PROVISION

The focus group discussions exposed considerable inconsistencies in the amount, type and perceived quality of the drug education that participants had received. This was particularly evident in the first round of focus groups conducted in 2001/2002. Here, disparities were not only evident between different schools and different year groups but also within individual year groups and, in some instances, between different participants within the same focus group. Participants reported receiving different degrees and packages of education (ranging from single classroom-based lessons to packages which included trips to local police stations and youth projects). Despite the provision of a rudimentary programme of drug education being a requirement of the national curriculum since 1995 (DfES Circular, 4/95), some participants claimed to have received no drugs education. In most instances, these differences were not explained by changes in school or by factors such as truancy or suspension, but instead appeared to reflect a structural patchiness in the provision of drugs education.

In the intervening years between the first and second series of focus groups, there does appear to have been some improvements in this situation. In Wales, there has been the introduction of the AWSLCP, delivered by police school liaison officers across Wales, which includes a drugs and substance misuse theme as one of three strands in a programme of lessons that deal with crime and disorder issues. The substance misuse strand is structured into five separate components delivered via PSE classes, which are intended to deliver a cumulative programme of education over key stages 1–4 (two of the components are delivered at key stage 2). In its annual report, this programme claimed to have accessed 93 per cent of Welsh schools in the period between 2004–5, and by 2007 coverage had increased to 97 per cent of Welsh schools (Markit Training and Consultancy, 2007). However, despite these developments there was a strong sense from all of the 2005 focus group participants that inconsistency was still an issue, that they would like more drug education classes, that drug education should start at an earlier age and that it should include a greater diversity of perspectives. Significantly, even in 2007 the evaluation of the AWSLCP continued to recommend 'greater consistency in terms of the delivery of the programme and the quality of the learning experiences' (Markit Training and Consultancy, 2007: 89).

**Style of delivery**
In both sets of focus groups the participants were frequently highly critical of the style in which their drugs education had been delivered. The core complaints in this respect were that drug education lessons were 'boring' and unimaginative. Thus, comments included:

'Too much to read'

'Bored of the same thing'

'They just read bits of paper'

'Just reading it from a book'

'They give us a sheet and tell us to do it'

'You feel like you're being lectured'

(2001/2002, 14–16 years, mixed)

Others struggled to recall something which had clearly had little long-term impact upon them:

'I can't remember really . . . one or two booklets and a visit to the police station'
(2001/2002, 14–16 years, mixed)

Where efforts had been made to make drug education more innovative and interactive through the use of modern information technology this was clearly welcomed, even if the audience ultimately disagreed with the message. This was illustrated in the first round of focus groups by a drama production made available to schools on video which depicted a young woman's 'descent' into drug use and her ultimate death as a result of taking ecstasy. When participants were asked about their experiences of drug education it was this drama production that was most consistently recalled and its innovative approach was generally well received. MacDonald and Nehammer (2003) report similar findings in their evaluation of a drama-based drug education programme, a pattern which has been replicated in evaluations of other drama-based approaches in other parts of the UK (Buckley and White, 2007). There is, therefore, quite strong evidence that this type of approach can be well received by its target audience. In our study, participants tended to be complimentary about the production values and entertainment value of the video and frequently recalled particular scenes from the production. They were, however, less positive about the quality of information presented in the video which was widely perceived as a repackaged version of a distorted and sensationalized abstinence message. One individual ultimately summarized the video as 'a bit crap really'.

A similar mixture of opinions was expressed by participants in 2005 focus groups, some of whom recalled a different video drama production which they had been shown. Some individuals clearly felt that the film was a useful component of their drug education:

'Our year's been to see a film about drugs called "Go", showin' what it could do to you and it can kill you.'

'it was action packed' – 'used shocking tactics to show you'
(2005, 15–16 years, mixed)

Others in this group, however, were less impressed and again focused on what they perceived to be the value laden nature of the underlying message. Consistent with these criticisms, these individuals also felt that a more factual documentary-based format would be more appropriate:

'It was a typical thing, like you're supposed to say no'
(2005, 15–16 years, mixed)

'Make it more serious with real people in it – like a documentary – show the effects'
(2005, 15–16 years, mixed)

Although the focus groups indicated that drug education packages which utilized a range of different delivery approaches would be best received by young people, a core underlying theme was that participants wanted more discursive and interactive approaches to their drug education. Participants in both studies often commented favorably about the interactive and discursive nature of the focus group format. Thus, as one remarked: 'There is ten of us here now, we can have a discussion instead of just being told' (2001/2002, 15–16-year-old, females).

From their perspective, such an approach respected the validity of their experiences, opinions and existing knowledge. As one group reported, 'in big classes you get bored, the teachers are talking to you. Here like you are treated better' (2005, 15–16 years, mixed). Moreover, a discursive approach was also seen as providing opportunities to ask their own questions about drug related issues. From the educator's perspective, a more discursive approach also creates opportunities to gauge levels and gaps in the knowledge in the group and therefore deliver information at appropriate levels and which is specific to the needs of the group. Similar criticisms of standard drugs education were noted in a government inspector's report on drugs education (OFSTED, 2000), which lamented the constrained opportunities for constructive discussion of the issues surrounding drugs, and the ways in which this frustrated involvement and lessened understanding.

## Personnel

A recurrent theme in both series of focus group discussions was that a wider range of external speakers should be brought in and that these people should be knowledgeable about, and have direct personal experience of their subject area. In other words, they should have what might be termed as credible expertise. The importance which young people attach to the credibility of drug education has also been noted in other research, such as by Orme and Starkey (1999) and Shiner and Newburn (1996). Building on earlier work, Shiner (2000) identifies four different types of credibility: personal characteristics; experience; knowledge; and approach/message. Although devised specifically in relation to peer education approaches, these categories provide a useful framework through which views expressed by participants in our research can be understood.

For example, participants often expressed positive views about the drug education they had received from police officers precisely because of their ability to draw their direct experiences and factual knowledge about issues such as different substances and the laws relating to them:

'Copper came in – he's a nice guy with little pots in the brief case ... told you about people getting beat up – showed us what it looked like so if you get offered it then you'll know what it is.'

'Believed him because he was a policeman, I didn't think he'd lie to me – it makes sense!'

'Good to get someone else in – he know what he was on about.'

(2005, 15–16 years, mixed)

However, it was clear that the participants also wanted to hear views from across the spectrum of those involved with substance misuse issues. This included individuals whose contact was on a professional basis, such as police officers, drugs workers and health professionals, and those with direct personal experience, such as former users and their family members. This finding reflects those of Buckley and White's (2007) review of research into the role of external contributors in delivering school-based drug education. They found that the use of external contributors generally coincides with more positive pupil experiences and increases in the effectiveness of drug education. Significantly, they also found that they were not able to distinguish between the effectiveness of different types of external contributors thus suggesting the need for a range of different contributors.

In our research, participants' support for this approach explicitly referred to the experiential credibility which they would attach to these individuals. This was particularly the case with former users:

'Someone who has taken drugs and knows what its like.'

(2001/2002, 14–16 years, mixed)

'People who have used it know what they are on about'

(2005, 15–16 years, mixed)

In the second round of focus groups, the researchers encountered groups who had received education from such an individual. This drug education had clearly impacted upon them and their recollections of this class were extremely positive.

'He had been through a lot and he told his story.'

'He made us aware that it affects not just you but a lot of people around you.'

'More of a real life person.'

(2005, 14–16 years, mixed)

Another group expressed similar sentiments: 'He was good because he said that he'd been on drugs and how what it was like to come off it, you could talk to him' (2005, 14 years, mixed). It is worth noting, however, that despite young people's evident enthusiasm for this approach, that professional drugs workers frequently expressed grave reservations about the use of either family members or ex-users in frontline education for reasons which included the potential for emotive content, glamorisation/sensationalism and lack of representativeness.

Worryingly, given the centrality of teachers in current policy guidelines for the delivery of drug education, participants in both series of focus groups were extremely sceptical about receiving drug education from teachers. The views expressed again related to the perceived credibility and teachers and many of the comments in this respect were scathing:

'[On women teachers] they know as much about drugs as they do about shaving.'
                                        (2001/2002, 12–14 years, males)

'They [teachers] don't know much.'
                                        (2001/2002,13–14 years , mixed)

'Teachers just chat shit to you.'
                                        (2001/2002, 14–16 years, mixed)

'How many people in a class room have actually stopped because a teacher said "no".'
                                        (2001/2002, 14–16 years, females)

'If a teacher tells you, you just – more often than not the teacher don't know what they are on about.'
                                        (2005, 15–16 years, mixed)

'It's really bad, teachers – they've never taken them.'
                                        (2005, 15–16 years, mixed)

'It's not the teachers place to tell you.'
                                        (2005, 14–15 years, mixed)

In part, the participants' negative perceptions of teacher's involvement in drug education may reflect a combination of the continued lack of training about substance use issues (Ofsted, 2005) and resultant caution in dealing with a controversial subject area. However, a further reservation about teachers delivering drug education classes relates to the power relationship that exists between teacher and pupil and the way in which it could inhibit opportunities to ask questions and discuss relevant issues openly. Such reservations were also expressed about other authority figures such as police officers delivering drugs education classes:

'No one would do it [ask questions].'

'The police make people feel uneasy.'
                                        (2001/2002 14–16 years, mixed)

'If he wasn't a policeman you could ask them.'
                                        (2005, 14–15 years, mixed)

'I just sat there and said nothing.'

'They're teachers as well so you don't want to talk to them.'

(2001/2002, 14–16 years mixed)

Underpinning this reluctance was the fear that asking questions could be regarded as suspicious. As one individual commented: 'The problem is if you know too much they [the police] assume you are on drugs' (2001/2002, 14–16 years mixed). Such fears were not expressed about education delivered by specialist drugs workers and this was a key part of the reason why these education packages were well received by those young people who had experienced them.

Finally, it is important to note that many expressed a preference for classes to take place in venues outside school premises. Those who had made use of local youth orientated projects such as a cyber cafe, or youth drop-in centres expressed very positive views about these facilities and the information that they provided. Interestingly, this type of community-based approach was also rated highly in White and Pitts (1998) review of drugs education, although they felt unable to draw any general conclusions due to a low sample size. An additional problem is presented by the diversity of groups involved in the design and delivery of community-based drug education, and the approaches and drug education packages which they have developed. Included within this diversity are groups which are continuing to promote the very hardline 'just say no' type of approach which the available evidence suggests is not only ineffective but positively harmful. However, those community-based approaches which are underpinned by the community development ethos with its emphasis on working with rather than for, and its concern with issues of user participation and empowerment, demonstrate a close fit with the concerns of the young people in our study. Other commentators have noted the potential of this type of approach in relation to such intractable issues as tobacco consumption in deprived communities (Black et al., 2003).

**Content**

The integrity of the content was clearly the single most important factor in participants' assessment of their drug education. As discussed above, there is a growing body of research evidence which suggests that shock tactics used to deliver simplistic abstinence messages provoke hostile reactions among their target audience and are likely to prove ineffective. In our research, this was exemplified by reactions to the educational video described above which, although being regarded favourably in terms of its delivery style, was ultimately criticized for its perceived sensationalism and lack of balance. Additionally, in the first round of focus groups participants were routinely scathing about the content of drugs education, which was seen as lacking in objectivity, being uninformative and primarily concerned with preaching an overly simplistic message of abstinence. As one group stated:

'Shoving it down your throat.'

'They don't say anything they just tell you to stay away from it.'

(2001/2002 12–14 years, males)

These criticisms were underpinned by the view that the information was minimal, unbalanced and would therefore be ultimately ineffective. Thus, participants remarked:

'If you don't tell the good effects people will use it for themselves anyway.' (2001/ 2002 16–17 years, mixed)

'It's no good just saying no all the time just don't do it, dying is the worst effect but they don't tell you about what is in the middle.'

(2001/2002 14–16 years, females)

'There's no point telling half the story.'

(2001/2002, 14–16 years, mixed)

Some participants appeared to actively rebel against this approach. One group of participants explained that 'they can't stop you anyway. If you're going to do it you're going to do it' (2001/2002 13–14 years, males).

In the second round of focus groups these criticisms were not as pronounced, but there was still widespread criticism that drug education lessons were pitched at too low a level. For example, in one group participants stated: 'The men we did have were a waste of time because they told us things we already knew' (2005, 14–16 years, mixed). Some participants interpreted this as being indicative of a general reluctance of educators to provide factual and balanced information on this subject: 'They give it you because they feel they have to give it to you. They don't really want you to know!' (2005, 14–15 years, mixed). For at least one of the drug workers interviewed in the second research project, and who had experience of delivering drug education in schools, this may have been a consequence of constraints placed upon educators by the national curriculum guidelines: 'The stuff on the national curriculum is bunkum. It is shock tactics rather than information. You are limited to the age level on what you can tell them in school, they knew more than I was telling them.' Although details vary, there is, therefore, a consistent theme of requests for accurate, balanced, comprehensive and relevant information among participants in both series of focus groups. Fundamentally, this is a request that many participants, particularly in the older age groups, felt was not being met.

It is important to note that requests for greater levels of information also included a desire to know more about the negative consequences of drug use. For example, many of the participants in both series of focus groups recalled photographs published in national newspapers and broadcast media of a young woman who had died of a heroin overdose. Given the recent history of drug education, it is scarcely surprising that such approaches are frequently criticized by professionals in the drug education field. For example, Roger Howard, Chief Executive of Drugscope, was reported to say that it is 'understandable that parents and teachers want images like this to be shown to highlight the potentially fatal effects of drugs, but there is little evidence that such shock tactics actually work in changing behaviour' (BBC, 2002). The participants in our focus groups were specifically asked about this and other prominent media examples and were even prompted with arguments about why such material might not be included. Almost without exception, they felt that this was a valid approach as such images were an integral part of the real life impact of substance misuse, its effect upon individuals and those close to them: 'When you look at it people still feel for her and they feel for her family' (2005,14–16 years, mixed). Rather than being intrinsically opposed to such materials, what appears to be crucial in determining young people's reaction to the use of shocking images is the extent to which they can be judged as authentic and embedded within a range of accurate and balanced content.

## CONCLUSION

From the research findings, there are a number of key conclusions to be drawn about the nature of schools-based drug education in Wales and the attitudes and preferences of young people in Wales towards drug education.

- There is continuing evidence of significant areas of ignorance, misunder-standing and confusion about substances and their effects, particularly in relation to alcohol and volatile substances.
- Although this appears to be an improving situation, there is continuing inconsistency in the nature, quantity and quality of the drug education delivered in Welsh schools.

- Blanket messages of strict abstinence and unbalanced or sensationalist information is poorly received and can provoke a hostile response.
- Imaginative and innovative approaches to the delivery of drug education were welcomed but this is not a substitute for accurate and objective information.
- Participants favoured more interactive and discursive approaches to drug education where they felt able to ask questions and air their own views.
- Participants preferred to receive drug education from individuals with direct personal or professional experience of substance use/misuse issues.

Collectively, these separate themes represent a rejection of the traditional 'just-say-no' approach, a finding which is shared by other similar pieces of research (see Crompton, 2003; Buckley and White, 2007) and many professionals in the substance misuse field. It is also a view which appears to be increasingly accepted by policy makers with current guidance advocating more pragmatic approaches to drug education and a corresponding commitment to evidence-based policy. This is perhaps best exemplified by the DfES funding a £7 million study into the effectiveness of the measures it recommends (McWhirter and Roberts, 2004). Moreover, at national, devolved and local levels, policy is also beginning to tackle other issues identified in this research. There is evidence to suggest that drug education is beginning to be delivered more consistently and coherently across schools and/or the necessary mechanisms are being established for this to be the case. Equally, at the local scale our research encountered instances where local authorities have worked in partnership with relevant agencies (including the police school liaison team) to develop the drug education packages delivered in schools and youth centers in that area. Moreover, there is tentative evidence of an increasing professionalization of drug education exemplified by such things as the requirement for police officers delivering the AWSLCP to complete a specially designed teacher training programme and by the inclusion of 3,000 funded places for in-service drug awareness training for teachers in the current DfES guidance.

In overall terms, therefore, it is possible to describe an improving picture in the development of drug education policy in England and Wales. However, the extent to which these policy developments actually impact on young people's experience and perception of school-based drug education remains to be seen. From the perspective of young people in Wales, our research found that there were some notable instances where perceptions of drug education were more positive in the focus groups conducted in 2005 than they were in 2001/2002. There was, nevertheless, considerable continuity in core criticisms relating to content, styles of delivery and personnel. The research also encountered considerable variation in the amount, nature and level of prioritization of drug education in different schools and in different local authority areas. Moreover, the research also encountered a number of instances, such as the use of shocking information and ex-users and/or their carers as educators, where young people's opinions were clearly at odds with those of professional drug workers and the developing trajectory of drug education policy.

## REFERENCES

Allot, R., Paxton, R. and Leonard, R. (1999). 'Drug education: a review of British government policy and evidence on effectiveness', *Health Education Research*, 14, 4, 491–505.

BBC, 1 March 2002. 'Heroin victim's death used as warning', *http://news.bbc.co.uk/1 /hi/education/1848092.stm*

Becker, J. and Roe, S. (2005). 'Drug use among vulnerable groups of young people: findings from the 2003 Crime and Justice Survey', Research, Development and Statistics Directorate, Home Office, *www.homeoffice.gov.uk* (accessed June 2005).

Black, M., McKie, L. and Allen, E. (2003) 'A community development approach to tobacco control', *Health Education*, 3, 2, 68–74.

Buckley, D. and White, D. (2007). 'A systematic review of external contributors in substance use education', *Health Education*, 107, 1, 42–62.

Coffield, F. and Gofton, L. (1994). *Drugs and Young People*, London: Institute for Public Policy Research.

Condon, J. and Smith, N. (2003). *Prevalence of Drug Use: Key Findings from the 2002/2003 British Crime Survey*, London: Home Office.

Crompton, L. (2003). *'It's Got to be Real . . . Really Real': Report on Consultations with Young People about Alcohol, Alcohol Education and School Policy*, London: Drug Education Forum.

Department for Employment and Skills (1995). 'Drug education in the curriculum', Circular number 4/95.

Department for Employment and Skills (2003). 'Drugs: guidance for schools', DFES/ 0205/2003.

Farrell, M. and Strang, J. (1998). 'Britain's new strategy for tackling drugs misuse shows a welcome emphasis on evidence', *British Medical Journal*, 316, 1399–400.

Fuller, E. (ed.) (2005). *Smoking, Drinking and Drug Use Among Young People in England 2004*, London: Health and Social Care Information Centre.

Gilvarry, E. (2000). 'Substance use in young people', *Journal of Child Psychology*, 41, 1, 55–80.

Hough, M. (1996). *Drugs Misuse and the Criminal Justice System: A Review of the Literature*, London: Home Office Drugs Prevention Initiative.

Johnston, L., MacDonald, R., Mason, P., Ridley, L. and Webster, C. (2000). *Snakes and Ladders: Young People, Transitions and Social Exclusion*, York: Joseph Rowntree Foundation/Policy Press.

Lloyd, C., Joyce, R., Hurry, J. and Ashton, M. (2000). 'The effectiveness of primary school drug education', *Drugs: Education, Prevention and Policy*, 7, 2, 109–26.

MacDonald, G. and Nehammer, S. (2003). 'An evaluation of a drug education play for schools in South Wales', *Health Education*, 103, 2, 83–7.

Manning, P. (2002). 'Comparing and explaining news discourse in the coverage of volatile substance abuse and ecstasy: how do some substances become "sexy"?', British Sociological Association and Political Studies Association Media Group Conference, University of Loughborough, 17 September 2002.

Markit Training and Consultancy (2007). *The National Evaluation of the All Wales School Liaison Core Programme: The Impact of the All Wales School Liaison Core Programme on Children and Young People*, Cardiff: Welsh Assembly Government.

McGrath, Y., Sumnall, H., Edmonds, K., Mcveigh, J. and Bellis, M. (2006). *Review of Grey Literature on Drug Prevention among Young People*, National Institute for Health and Clinical Excellence, *www.publichealth.nice.org.uk*.

McWhirter, J. and Roberts, M. (2004). *Beyond Just-Say-No: New Drug Education Guidance for Schools*, London: Drugscope and Childright.

National Assembly for Wales (2002) 'Substance misuse and young people', National Assembly for Wales, Circular No. 17/02.

Office for Standards in Education (2000). 'Drug education in schools: an update', *www. ofsted.gov.uk*.

Office for Standards in Education (2005). 'Drug education in schools', *www.ofsted.gov.uk*.

Orme, J. and Starkey, F. (1999). 'Peer drug education: the way forward?', *Health Education*, 1, 8–16.

Parker, H., Aldridge, J. and Measham, F. (1998). *Illegal Leisure*, London: Routledge.

Parker, H. and Measham, F. (1995). 'Pick 'n' mix: changing patterns of illicit drug use among 1990s adolescents', in C. Martin (ed.), *Dealing with Drugs: A New Philosophy?*, London: Institute for the Study and Treatment of Delinquency.

Parkin, S. and McKeganey, N. (2000). 'The rise and fall of peer education approaches', *Drugs: Education, Prevention and Policy*, 7, 3, 293–310.

Pearson, G. (1987). *The New Heroin Users*, Oxford: Basil Blackwell.

Powis, B., Griffiths, P., Gossop, M., Lloyd, C. and Strang, J. (1998). 'Drug use and offending behaviour among young people excluded from school', *Drugs, Education, Prevention and Policy*, 5, 3, 245–6.

Roberts, C., Moore, L., Blakey, V., Playle, R. and Tudor-Smith, C. (1995). 'Drug use among 15–16-year-olds in Wales, 1990–94', *Drugs: Education Prevention and Policy*, 2, 3, 305–16.

Shildrick, T. (2002). 'Young people, illicit drug use and the question of normalization', *Journal of Youth Studies*, 5, 1, 35–48.

Shiner, M. (2000). 'Doing it for themselves: an evaluation of peer approaches to drug education', Public Policy Research Unit, Goldsmiths College, University of London.

Shiner, M. and Newburn, T. (1996). 'Young people, drugs and peer education: an evaluation of the Youth Awareness Programme (YAP)', London: Home Office.

Shiner, M. and Newburn, T. (1997). 'Definitely maybe not? The normalisation of recreational drug use among young people', *Sociology*, 31, 3, 511–29.

Smith, C. and Nutbeam, D. (1992). 'Adolescent drug use in Wales', *British Journal of Addiction*, 87, 227–33.

Sutton, M. and Maynard, A. (1992). *What is the Size and Nature of the 'Drug' Problem in the UK?*, York: Centre for Health Economics, University of York.

White, D. and Pitts, M. (1998). 'Educating young people about drugs: a systematic review', *Addiction*, 93, 10, 1475–87.

Wright, J. D. and Pearl, L. (1995). 'Knowledge and experience of young people regarding drug abuse', *British Medical Journal*, 309, 20–4.

# 9. GANGS? WHAT GANGS? STREET-BASED YOUTH GROUPS AND GANGS IN SOUTH WALES

## Jennifer Maher

### ABSTRACT

*In recent years the British mass media have 'discovered' a new and urgent social problem – the youth gang. Images of young people submerged in cultures of crime and drugs have combined with a growing fear of youth street presence and violence to create a disturbing picture of modern UK youths. The widespread public perception of street youth groups as problematic is evident across the UK, and further confirmed by the increased introduction of what are arguably anti-youth behaviour policies (e.g. ASBOs). Youth gang activity has been reportedly prevalent across the UK, with serious gangs documented in some UK cities (e.g. Manchester, Birmingham and London). With the predominant focus on English gangs, little is understood about the nature and prevalence of troublesome youth groups in Wales. Essentially, do Welsh youth groups reflect the prevailing UK image of gang-involved, violent and criminal youth? The following article presents the findings of a three-year multi-method, multi-site investigation into youth gangs and troublesome youth groups in south Wales, the principal aim of which was to identify what type of street youth formations exist and to explore whether these formations could be considered gangs. Central to this is the identification of group characteristics and factors associated with gang membership. A profile of south Wales youth street groups based on these characteristics is presented. The author concludes that this study has identified a proliferation of troublesome street-based youth groups that could be considered to be embryonic and emergent gangs across both urban and semi-urban areas of south Wales.*

## INTRODUCTION

There has been a notable rise in both political and public concern in the United Kingdom over youth groups and youth violence. In recent years, the British mass media have reported new and urgent social problems of 'ASBO' youth (Mulholland, 2007), 'Yobs' (Doward, 2007), 'Hoodie' youths and 'Gangs' (Akwagyiram, 2008). Most recently, attention has turned to problematic alcohol misuse (Wintour, 2008) and weapon use (Asthana and Slater, 2008) among young people. These combined images fuel a growing fear of young people and portray a UK epidemic of dangerous street-based youth formations, as evidenced by media headlines such as 'Marginalised British youngsters leave adults living in fear, says US magazine' (Dodd, 2008) and 'Youth gangs triple child murder rate' (Wynne-Jones and Leapman, 2008). This notion of a scourge is sustained by the increasing body count of young people falling victim to peer gun and knife attacks – increasingly identified as *gang* related (*Guardian*, 2008). Beyond the high profile media coverage and generic police statistics, little is known about the nature or characteristics of UK 'gangs'. Two main barriers to understanding these formations exist: the absence of a consistent identifier or definition of gangs or gang behaviour *and* the focus on extreme cases of youth formations and youth violence instead of wider youth experiences of participation in street-based youth groups.

Although numerous UK studies into youth formations and criminality exist, there is a notable deficit in knowledge and research specific to the gang and other modern street-based youth groups. Efforts to estimate gang prevalence support the premise that youth gangs have become part of the UK youth culture (Bennett and Holloway, 2004). Nonetheless, there is a notable absence of research, policy and practice geared towards this phenomenon in south Wales and the UK more generally. Like the US, the UK lacks a unified gang definition – although the work of Sharp et al. (2006) and the Eurogang group (Klein, 2006)[1] goes some way towards remedying this. The absence of an agreed working gang definition or gang-centred UK youth research gives rise to numerous problems in identifying the existence and prevalence of UK gangs or gang-like youth formations. From a brief overview of a century of US gang research and literature, it is evident that US gangs have been reportedly 'everywhere' and 'nowhere' depending on the definition used, the definer, the type of research, the focus of the research and the social and political context at the time. Simply, US gangs vary so significantly as to defy a single comprehensive definition. As a result, identifying UK gangs from the quagmire of US definitions is almost impossible. A further problem exists for UK gang definitions – a general resistance among officials and academics to employ gang terminology or the gang focus which dominates US youth research (Bennett, 2007). This resistance stems from important debates surrounding the historical variations in UK and US youth research and culture (Muncie, 2004), along with concerns over the usefulness of adopting the ambiguous and problematic term 'gang' (Sharp et al., 2006). The term carries negative connotations and potentially stigmatizes and stereotypes young people (Katz and Jackson-Jacobs, 2003). Furthermore, the ontological validity of the terminology continues to be questioned both here and in the US (Ball and Curry, 1995; Sullivan, 2006). The resulting paradox is that UK gangs (like those in the US) are reportedly 'everywhere' (according to the media) and 'nowhere' (according to many academics and, until recently, political debate).

Although academics and agencies have highlighted the problem of defining and researching gangs in the UK, there remains a case for using the term 'gang' to describe certain UK youth formations. The rationale for using the term, given the aforementioned criticisms, is two-fold. First, although the term is identified as foreign (largely north American), it originated within the UK context and culture – in the late nineteenth century – to describe street-based youth groups involved in delinquency and violence (Pearson, 1983). Thrasher's (1963) seminal US gang study also identified gangs within this context (delinquent youth street-based groups) rather than organized and violent contemporary US gangs. Taking the original use of the term, gangs are foremost identified as distinct from non-gangs in terms of their *'street presence'*, involvement in *criminal and/or nuisance behaviour* and the *group's identity* as a *durable* youth formation. These initial characteristics have been used to define youth gangs in south Wales. Second, the term is not used here as a single entity, but as representing a body of units. In essence, a typology was constructed from the research analysis detailed herein to reflect the various levels of development evident among the street-based youth formations (which had a significant influence on their behaviour, structure, organization and cohesion) (see Maher, 2007).

In Maher (2007), a typology of four gang-like (from Contemporary – most gang-like – to Traditional, Compressed and Wannabee) and two non-gang (Sub Cultural and Friendship) categories emerged. The typology utilized a comprehensive set of gang dimensions (level of development being the central thread) to classify the street groups into independent categories. The typology is based on the 106 street groups identified, of which 58 per cent are represented in the four gang-like categories. Although the characteristics and behaviour of these groups vary, each of these groups could be viewed as a gang as they possess a somewhat durable gang identity that includes participation in criminality and violence. As the vast majority fall into the lower gang-like categories, this paper profiles the 'lesser' troublesome youth groups rather than 'conventional' gangs conceived in US research.

The purpose of this paper is to take stock of the types of street-based youth groups in south Wales, present an accurate account of their nature and characteristics and link this to existing gang literature. The paper considers conventional gang characteristics which have laid the ground for most definitional debates, such as structure, organization, cohesion, territoriality and criminality (Klein et al., 2001) to measure the gang-likeness of south Wales's youth groups. The paper begins by placing the research in context, with a brief description of the study area and design. Thereafter, a general profile of youth groups in south Wales is presented. Finally, drawing on some general conclusions, the implications of this study and key debate are discussed, namely whether these groups constitute gangs now or will in the future.

## BACKGROUND

The Index of Multiple Deprivation (WIMD) identifies both the major cities and coalfields of south Wales – the research location – as two of the most deprived areas in Wales (Data Unit Wales, 2005). Beginning in the 1980s, de-industrialization brought about the closure of all south Wales collieries (BBC, 2008), which resulted in the fragmentation of communities, large scale unemployment and general community decline (including the loss of many services). In its place, south Wales now supports a growing service industry; the type of employment unlikely to attract young working class males. Young people growing up in south Wales continue to experience the Valleys in decline – characterized by rundown housing estates, depopulation, breakdown in family and social ties, under-performing schools and decaying amenities. Like their parents, young people have had to adapt to a different way of life from the generations that have preceded them, with limited employment opportunities and aspirations, dramatic social change and little safety in their community or certainty about their futures. Additionally, while the UK is the fourth largest economy in the world, it has one of the highest levels of child poverty of all industrialized countries. Recent figures show that Wales continues to have the highest rate of child poverty in the UK and has comparatively above average rates within EU15 and EU25 (Children in Wales, 2007; see Thomas and Crowley, 2006 for further discussion on youth poverty in Wales).

The broad research location facilitated the documentation of young people's experiences from *semi-urban* locations (which are often neglected in youth studies), as well as *urban* areas. While the research was located in many areas with high levels of deprivation, participants were from locations representing the various levels of the deprivation index (Data Unit Wales, 2005). Thus, the research location was chosen to reflect the varying experiences of young people from different economic and social backgrounds. Further details of sample selection are given below.

**Methodology**

The research comprised three distinct methods, each conducted in multiple post-industrial cities and towns across south Wales. Stage one involved conducting semi-structured interviews and self-completed attitudinal and behavioural questionnaires using a sample of fifty-four 'at risk'[2] pupils from five school cohorts (Table 9.1). Stage two involved the identification of 106 youth groups in a city (urban) and various towns (semi-urban) around south Wales. This paper is based on the thirty-four groups (sixteen semi-urban and twenty-three urban) observed in detail through ethnographic field research over a thirteen-month period (Table 9.1). The data from stage one provided an external attitudinal and behavioural perspective which was used to validate and complement the ethnographic findings.

Detached youth workers facilitated access to the field for observation and assisted in the collection and corroboration of data on core features of the groups identified. Observing, listening and eliciting through informal conversation, generated much of the data recorded. Over 200 hours were spent in the field observing semi-urban street groups and almost 180 hours observing urban street groups. This involved repeated observation over a continuous six-month period in semi-urban areas at the beginning of the research and one-month period at the end of the research (see Table 9.2 for additional information). Urban groups were observed for a continuous seven-month period (the final month overlapping with semi-urban observations). All but two of the thirty-four 'observed' groups were engaged (observation or conversation) with more than twenty times,

**Table 9.1**
**Sample summary from multi-method and multi-site research methods employed**

| Method | Semi-urban | Urban |
|---|---|---|
| Semi-structured interviews and self-completed questionnaires | 29 youths | 25 youths |
| Ethnographic observation of street groups | 32 identified *16 observed* | 74 identified *23 observed* |

Table 9.2
Summary of observation in semi-urban and urban locations

| Observation setails | Semi-urban | Urban |
|---|---|---|
| Period of observation | January–June and January | July to January |
| Total group contact time | 200 hours | 180 hours |
| Sessions in a week | 3–5 (Monday to Friday) | 3–5 (Monday to Saturday) |
| Hours per session | 4–5 hours | 3–5 hours |
| Periods of absence | Easter school holidays | Mid-term and Christmas break |

for approximately twenty-five minutes each time. Some group observations were consolidated through four weekend residentials organized by detached youth workers. Arguably, the observation period may appear to be short for an ethnographic study; it was in fact immense when one adds the additional time in the field not recorded above. This included many evenings when areas were visited but no groups were observed or interacted with. These periods provided additional important information on group cohesion and the frequency of group behaviour.

These observed groups were chosen for a number of reasons: (i) their location was covered by the detached team, (ii) they regularly frequented their area, (iii) they appeared to accept the researcher's presence and (iv) as a whole, the sample reflected the spectrum of characteristics evident in the groups identified (e.g. age, gender, behaviour).

The research was approached with few assumptions, allowing the young people themselves to paint a picture of their group. That said, the field was approached with an 'open, not empty mind' (MacDonald, 2001). Taking heed of Short's (2006) warning about 'blind spots' in gang research and the confusion over the spread of gang culture as opposed to gang organizations, the study purposefully included all street-based youth groups as units of analysis. The initial aim of the research was to observe all towns/estates in each locality. However, as this was reliant on the detached workers (for safety and access) some concessions were necessary. The detached workers' remit involved randomly making contact with groups from all locations (i.e. not specifically problem areas or referrals from officials). Therefore, if an unknown group was identified through the research the detached youth workers were often eager to facilitate observation in that area also. During the final months, the detached youth workers were invited to comment on the profile of each group identified, which included a geographical profile of the groups in each locality and general group characteristics (e.g. number, gender, behaviour). When discrepancies arose, the final month's observation was used to validate the researcher's information and eliminate discrepancies.

Although street-based youth groups are a difficult population to research and the data collected hard to authenticate (it is always difficult to distinguish between reality and young people's assertions), the integration of in-depth fieldwork, interviews and surveys proved a successful and complementary way to study them and their behaviour. As Vigil (2003, p. 237) posits, 'large numbers count, but it is in the details that human complexity is better examined and understood'. The following section presents a brief introduction to the sample achieved.

**Demographics**
The age of the groups observed ranged from 11 to 25 years. Due to the difficulty of recording each member's[3] age, the age range of each group was recorded instead – that is, the difference between the youngest and oldest members (see page 187 for types of membership). The average age range of semi-urban groups was five years, compared to three years for urban groups. Although the sample was taken from a wide geographical area, only two groups had members who were born outside of Wales. Two urban and one semi-urban group had non-white members, which is consistent with the small minority ethnic composition reported in Wales (2.12 per cent: 8.4 per cent urban and 1.1 per cent semi-urban – ONS, 2004). The majority of urban (59 per cent) and semi-urban groups (53 per cent) identified had a mixed gender membership followed by male-only youth groups (33 per cent urban and 44 per cent semi-urban). Female-only groups were twice as common in urban locations than semi-urban; nonetheless, this made up less than 10 per cent of all urban groups identified. The male-only and female-only groups were identified as such due to the complete absence of the opposite sex. Also, members did not identify existing girlfriends or boyfriends as part of their group. It is worth noting, too, that mixed gender groups were always male-dominant.

In summary, the groups identified were largely characterized as white, male or mixed gender with members predominantly aged between thirteen and seventeen. The following profile of youth street-based groups is based upon 39 of the 106 groups identified.

## STREET-BASED YOUTH GROUPS PROFILE

The following section describes the characteristics and behaviour of south Wales's youth street-based groups (identified hereon as 'group(s)'). Of particular interest here are issues of group formation and development, structure and organization, and lifestyle and behaviour; these are recurrent themes in gang literature.

## Formation and development

How gangs form and develop is central to their character. Gangs that develop from local friendship groups (Thrasher, 1963) differ significantly from those formed through displacement and immigration (Vigil, 1988). The groups identified in south Wales predominantly developed through local or school friendship groups. Despite this, the impact of US gang culture was evident among a number of groups, who adopted the gangsta-rap image and attitude on the street. The US gang image, while clearly symbolic, may influence the development of more structured and gang-like group formations in the future. However, currently, group formation is presented by most young people as a haphazard occurrence. Groups either naturally evolved from diffuse and loosely organized friendship groups into a more solid collective or youths from dissolved groups merged together to form a new local group. Few youths actually spoke about officially 'joining' their group. Becoming a group member is seldom a conscious decision or a marked occasion. That said, the longest formed groups reported having some basic rules or rituals in place for prospective members, such as fighting the toughest group member.

Unlike much US gang research, the groups observed did not form on the grounds of ethnic conflict. Instead, the existence of pockets of ethnic minority communities (e.g. Somali and Asian) in the research locality encouraged cohesion among some groups who viewed these communities as a common enemy. Area or cultural group rivalries were more likely to be expressed as the reason for youths joining a group or for a number of groups merging together. One skater group, for example, was formed from several separate groups. Conflict with other youth groups (e.g. Chavs and Townies) and the need for protection led to the formation of one large group. Protection (e.g. from school or area rivalries), status elevation and respect (e.g. being the toughest group in the area), belonging to a friendship network (e.g. hotspot where young people 'hang-out'), access to financial or other resources (e.g. members of the opposite sex, alcohol or drugs) and the ability to 'let off steam' or have fun were commonly cited by youths when asked why membership of a group was desirable. Additionally, given the rules and restrictions characterizing other available social groups (e.g. youth clubs, sports clubs), the youth group was deemed less effort and a more attractive alternative.

The majority of groups were dominated by boys, but often developed through their heterosexual relationships. Boys tended to form groups earlier and remain in the group longer than girls (who appeared to move on by their late teens) – which may explain their larger numbers. Boys also differed from girls in that they more often reported a poor educational history, limited job skills and little motivation to leave the comfort zone of their group – which may account for their prolonged membership. Males, especially older boys, played the key role in group (except girl-only) formation and the group's drift towards deviance. In particular, groups with veteran (older) boys often reported participation in more sophisticated offending and increased drug consumption and sales. These males also helped attract young girls into the group. For many girls an older boyfriend was status enhancing, providing easier access to alcohol and transport. The nature of these relationships was troubling given the age difference and 'role' of female members suggested by many males. According to the boys, girls fulfilled one of four roles in the group – the entertainment, a commodity, a sex object or, least likely, an active 'soldier'.

Boys often played down the position of female members and described them as insignificant in the formation or development of their group. Indeed, female members often had to contend with glaring double standards – often referred to by boys as 'slags' (sexually available), 'lads' (non-sexual, tough, active gang member) or 'good girls' (not readily sexually available, but desirable and feminine). Observation of male and female roles presented a somewhat different picture. The presence (or availability) of females was an important commodity in mixed groups and played a significant factor in the development and durability of the group. Essentially, the group's popularity and status among local youths increased when girls became members. The control and influence of females in inciting and organizing conflict (e.g. group rivalries) and thereby enhancing group cohesion also conflicted with the girl's trivial role as reported by males. Girls were observed on many occasions phoning male friends to demand retaliation for a slight by another boy, passing on personal insults from another youth and organizing support for group fights. Additionally, if a girl became attached to a male in another group, her female friends often left with her (instantly reducing group numbers and passing resources to another group). Single-sex groups often consisted of mostly younger or older youths, the former usually childhood friends with little interest in the opposite sex and the latter more purposeful groups who disregard the opposite sex as too troublesome (thereby keeping their group and their relationships apart).

The life cycle of groups varied greatly. Although few terminated during observation, there was a noticeable fluctuation in the membership and behaviour of some groups. The maturity or 'coming of age' of some members (in terms of them legally being able to drive, drink alcohol and leave school) altered group dynamics. A wider territory and more resources often became accessible to boys of this age (16+ years), which resulted in some group fragmentation and movement to remote areas or indoors to the 'local' (public house). Females were more likely to develop interests outside of the group, for example, by establishing a serious relationship or family, or finding a job. Four main personal scenarios were commonly identifiable when groups dispersed or members left: interest in establishing a sexual relationship or family; leaving education and/or joining the workforce; access to driving; and access to licensed premises. In addition, a number of external factors influenced group behaviour, such as police or council crime prevention measures and (poor) outdoor conditions. The inability of some youths (especially boys) to make a socially acceptable transition into adulthood, due to unemployment and limited finances, may explain why some groups have an extended life cycle (with members over twenty-five).

## Structure and organization

US gang research suggests that street groups develop into serious gangs through increased cohesion, structure and organization (Sanchez-Jankowski, 2003). However, many of the groups observed appeared too disorganized to develop to this stage. In particular, their life cycle was short when compared to that of many US gangs (Moore, 1991). The term 'fluid' is used to indicate the loosely structured and disorganized nature of groups. Most groups possessed little formal or permanent structure or role differentiation. All groups had a membership of two to five *'core'* members, which were found regularly in the same location, supplemented by a number of *'peripheral'* members whose presence was less predictable or frequent. The fluidity observed was often influenced by changing sexual relationships (a new partner), the weather, the time of day or season, group finances and 'maturity'. Accordingly, the groups grew or shrunk throughout the period of observation. This fluidity benefited the group when they required a larger 'crew' to call upon for organized fights with rival groups. It is important to note that although membership and structure appeared fluid and weak, a number of groups exhibited durability. Although both youths and detached workers had difficulty identifying how long their group had been in existence, just under half of these groups (usually through the core members) had existed in their location for between one and four years. Both the aforementioned absence of a formal formation process and the general lack of cohesion evident among groups made accurately 'aging' each group unfeasible.

Cohesion is central to the nature and organization of gangs. Gangs are often characterized by their focus on loyalty and solidarity – with group loyalty overriding individual conscience (Campbell and Muncer, 1989). South Wales's gangs were characterized by their dynamic nature, which included both fragile and somewhat intense group cohesion. Interpersonal relationships between peripheral members often appeared tenuous, shallow and superficial. Core members, in contrast, presented close, loyal and warm friendships. Cohesion was enhanced in groups involved in group rivalries. A long history of area and school rivalries was evident in south Wales, many of which have been internalized by local groups. Fighting against a common enemy provided groups with a strong identity and history, and thereby group cohesion. In particular, protecting the group or area reputation and physical wellbeing was reported as central to being a 'member'. Those groups involved in more serious criminality and violence displayed stronger cohesion and less fluidity (evident by their widespread reputation and lengthy existence).

Although a litany of structural characteristics are provided in gang literature (Klein et al., 2001), membership and territory would appear to be the central component in understanding the diverse nature and structure of the groups researched. Any estimation of membership numbers is influenced by what one chooses to count. For example, this research included core and peripheral members but not other 'associates'. On average, the groups observed had a frequent membership of six to seven youths (including core and peripheral members). Groups and detached workers reported membership up to four times this number on weekends and during organized fights. The largest urban group recorded sixty-five regular members, while the largest semi-urban group reported fifty regular members. Whatever the size, most groups were characterized as a single cluster with a diverse membership. A small number of sub-groups – age-graded or locality-linked (groups who tend to share affiliation, but not the specific locality) – were also observed. These sub-groups were identified as members, but spent most of their time away from the core group. The ability to call on sub-groups from other areas to boost numbers in violent encounters was of great benefit to groups. Age-graded cohorts – found in both urban and semi-urban locations (e.g. the Preston Youth and Preston Boys) – benefited younger members providing protection and a public display of maturity, as well as access to more serious criminality and violence.

Territory has been recognized as a significant US gang characteristic and is frequently used to identify and measure levels of seriousness (Maxson and Klein, 1995). Territoriality is not a distinctive feature of south Wales groups. Defence of a specific 'turf' was identifiable in two groups who were also associated with drug sales and serious violence. Specific territories (a location with clear boundaries which other gangs could not cross) were not commonly identified; instead, violent encounters erupted as a result of rival group's provocation, disrespect towards their area or a group member or attempt to take a resource (e.g. females). These encounters often revolved around disputes older than the gang members themselves; based on area identity, old football rivalries, subcultural group conflicts, urban/semi-urban divides, social class and school divisions. Supporting and defending one's local traditions and reputation was an important source of pride and status within the group. On occasion, large scale school and area rivalries reportedly involved the organization of hundreds of youths. Mobile phones and Internet chat rooms are used to pass fight details to interested groups. Interestingly, local rivalries were often abandoned when facing a common enemy or outsider – depending on the perceived enemy at the time, the social geography (relationship between rival locations) could change.

The importance of organization, once deemed to be a significant characteristic of youth gangs, is now widely debated (Klein, 1995). Organization in the gang is often assessed by the presence of a gang name and identity, gang roles, leadership and formal and informal controls. Although most gangs demonstrated some level of elementary organization (e.g. purchase and low-level sale of drugs), the majority of youths rejected the idea of group organization. Locality names – either chosen by the youths themselves or assigned by others – were often used to identify groups in south Wales. No gang signs (colours), symbols (clothes, jewellery) or other specific group identifiers were observed or recorded during the research. While these groups had few defined roles, there were 'leaders' – usually the toughest/hardest, best fighter. The identity of the leader changed in some groups according to the nature of their activities and presence/absence of certain key members. Typically, organization varied from elementary to more sophisticated, suggesting various stages of development among the groups observed. The three groups demonstrating cohesion, durability and involvement in more serious levels of crime and violence also reported a hierarchy and set roles within their group.

**Lifestyle and behaviour**
Criminality and violence are a focal concern for gang researchers (Decker and Van Winkle, 1996; Huff, 1996), yet these behaviours represent only a small part of group life. For a complete group profile, it is important to look at the everyday activities of its members. Generally, those members not involved in education (over 16 years) were unemployed or employed part-time. Their routine involved sleeping until midday, meeting friends in the early evening, then returning home to sleep, eat and play video games. Those still attending school followed a similar routine of meeting friends after school in public and remaining there until the late evening. Core members appeared to spend little time with people outside the group, as evenings were spent with their group and conversations usually revolved around activities with these group members. Football, shooting

(air rifles) and boxing were the main sports discussed by boys (girls seldom reported participating in sport). Football was a prestigious activity, especially among semi-urban youth as this ability was eagerly supported by their wider community. Being a successful footballer often raised the profile of a youth in their group and discharged the further need to demonstrate their toughness and/or fighting prowess. Shooting (air-rifle) and boxing, when practiced, often took place outside of a controlled environment (e.g. club) and were reportedly misused (causing injury to willing and/or unwilling victims). Boxing (or other martial art) could also establish respect and masculinity within the group, as youths could use their skills in violent encounters (a reason some gave for learning the skill).

As previously discussed, belonging to a locality was important to the group identity. Therefore, it was important to be 'seen' by others (e.g. older youths or outsider groups) as belonging there. Although groups craved the freedom of unsupervised and unregulated areas, they also enjoyed being visible to other peers and being present in areas most likely to create some excitement (such as shopping areas, leisure centres or the entrance to an estate). Movement to more remote areas usually facilitated avoiding the police or partaking in illegal activities, usually drug consumption or organized conflict. Although many of the groups reported involvement in low-level criminality only, their street presence, in particular, exposed them to a criminal label (labelled by peers, the community and the police). Street presence also exposed groups to numerous situations in which trouble could arise and provided a variety of opportunities for becoming a victim or offender (e.g. encounters with drug users, homeless people or rival groups). Youths reportedly turned to drug use (e.g. alcohol, cigarettes and cannabis) to fill periods of boredom. This activity provided a positive identity (within the remit of their peers), aided group cohesion and the youths saw this as a transition from childhood to adulthood. Boredom was identified as a precursor to anti-social and criminal behaviour, while alcohol was a regular precursor to violent behaviour. As a result, the majority of groups reported participation in some form of criminality – which ranged from anti-social behaviour to serious violent offences (see Table 9.3). Drug offences and anti-social behaviour was observed, while arson, theft, motor vehicle offences and violent offences were documented in conversation with youths and confirmed by other groups or group members.

The link between criminality and group membership was not straightforward. In particular, there was a need to differentiate between *group-motivated* and *group-affiliated* criminality. Group-motivated criminality requires the participation and/or support of members in an offence. Group-affiliated criminality, in contrast, describes a group member engaging in crime, alone or with other youths, for

**Table 9.3**
**Reported involvement in criminal and anti-social behaviour among**
**semi-urban and urban gangs observed**

| Behaviour | Semi-urban | | Urban | | All | |
|---|---|---|---|---|---|---|
| | N | % | N | % | N | % |
| Arson | 3 | 19 | 3 | 13 | 6 | 15 |
| Motor vehicle offences[2] | 5 | 31 | 6 | 26 | 11 | 28 |
| Theft[3] | 5 | 31 | 7 | 30 | 12 | 31 |
| Other crime[4] | 11 | 69 | 14 | 61 | 25 | 64 |
| Anti-social behaviour | 14 | 88 | 22 | 96 | 36 | 92 |
| Supply of contr. drugs | 1 | 6 | 7 | 30 | 8 | 21 |
| Use of drugs: cannabis. | 12 | 75 | 16 | 70 | 28 | 72 |
| Use of drugs: other[5] | 8 | 50 | 13 | 57 | 21 | 54 |
| Use of alcohol | 16 | 100 | 19 | 83 | 35 | 90 |
| Interpersonal violence | 9 | 56 | 13 | 57 | 22 | 56 |
| Previous incarceration[6] | 3 | 19 | 4 | 17 | 7 | 18 |
| *Total[7]* | *16* | *100* | *23* | *100* | *39* | *100* |

Note:
1  Based on the observation sample (N=39)
2  Includes offences such as dangerous and careless driving, unlawful use of vehicle, speeding, driving under the influence, theft of and from motor vehicle.
3  Includes theft and handling of stolen goods, shoplifting, fraud and forgery, mugging, burglary and robbery from domestic households and businesses
4  Includes offences such as criminal damage, wasting police time, vandalism, malicious mischief, breach of the peace.
5  Other drugs: any other drugs reported with the exception of alcohol and cannabis use.
6  Includes incarceration in juvenile detention or adult prison, or other restrictions to their liberty (e.g. curfew and electronic tag.).
7  More than one response given.

personal gain. Group members reported offending with another group member, but not necessarily for the benefit of or with the knowledge of the group. Conversely, it was often documented that criminal gains from individual (non-group) offending was pooled together for the groups benefit (to pay for activities and drug use). This is a complex matter. It is notable that the groups exhibiting more cohesion, durability and organization also tended to participate in higher rates and more serious types of criminality. This suggests that group membership, especially the most gang-like, is linked to increased participation in and seriousness of criminal behaviour.

Generally, youth offending appeared to be more motivated by social capital or street currency than material profit. This is supported by the often unplanned, 'cafeteria-style' (Klein et al., 2001) offending rather than organized criminality. Violent conflict reportedly produced substantial 'capital' for boys. Partaking in violence ensured group acceptance and prestige, while avoidance was reported in some groups to result in punishment beatings from fellow members. The importance placed by all youths on honour and reputation in conflict cannot be understated – as evidenced by the 'leader' status. Violent encounters (except those with a financial motivation) were apparently governed by rules, conditions and etiquette. Weapon use was not commonplace among most groups observed (although knife and blunt weapon *ownership* was observed on many occasions). However, in particular, the use of weapons during conflict was reportedly covered by a code of honour, agreed by the different groups prior to the conflict. Although youths reported severe penalties for breach of these rules, the use of knives was occasionally reported. Youths often referred to the 'stupidity' of using serious weapons (e.g. firearms), due to the possible negative consequences (evident in media coverage of UK and US youth homicide). This view of lethal weapons and general weapon use was fuelled by the idea of honour and machismo in the locality. Essentially, there was greater prestige attached to 'winning' conflicts without recourse to weapons. The almost complete absence of firearm usage was linked to the limited availability of these weapons in the research location (even among adults). Participation in some level of violence was evident in the majority of groups; however, weapon use and serious violence was only reported among those few groups exhibiting stronger cohesion, structure and durability. Serious violence and weapon use appears to be a key identifier of gang-like groups.

## CONCLUSION

The gang is a multifaceted phenomenon, demanding detailed and broad enquiry, with careful consideration given to the research focus and purpose. Sherif and Sherif (1964) argued that the study of gangs should not be separated from the study of adolescent groups in general. This research did not set out to find gangs specifically. It explored the nature of youth street formations and the possible existence of gangs and other troublesome youth groups. Although exploratory in nature, it expands the limited knowledge available on youth street-based groups and gangs in south Wales, in particular, and the UK more generally. Given the dearth of UK knowledge and chaos surrounding gang definitions, it was perhaps to be expected that investigating the existence of gangs in south Wales would produce more questions and lines for further enquiry than definitive answers. That said, two important conclusions are presented here on defining gangs and whether they exist in the UK.

Increasingly, gang research suggests that the modern use of the term gang is, in fact, a rigid and outdated concept. Perhaps it *is* more helpful not to conceive of the 'gang', but groups (as presented in the typology) that clearly display orientations of gangs which may become less fluid and more solid, less fragmented and more organized, less playful and more violent. The idea of a variety of groups demonstrating 'gang-likeness', as opposed to adhering to a singular gang definition, provides a path out of the definitional quagmire. Since so much youth activity takes place in groups and in public, it is important for future research to distinguish legitimate group activity from that of deviant or illegal group activity – whilst recognizing that the two might sometimes overlap. The key is to focus on what links most gang research together: the presence of street-based socially disadvantaged and marginalized youths who appear to normalize violent behaviour.

There are evidently elements of traditional youth gangs in south Wales which should be linked to the substantial ongoing gang debates. Equally, there are differences which raise many questions and concerns. Clearly, we are not dealing with the 'supergangs' evident in parts of the US. Nonetheless, the research has uncovered a proliferation of troublesome street-based youth groups that could be considered to be embryonic gangs across both urban and semi-urban areas. Many of these groups do not appear to be like the stereotypical images of contemporary US gangs (and rightly so since they are less structured, organized and violent). Their patterns of behaviour, the practice of living life on the street, and the method of acquiring income and honour, are nevertheless suggestive of elements of traditional (possibly some contemporary) gang formations. In answer, then, to the question 'are there gangs?', we might say that, yes, there are, but few conform to the conventional singular use of the word.

## NOTES

[1] 'A street gang is any durable, street oriented youth group whose own identity includes involvement in illegal activity' (Klein, 2006, p. 129).

[2] 'At risk' youths are identified by the Local Education Authority. Often they are young people expelled from or are unable to attend mainstream schools. Pupil Referral Units (PRU) provide these young people with work placements, college courses and primary education level usually up to GCSE qualifications.

[3]  Membership was identified during observation in two ways: those young people most frequently observed in the group and by asking core members who was part of their group. This included both core and peripheral members.


## REFERENCES

Akwagyiram, A. (2008). 'Killing highlights gang culture', *BBC News*, *http://news.bbc. co.uk/1/hi/uk/7232344.stm* (accessed 9 May 2008).

Asthana, A. and Slater, R. (2008). 'In their own words: Why young men carry knives', *The Observer*, *www.guardian.co.uk/uk/2008/may/18/ukcrime2* (accessed 3 June 2008).

Ball, R. A. and Curry, D. G. (1995). 'The logic of definition in criminology: purposes and methods for defining "gangs"', *Criminology*, 33, 2, 225–45.

BBC News. (2008). 'Knives affect ,one in 10 youths', *BBC News Online*, *http://news. bbc.co.uk/1/hi/uk/7351207.stm* (accessed 16 April 2008).

Bennett, R. (2007). 'They are a loose collection of fragile kids – not gangs', *The Times Online*, *www.timesonline.co.uk/tol/news/uk/crime/article1832240.ece* (accessed 24 May 2008).

Bennett, T. and Holloway, K. (2004). 'Gang membership, drugs and crime in the UK', *British Journal of Criminology*, 44, 305–23.

Campbell, A. and Muncer, S. (1989). 'Them and us: a comparison of the cultural context of American gangs and British subcultures', *Deviant Behavior*, 10, 3, 271–88.

Children in Wales. (2007). *Updating and Revising the Welsh Index of Multiple Deprivation, prepared by the End Child Poverty Network Cymru*, *www.childreninwales.org.uk/ 4673.file.dld* (accessed 12–13 August 2007.

Dataunitwales.gov.uk (2005). *Welsh Index of Multiple Deprivation 2005*, *www. dataunitwales.gov.uk/ProductsServices.asp?cat=234* (accessed 23 May 2008).

Decker, S. H. and Van Winkle, B. (1996). *Life in the Gang: Family, Friends, and Violence*, Cambridge: Cambridge University Press.

Dodd, V. (2008). 'Marginalised British youngsters leave adults living in fear, says US magazine', *The Guardian*, *www.guardian.co.uk/uk/2008/mar/29/ukcrime.children* (accessed 21 May 2008).

Doward, J. (2007). 'Britons fear the rise of the yob'. *The Guardian Unlimited*, *www. guardian.co.uk/society/2007/aug/19/drugsandalcohol.crime* (accessed 19 August 2007).

Guardian. (2008). London teenage violence: The death toll', *The Guardian*, *www.guardian. co.uk/uk/2008/jun/02/knifecrime.ukguns1* (accessed 3 June 2008).

Huff, C. R. (1996). *Gangs in America*, CA: Sage.

Katz, J. and Jackson-Jacobs, C. (2003). 'The criminologists' gang', in C. Sumner (ed.) *The Blackwell Companion to Criminology*, Oxford: Blackwell.

Klein, M. (1995). *The American Street Gang: Its Nature, Prevalence and Control*, Oxford: Oxford University Press.

Klein, M. (2006). 'The value of comparisons', in J. F. Short and L. A. Hughes (eds) *Street Gang Research. Studying Youth Gangs*, New York: Rowman & Littlefield.

Klein, M., Kerner, H-J., Maxson, C. and Weitekamp, E. (eds). (2001). *The Eurogang Paradox: Street Gangs and Youth Groups in the U.S. and Europe,* Amsterdam: Kluwer Press.

Maher, J. (2007). 'Angels with dirty faces: youth gangs and troublesome youth groups in south Wales', unpublished PhD Thesis, University of Glamorgan.

Maxson, C. and Klein, M. (1995). 'Investigating gang structures', *Journal of Gang Research,* 3, 1, 33–40 .

Macdonald, N. (2001). *The Graffiti Subculture: Youth, Masculinity and Identity in London and New York,* Hampshire: Palgrave.

Moore, J. (1991). *Going Down to the Barrio: Homeboys and Homegirls in Change,* Philadelphia: Temple University Press.

Mulholland, H. (2007). 'ASBOs encouraging more crime, Thinktank claims', *The Guardian, www.guardian.co.uk/politics/2007/dec/10/immigrationpolicy.ukcrime* (accessed 10 December 2007).

Muncie, J. (2004). *Youth and Crime,* London: Sage.

Office for National Statistics (2004). *Census: The Census in England and Wales, www.neighbourhood.statistics.gov.uk/dissemination/AreaListMapSelection.do* (accessed 10 February 2008).

Pearson, G. (1983). *Hooligan: A History of Respectable Fears.* London: Macmillan.

Sanchez-Jankowski, M. (2003). 'Gangs and social change', *Theoretical Criminology,* 7, 2, 191–216.

Sherif, M. and Sherif, C. (1964). *Reference Groups,* Washington, DC: Harper and Row.

Sharp, C, Aldridge, J. and Medina, J. (2006). *Delinquent Youth Groups and Offending Behaviour: Findings from the 2004 Offending, Crime And Justice Survey,* London: Home Office.

Short, J. F. (2006). 'Why study gangs? An intellectual journey', in J. F. Short and L. A. Hughes (eds) *Street Gang Research. Studying Youth Gangs,* New York: Rowman & Littlefield.

Sullivan, M. L. (2006). 'Are "gang" studies dangerous? Youth violence, local context, and the problem of reification', in J. F. Short and L. A. Hughes (eds) *Street Gang Research. Studying Youth Gangs,* New York: Rowman & Littlefield.

Thrasher, F. (1963). *The Gang,* London: University of Chicago Press.

Thomas, N. and Crowley, A. (2006). 'Children's rights and well-being in Wales in 2006'. *Contemporary Wales,* 19, 161–79.

Vigil, J. D. (1988). *Barrio Gangs,* Austin: University of Texas Press.

Vigil, J. D. (2003). 'Urban violence and street gangs', *Annual Reveiw of Anthropology,* 32, 225–42.

Wintour, P. (2008). 'Parents, police powers and ID targeted in new crackdown on teenage binge drinkers', *The Guardian, www.guardian.co.uk/society/2008/jun/02/drugsandalcohol.health* (accessed 3 June 2008).

Wynne-Jones, J. and Leapman, B. (2008). 'Youth gangs triple child murder rate', *Telegraph, www.telegraph.co.uk/news/uknews/1576698/Youth-gangs-triple-child-murder-rate.html* (accessed 21 May 2008).

# 10. IDENTITY, BRAND OR CITIZENSHIP? THE CASE OF POST-DEVOLUTION WALES

*William Housley, Kate Moles and Robin Smith*

## ABSTRACT

*During the course of this article we explore three dimensions of subjectivity in relation to post-devolution Wales. The space of subjectivity is something that is experienced by individuals but also shaped by wider sociological, historical and economic forces. The article does not aim to provide an empirical analysis of this process per se but rather to outline three ways in which 'Welsh subjectivity' and 'ways of being Welsh' can be currently understood in terms of the post-devolution landscape. This is of importance due to the fact that the political landscape of Wales is undergoing radical transformation within a context of globalization and increasingly complex flows of capital and labour. The ways in which general frames of Welsh subjectivity are being mobilized and shaped by the new regime of devolved governance and other sub-state actors requires consideration as it impacts upon patterns of participation, cohesion and representation within the territory.*

## INTRODUCTION

Discussion on Welsh identity has proliferated in recent years. This is due to two principal processes: first, the emergence of identity politics through the twin, but not always related, forces of nationalism and culturalism, and second, political processes such as devolution and the restructuring of governance in response to a perceived crisis of democratic legitimacy and the centralized state. The German philosopher Hegel noted that Enlightenment-based social forms were characterized by two forms of politics: first, the politics of redistribution characterized by attempts to ameliorate differential economic circumstances generated through exploitation and oppression and, second, the politics of recognition in which attempts are made to ameliorate differential life chances generated through subjugation and repression (Fraser, 1995). Identity politics can be seen to be a product of the latter form of political action. However, processes associated with the formation and maintenance of social identity also have another political and sociological dimension, namely as a resource through which technologies of societal integration can be mobilized. In more contemporary parlance this dimension of identity can be understood through debates surrounding social cohesion within national territories.

In this paper we note how discussion of Welsh subjectivity has been dominated by discussions of identity. However, we also note how identity issues and the forms of subjectivity they describe are being reconfigured through the transformation of identity and its related subject positions through branding and the marketing of space and place. Finally, we consider how these moves relate to alternative forms of subjectivity (e.g. devolved citizenship) that is emerging within the political arena due to the process of devolution. We make the claim that these frames can be understood in terms of identity, branding and citizenship as they relate to the contemporary (rather than historical) repackaging and reconstitution of Wales as a devolved social, cultural, economic and political territory within the UK. The ways in which these three discursive frames relate to the current re-imagining of nation is, we claim, of consequence to issues of inclusion, exclusion and the social integration of persons with emerging devolved state institutions.

## WELSH IDENTITY

Welsh identity has been explored from a number of perspectives. These include: the notion of a 'romantic', historically uninterrupted identity located within and through language; specific forms of cultural practice – on the one hand, forms of identity expressed and realized through particular forms of political economy and industrial organization – on the other, an historical reading of identity where the Dragon has two tongues. More sociological forms of commentary concerning national identity and 'Welshness' (e.g. Fevre and Thompson, 1999) have recognized the ways in which such forms are in some sense characterized by social processes that are 'invented' (Kedourie, 1960; Gellner, 1983) 'imagined' (Anderson, 1991) or reconstructed (Smith, 1991). Nationalism and national identity in Wales has often been explored as a social construction where the activities of nationalist groups and organizations are seen in terms of the protection of monopolies in social and economic resources (Fevre, Borland and

Denney, 1997; Fevre and Thompson, 1999). The relationship between configurations of Welsh identity and the challenge of 'inclusive politics' within new devolved political frameworks (Chaney and Fevre, 2002) has also been explored from this approach. Further work has explored the construction and negotiation of Welsh national identity within primary schooling and childhood where notions of national identity are related to an emerging devolved civic sphere in Wales (Scourfield, Davies and Holland, 2004). In addition, the more mundane aspects of nationalism (Billig, 1995) and its interactional and situated characteristics in relation to Wales, Welsh identity and the UK have also been examined (Housley and Fitzgerald, 2001).

Earlier accounts of Wales and national identity utilized Hechter's theory of 'internal colonialism' in relation to a Marxist theory of underdevelopment. Whilst this approach remains contested (e.g. Levering and Lovering, 1978; Day, 1980; Adamson, 1991), it still has explanatory resonance as a political form of articulation beyond the confines of Welsh social and economic history. The strength of a concept such as internal colonialism is that it highlights uneven developments within different regions and territories, but what it does not take into account is issues surrounding culture and hybridity that exist as part of the colonizing process. The internal colonialism position argues that society is replicated through specific class structures which reproduce the colonial through internal relationships that are based on political and economic inequalities between regions within a single society. This is problematic, as it is impossible to distinguish between the cultural ramifications of colonialism and the economic and political ones, or indeed to isolate specific cause and effect outcomes associated with colonialism. Thus, whilst the analysis of uneven development may well be contestable, its narrative power has a legitimating effect within the discourse of Celtic nationalism (Edwards et al, 1968).

More recently, questions of diversity and matters of gender and ethnicity have transformed the way in which Welsh identity has been thought about. As Charlotte Williams (2002) notes in relation to the autobiographical life history *Sugar and Slate*, 'there are many ways of being Welsh'. The emerging multiple readings of Welsh identity have only recently come to the fore. In doing so they provide challenges and opportunities to the perception of ourselves at this point in time in relation to the past and the future. This process of cultural modernization has identity at the fulcrum where debates between ancient traditions, political economy and lived experience intersect with biography, institutions and history. However, more recently questions of identity have become enlivened in the context of devolution through which the emergence of Welsh democratic institutions has become a reality. Consequently, the imagined community has become subject to the gaze of emerging democratic processes within which definitions of identity, participation and inclusion are matters of political scrutiny and are redefined in the language of democratic engagement. When the nation begins to assemble state-like institutions, the imagined community has boundaries and suddenly 'who's in' and 'who's out' are pressing issues. The use of identity position as a means of restricting labour markets and recruitment to professional groups and elites and their associated resources becomes harder to sustain within the context of the democratic gaze. The extent and direction of this process remains a moot point that would benefit from longitudinal empirical investigation. However, the logic of democratic institutions and representation suggests it will come to the fore within the emerging public sphere in Wales as part and parcel of the wider constitutional and democratic settlement. However, before exploring this matter through the lens of emerging contours of Welsh citizenship, one of the other ways in which the 'Welsh subject' has been significantly re-engineered in the post-devolution era is through the technology of the 'brand' and the associated techniques of marketing.

## BRANDING THE NATION?

'Cool Cymru' and the marketing of Wales and Welshness in the last decade have received attention within academic journals (Pritchard and Morgan, 2001; Kompotis, 2006) and Welsh public life (Smith, 1998). It is worth noting that whilst the technology of marketing makes use of the cultural resources provided through history and contemporary interpretations of said history, it entails a different mode of subjectification. However, it is not merely a distinct or isolated mode of subjectification as it involves the active political and economic transformation of Welsh identities into marketing brands. This process repositions supposedly 'organic' forms of Welsh identity and repackages these cultural resources into flows of representation that promote the marketing of goods, services and the territorial space as a site of consumption and material exchange. The marketing of Welsh identity by the Assembly Government, the Welsh tourist board and various agents of economic development partake in what has been called the aesthetics of neo-liberalism (Boltanski and Chiapello, 2005) which, from a Marxist perspective, can be understood as a reflection of the hegemonic demands of positional competition among other economic territories of governance within the UK, Europe and further afield. This is of course not without consequences in relation to two principle paradigms for conceptualizing Wales as nation. First, from the point of view of realist readings of romantic history and organic cultural practice sustained in the face of colonial subjugation branding represents a challenge to the very ontological foundations and legitimacy of such an enterprise as a genuine and authentic process of cultural reproduction. Second, from the point of view of social history, branding of certain practices through heritage enterprises and the repackaging of industrial experience and struggle often involves a process of reinterpretation where the historically important and innovative forms of social change and vision are relegated and sometimes elided within a narrative of consuming the past (Dicks, 2008). Thus, in both cases the Dragon's tongues are presented with the same tastes of today's restricted menu.

The relationship between nation and brand has a long history. As O'Shaughnessy and O'Shaughnessy (2000) note, Ernest Williams (1896) observed that the 'Made in Germany label' was an advantage. This speaks of a modality in which a nation's 'brand' entailed a more direct relation between production and industry within that country and populist notions about the nation itself (O'Shaughnessy and O'Shaughnessy, 2000). A clear example of this relation in our case is the inextricable tie between the mining of coal and the identity of the working classes of Wales; the coal acting as a national symbol but also a process imbued with meaning understood to represent specific characteristics and world view. However, the well-documented decline in production and the shift in economic and societal organization from a focus on production to an emphasis on consumption (Bauman, 1998) has heralded a change in this relation. Increasingly, the nation as a brand is tied to positioning the country as a site attractive to investors and commerce at one level and consuming tourists and visitors at another; a process which is known as 'destination marketing' (Fan, 2006).

The central distinction between the categories of identity discussed in the previous section and 'Welshness' as it is realized within the practices of branding is that, in the case of the latter, this identity is specifically tailored to be externalized. That is to say within a globalized neo-liberal economy in which places, localities and nations are increasingly in competition with one another (Swyngedouw, 1992), the way in which a given socio-geographical location is perceived is increasingly important. This externalization and projection of a national imagery entails a reconfigured relation between State, nation and citizenry in that the practices of the agents responsible for the creation and distribution of the popular imagery with which to represent the territory are, by and large, aligned with a gaze positioned outside the locale which the symbols represent. Whereas in the past, the Great Exhibition of 1851 being a particularly salient example, the identity of the global British Empire would be displayed to sovereign subjects, in the contemporary era the identities of the citizenry (and the objects and symbols with which they associate and perform their identity) are taken up, re-packaged and displayed to a global audience. Thus, in the production of a competitive representation of 'Welshness', the people of Wales and aspects of their culture are made both object and subject.

The branding of a nation in this manner is problematic as it not only selectively incorporates and submerges particular aspects of socio-cultural history but it also assumes, and then reproduces, an inter-subjective position of a generic Welsh brand within which persons and practices are increasingly subsumed. The practice of nation branding also entails a dual process, namely the production of symbols that must both identify a 'New Wales' to an imagined global periphery and create a sense of association and attachment within and between people inhabiting the territory. Clearly the process of branding cannot maintain equilibrium between the dual demands and, as Eisenger (2000, p. 322) has argued with regard to the re-structuring of cities, the process tends to prioritize appeals to the 'visiting class'.

The branding and promotion of the 'New Wales' ('new' in terms of devolved democratic status and as an emerging symbolic identity within the markets of global tourism and investment) exhibits various tensions within the way in which 'Welshness' is conceptualized historically and socially within Wales itself. The process of the branding of Wales and the production of a new register of marketable symbolic imagery is largely concerned with the construction of a recognizable, and readily accepted, smooth narrative of Welshness. Within this branding of the 'New Wales' there is an apparent awareness of the way in which the existing national imagery of Wales is perceived in the global market place. What we see in the branding of Wales is a re-representation of the nation, a 'creative destruction' (Brenner and Theodore, 2002) of Wales as socio-geographical place and an emphasis on the production of a globally recognizable, acceptable and ultimately consumable identity. The branding of a nation necessarily involves the construction of a smooth socio-historical narrative, yet in the case of Wales, 'Welshness' and the 'New Wales', there are further influences to take into consideration.

Welsh identity, as we have already discussed, is problematic. Historically, Wales has been a site of struggle, cultural oppression and social change from below, yet within the primary frame of neo-liberal marketing practices Welsh identity, along with significant aspects of the nation's symbolic register, is being constrained. The rich social history of Wales is confined both conceptually and physically within heritage centres, such as St. Fagan's or the Rhondda Heritage Park (see Dicks, 1997), where whilst visiting the 'New Wales' tourists can take a step in to the carefully re-packaged and re-presented 'Old Wales'. As Dicks (2003, p. 1) states:

Places today have become exhibitions of themselves. Through heavy investment in architecture, art, design, exhibition, space, landscaping and various kinds of redevelopment towns, cities and countryside proclaim their possession of various cultural values – such as unchanging nature, the historic past, the dynamic future, multiculturalism, fun and pleasure, bohemianism, artistic creativity or simply stylishness.

Dicks describes the way in which the socio-historical culture of a place or setting is utilized to increase an area's 'visitability'; its attractiveness to visitors, local residents, and employers and employees alike. Facets of cultural practices and forms of life are re-packaged and commodified within these spaces of display. As Dicks (2000) notes, the kind of tourism that is being promoted in post-industrial times is centred upon 'spectacle and display', falling under various 'tourist gazes' (Urry, 1990). These are constructed sites of experience in which a particular past can be readily understood and consumed, and contours of identity are reconfigured. Furthermore, the branding of Welshness and Wales within the landscapes of consumption also provides a means of re-engineering the concept of the nation as an instructive historical frame into a performative resource that is of value in stimulating patterns of consumption. As has been previously recognized (Aaron and Williams, 2005), incorporating a view from postcolonial theory is useful in informing debates surrounding subjectivity and Welshness.

The postcolonial theorist Homi Bhabha suggests the idea of the nation is continually being split by a 'conceptual ambivalence' (Bhabha, 1994, p. 145) that emerges due to two contradictory modes of representation; Bhabha identifies these as pedagogic and performative. This disruptive 'double narrative moment' (Bhabha, 1994, p. 145) means that nationalist discourses are continually split and pulled apart. The pedagogic discourse of nationalism claims a fixed origin for the nation, and asserts a continuous linear timeline of history. It is pedagogical in that it warrants the authority, legitimacy and primacy of the nation as the central political and social frame within which the 'people' are unified and collected. The people are the object of the pedagogic discourse; they are the body which nationalism constructs and upon which it acts. However, with the performative aspect of nationalist discourse, the position of the people in relation to the discourse is inverted. In this mode of representation, which Bhabha (1994) states exists simultaneously with the pedagogic, the people are the subjects of nationalist discourse, as they are constantly involved in the ongoing production and rehearsal of nationalist icons and popular signs. 'The scraps, patches and rags of daily life must be repeatedly turned into signs of a coherent national culture' (Bhabha, 1994, p. 145) by the performance and repetition of aspects of national identity.

The ambivalence that these differing, though simultaneous, forms of representation have within the understanding of nation is extended. For the pedagogic, there is a fixed, original essence, linked with a teleological sense of the past. However, the performative, through the repetitious and recursive construction of the nation, holds the nation as something made through the people, and therefore lacking a fixed 'nation', instead constantly being recast and rediscovered through the performance of traditions and the rehearsal of meanings. This leads to a problematic position, whereby the plurality of the performative discourse destabilizes the singularity of the pedagogic and we 'are confronted with the nation split within itself, articulating the heterogeneity of its population' (Bhabha, 1994, p. 148).

The ambivalence that exists within the very notion of nation for Bhabha makes it impossible to construct something accessible, meaningful and representative of the group of people this abstract term is meant to denote. The performative displays of nation, such as heritage centres which depict 'Welsh life', and the discursive construction of a passive and linear history must converge to present an acceptable authenticity for both the people of the territory and the 'visitor class' of consumers. In this way, an acceptable and selected face of the 'Old Wales' is utilized as a foundation for and the promotion of the 'New Wales'. We can also theorize this process by engaging with Hannerz's (1991) discussion of organizational frames through which flows of meaning and culture are arranged and understood. Hannerz (1991) identifies four primary social frameworks within a globalized and globalizing culture,[1] the second of which is that of the state as an organizational form. Hannerz states that within this frame the central objectives of the states' 'cultural engineering' is to culturally construct subjects as citizens, create a degree of homogenization among the citizenry and to provide means by which actors may develop reflexive stances toward themselves and their world. In the case of post-devolution Wales, practices of cultural engineering appear to have a diminished regard for connecting and appealing to people within the territory as citizens, rather positioning them as subjects (and ultimately, through the process of branding and commodification, objects) within what it is ultimately constructed as a product in the global shop window. However, as we have already alluded, in the case of post-devolution Wales, the practice and process of branding also incorporates and demonstrates a reflexive awareness of perceived negative associations with traditional Welsh symbolism held by those at the periphery. With the branding of the 'New Wales', there is a distinct rupture in the linear historical progression of the nation and whether this history is seen to be authentic or not now becomes moot. In shaping the contours of identity within Wales, and the presentation of this identity to the 'other', there is a manipulation of the national imaginary and a visible re-organization of Welsh subjectivity. To illustrate this point further, let us consider developments within Cardiff, 'Europe's Youngest Capital'.

## CARDIFF, CAPITAL AND WALES

Cardiff is, of course, no longer 'Europe's Youngest Capital'. It became capital of Wales in 1955, its claim for youngest capital lapsed in the early 1990s with the establishment of a unified Berlin as capital of Germany in 1990, and again in 1992 when Bosnia and Herzegovina gained independence from Yugoslavia with Sarajevo as the capital, and yet this slogan was key in the city's bid for the 'Capital of Culture 2008' which was awarded to Liverpool. The branding of the capital city as 'European' and 'Young' fits neatly within the discourse of a New Wales, which started with the 'Cool Cymru' promotion of Welsh music (itself a media response to 'Brit Pop' and 'Cool Britannia' which was predictably Anglo-centric) and which has now taken on a new dimension and form.

In February 2008 the Welsh capital revealed its logo which, designed by Cardiff and Co., was intended to mark a break with 'stereotypical images of daffodils and dragons'. Cardiff's previous logo (Figure 10.1) is in marked contrast to its new symbol (Figure 10.2).

A statement from the company's chairman, Bill Savage, clearly displays the neo-liberal discourse of marketing and the functioning of such branding:

> We are confident that we have created a distinctive brand for Cardiff that has the potential to give the Welsh capital a competitive advantage that will stand out on the world stage. The place brand is a banner under which the city can rally to spread

| **Figure 10.1** | **Figure 10.2** |
|:---:|:---:|
| **Cardiff's previous logo** | **Cardiff's new logo** |

our message to the world – our ambitious, young capital can compete with the great cities of the world as a place to live, work, visit, invest and study. The brand has been developed after extensive research and consultation to ensure that it is a tool which the people of Cardiff will be proud to use.[2]

Within this statement is a clear and intentional move to position the Welsh capital city away from the stereotypes of the past and locate it within a global marketplace in which cities and nations compete for globally mobile capital, investment and tourism. To achieve this positioning of Cardiff, there has been a complete disconnection with the traditional symbols of Welsh identity; only the language remains, although note that 'Caerdydd' is positioned outside of the coloured 'circle' of Cardiff. Of course at this point we could well be criticized for focusing upon Cardiff as an example, and rightly so; however, it may be argued that the construction and branding of the 'New Wales' as a nation in the global shop window is increasingly centred around three new architectural icons, all of which are located in Cardiff: the Millennium Stadium, the Wales Millennium Centre and of course the Senedd. Whilst the Millennium Centre contains within its design certain representations of Welsh identity, most notably the bi-lingual text which adorns its front, there is a notable absence of Welsh symbolism on the exterior of the Senedd; in fact, the building does not even fly the Welsh flag. Instead the 'Welshness' of the Assembly building is displayed in the use of slate materials in the public exterior and entrance areas (Housley and Wahl-Jorgensen, 2008). The branding of the nation of Wales is increasingly focused upon breaching with tradition, history and culture as part of a marketing and branding exercise oriented to the notion of a new, 'fresh and forward looking' representation.

The hegemonic relation of place and nation branding is arguably central to practices relating to the 'new spirit of capitalism' (Boltanski and Chiapello, 1999 and 2005). This 'new spirit' refers to the way in which criticism against neo-liberalism has precipitated opportunities for new forms of ideology; an ideology increasingly concerned with instilling an enthusiasm for capitalism. This formulation goes some way in identifying how practices of branding may emerge from and are, in fact, strengthened by the tensions and 'hidden injuries of class' (Sennett and Cobb, 1972) that have been experienced in Wales. The promotion of Wales as a 'forward looking' 'vibrant' nation of commerce and tourism, and the current breaching with the symbols of the past, act to submerge the changes in the relationship between labour, production and employment that occurred with the changes in the Welsh economy. Thus, the branding of the nation is not only concerned with the re-representation of the past but also with the portrayal of a particular future which encompasses new forms of classification and categorization that may be used to perform a certain branded form of 'Welshness' in the post-devolution era (Housley and Fitzgerald, 2001). What we have argued in this section is that the reconfiguration of the popular imagery of Wales in accordance with an interpretation of the gaze of the periphery in the global market place marks a reconfiguration of the relationship between Welsh subjectivity, nation and the emerging devolved state apparatus. Furthermore, the processes described here may not only describe the branding of Welsh identity but possibly the blanding of it as a consequence of the pursuit of an increasingly homogenized 'corporate image'.

## DEVOLVED CITIZENSHIP?

The case of Welsh citizenship has only recently arrived as a political fact. In many respects it is a product of radical liberal thought and is grounded in established and evolving institutions. Welsh citizenship is currently characterized by developing patterns of taxation, the vote to a national legislature with limited but developing executive power and a new relationship of well-established national institutions with emerging democratic structures. Citizenship backed by democratic franchise represents a challenge to both 'brand' and 'identity' in relation to class, status and party. In the case of 'identity', claims to an authentic or indigenous subject position become reconfigured through the language of rights and obligations. This is not to say they are made redundant, merely that cultural particularism becomes part of a wider pattern of diversity and recognition in relation to Welsh society and the principles and processes of democratic universalism. It only has purchase on representation through the limited demands of exclusivity and exclusion unless it reconfigures such practices within a culture of reciprocity and respect. Within the context of the democratic gaze a democratic culture is, by definition, open and inclusive. This is the challenge of the current cultural dialogue between the many ways of being Welsh that will, it is hoped, formulate a cultural dimension of Welsh citizenship where the ancient and the contemporary are synthesized through dialogue and debate and where the boltholes of an imagined past or the path of ignorance in relation to history are overcome through a mutual requirement to make democratic decisions within the territory; a discourse of universal citizenship as opposed to the politics of status security and its predication through privileged access to limited resources. In many respects this constitutes some of the core challenges that are central to the promotion of inclusive politics in post-devolution Wales (Chaney and Fevre, 2002).

In the case of 'brand', contours of citizenship represent a challenge to aesthetics of neo-liberalism and the stripped down model of society where the individual consumer and market are of primary importance. Citizenship provides the raw material through which the securing of rights and a wider vision of social relations and community can be realized, albeit within the strictures of a form of governance heavily shaped by neo-liberal conceptions of regional governance within a single market. To brand Wales is a marketing strategy through which to compete within the global market place and attract investment and consumers; branding subjects us to the marketization of the social and all that it entails. It also represents a subject position that fulfils hegemonic economic imperatives whilst occluding social, cultural, economic and other rights within a fully formed rubric of citizenship. The development of a devolved state apparatus means that national identity in Wales must now be conceptualized in different terms. If a person can vote in Wales they are contributing to the political arena, and as such can expect to be regarded as a citizen. However, the idea of national identity exists beyond and before this concept. For a long time Wales, with its own culture, language, religion and literature, was a nation without a state. Welsh national identity was expressed in ways that did not incorporate political positions (nationalism notwithstanding within which left and right were subsumed). Indeed, it can be argued that this led to the development of a particular kind of cultural, romantic conceptualization of national identity that was grounded in claims of authenticity. This is not to suggest that authenticity has followed where Welsh culture has led, ideas of authenticity have underpinned popular ideas about Welsh culture for many years, making it almost indistinguishable from ideas of Wales and the culture present today.

With reference to Ireland, Graham (2001, p. 135) discusses how 'a focus on authenticity takes us to the verge of seeing Irish material history as an unravelling backwards in time, detecting signs which plough against the linearities we know from political history'. In this way, tracing ideas of authenticity requires a retrospective gaze to try and identify the influences which led to the emergence of the concept of the authentic, while they are being continually wiped out by the processes they produce. The authentic cannot be seen as having a moment of construction, as it moves beyond that into claims of naturalness, an expression of the 'real', the obvious. As such, these ideas underpin the notion of the nation, the reason for its being. The nation's logic of existence is the claim to an undeniable essence as a pure expression of the 'real'. It is partly out of a way of replicating this essence that authenticity arises as a way of facilitating yet controlling the replication of a single essence (Graham, 2001). For Adorno (1964), the authentic is something socialized and popularized, it is a jargonized system, falsely constructing itself as essence and origin. His famous critique of authenticity hinges on disrupting the edges of its claims to wholeness and organicism, and its ability to become a self-sufficient ideology and way of speaking. However, critically, not everyone can be a part of a Welsh authentic national identity, or it loses its strength of meaning. This is problematic when conceptualizing a Welsh citizenship which aims to incorporate abstract concepts of the nation and national identity alongside political, social, cultural and economic rights.

Whilst the rebranding of Wales can be seen to be inclusive in the sense that, providing you have the money or have ownership of parts of the economy which this branding serves, everyone has the opportunity to consume and exchange. It *also* constitutes Welsh subjects primarily as consumers in a globalized market place at the expense of other ways of being. In the age of devolution and the credit crunch, these economic imperatives may also need to embrace citizenship as a form of subjectivity that is able to rise to the social, political, cultural and economic challenges that small nations in the twenty-first century face. In the final analysis, in terms of the shaping of new devolved institutions and Welsh subjectivity, discourses of citizenship may well promise some form of participation and inclusion rooted in firm democratic credentials over and above the market place or claims to 'authentic identity' (and hence legitimacy within devolved space). It might also be the case that emerging forms of devolved citizenship are more progressive vehicles for integrating subjects with the imagined life of the nation within devolved state organization. Citizenship, as opposed to 'brand' or 'identity', provides a set of resources that can be mobilized as a means of negotiating history and future aspirations through devolved democratic processes. It remains to be seen which discursive frame is most influential in shaping our new devolved institutions and the way in which we choose to politically and reflexively understand ourselves in relation to that particular process.

## NOTES

[1]  Hannerz (1991) identifies these four frameworks as the market, the state, forms of life and movements.

[2]  *www.cardiff.ac.uk/news/articles/launch-of-first-city-brand.html* (accessed 27 August 2008).

# REFERENCES

Aaron, J. and Williams, C. (2005). *Postcolonial Wales*, Cardiff: University of Wales Press.

Adorno, T. (1964). *The Jargon of Authenticity*, London: Routledge & Kegan Paul.

Adamson, D. L. (1991). *Class, Ideology and the Nation: A Theory of Welsh Nationalism*, Cardiff: University of Wales Press.

Anderson, B. (1991). *Imagined Communities: Reflections on the Origins and Spread of Nationalism*, 2nd edition. London: Verso.

Bauman, Z. (1998). *Work, Consumerism and the New Poor*, Buckingham: Open University Press.

Bhabha, H. (1994). *The Location of Culture*, London: Routledge.

Billig, M. (1995). *Banal Nationalism*, London: Sage.

Boltanski, L. and Chiapello, E. (1999). *The New Spirit of Capitalism*, Paris: Gallimard.

Boltanski, L. and Chiapello, E. (2005). 'The new spirit of capitalism', *International Journal of Cultural Sociology*, 18, 161–88.

Brenner, N. and Theodore, N. (2002). 'Cities and the geographies of actually existing neoliberalism', *Antipode*, 34, 3, 349–79.

Chaney, P. and Fevre, R. (2002). 'Is there a demand for descriptive representation? Evidence from the UK's devolution programme', *Political Studies*, 50, 5, 897–915.

Day, G. (1980). 'Wales, the regional problem and development', in G. Rees and T. Rees (eds), *Poverty and Social Inequality in Wales*, London: Croom Helm.

Dicks, B. (1997). 'The life and times of community: spectacles of collective identity at the Rhondda heritage park,' *Time & Society*, 6, 2–3, 195–212.

Dicks, B. (2000). *Heritage, Place and Community*, Cardiff: University of Wales Press.

Dicks, B. (2003). *Culture on Display: The Production of Contemporary Visitability*, Buckingham: Open University Press.

Dicks, B. (2008). 'Performing the hidden injuries of class in coal-mining heritage', *Sociology*, 42, 3, 436–52.

Edwards, O. D., Evans, G., Rhys, I. and MacDiarmid, H. (1968). *Celtic Nationalism*, London: Routlege & Kegan Paul.

Eisenger, P. (2000). 'The politics of bread and circuses', *Urban Affairs Review*, 35, 3, 316–33.

Fan, Y. (2006). 'Branding the nation: what is being branded?', *Journal of Vacation Marketing*, 12, 5, 5–14.

Fevre, R., Denney, D. and Borland, J. (1997). 'Class, status and party in the analysis of nationalism: lessons from Max Weber', *Nations and Nationalism*, 3, 4, 559–77.

Fevre, R. and Thompson, A. (1999). *Nation, Identity and Social Theory: Perspectives from Wales*, Cardiff: University of Wales Press.

Fraser, N. (1995). 'From redistribution to recognition? Dilemmas of justice in a "post-Socialist" age', *New Left Review*, 122, 68.

Gellner, E. (1983). *Nations and Nationalism*, Ithaca: Cornell University Press.

Graham, C. (2001). *Deconstructing Ireland: Identity, Theory, Culture*, Edinburgh: Edinburgh University Press.

Hannerz, U. (1991). 'Scenarios for peripheral cultures', in A. D. King (ed.), *Culture, Globalization and the World-System*, Minneapolis: University of Minnesota Press.

Housley, W. and Fitzgerald, R. (2001). 'Categorisation, narrative and devolution in Wales', *Sociological Research Online*, 6, 2.

Housley, W. and Wahl-Jorgensen, K. (2008). 'Theorising the democratic gaze: visitors' experiences of the New Welsh Assembly', *Sociology*, 42, 4, 726–44.

Kedourie, E. (1960). *Nationalism*, Oxford: Blackwell.

Kompotis, P. (2006). 'Marketing the City of Cardiff: is the Red Dragon white and middle class?', *Contemporary Wales*, 18, 167–90.

Levering, J. and Lovering, J. (1978). 'The theory of the "internal colony" and the political economy of Wales', *Review of Radical Political Economics*, 10, 3, 55–67.

O'Shaughnessy, J. and O'Shaughnessy, N.J (2000). 'Treating the nation as a brand: some neglected issues', *Journal of Macromarketing*, 20, 1, 56–64.

Pritchard, A. and Morgan, N. (2001). 'Culture, identity and tourism and representation: marketing Cymru or Wales?', *Tourism and Management*, 22, 167–79.

Scourfield, J., Davies, A. and Holland, S. (2004). 'Wales and Welshness in middle childhood', *Contemporary Wales*, 16, 83–100.

Sennet, R. and Cobb, J. (1972). *The Hidden Injuries of Class*, New York: Vintage Books.

Smith, J. (1998). *The Welsh Image*, Cardiff: Institute of Welsh Affairs.

Smith, A. D. (1991). *National Identity*, Harmondsworth: Penguin.

Swyngedouw, E. (1992). 'The mammon quest: "glocalisation", interspatial competition and the monetary order', in M. Dunford and G. Kafkalas (eds), *Cities and Regions in the New Europe*, New York: Guilford.

Urry, J. (1990). *The Tourist Gaze: Leisure and Travel in Contemporary Societies*, London: Sage.

Williams, C. (2002). *Sugar and Slate*, Ceredigion: Planet.

Williams, E. (1896). *Made in Germany*, London: Heinemann.

# BOOK REVIEWS

Colin H. Williams (ed.) (2007) *Language and Governance* (Politics and Society in Wales), Cardiff: University of Wales Press
ISBN 978-0-7083-2112-6

Edited volumes are sometimes open to the accusation of a lack of coherence and unity. Attempts to apply diverse viewpoints and theories to a core debate can lead to a lack of focus. In such cases, it is not always clear whether conceptual coherence or empirical manifestations of the core debate take prominence. On the other hand, the possibility of a lack of coherence may provide the necessary space with which to help readers formulate the role and purpose of the volume, all the more so if seemingly disparate literatures are synthesized in a way that acknowledges their interdependence. Such interpretations are the stuff of Colin Williams's *Language and Governance*.

Williams' thesis is strikingly simple. It emphasizes the need to apply language-equality policies to contexts which are increasingly multicultural and inter-dependent. Thus the volume focuses on the decision-making processes in polities where 'minority' languages have a prominent socio-cultural role. For Williams, language policies and language rights are not *sui generis*. He explains his standpoint in the introduction to the volume when he states that he is not an apologist for the empowerment of speakers of these languages but rather is a 'critical participant' (p. 4) who has been both observer and contributor to the development of language policy in Canada and Wales. Williams's own academic work on these two countries, anchored to the deep-held conviction that there has been a dearth of critical and comparative study of language policies, has led to a series of publications that deal with how language policies are mediated in evolving federal and devolved systems, which are in turn influenced by external global, economic and societal pressures. In *Language and Governance,* he explores such developments in relation to six overarching themes: belonging, globalization, democracy, language policy, languages and governance.

The volume is divided into four sections that focus on the constituent nations of the UK, Ireland and Canada; contributors to the volume include academics, civil servants, political advisers and politicians. Indeed, the fact that Williams includes highly informative contributions from elected politicians says much for his commitment to the cross-cutting reach of language policy as much as the comprehensive nature of the volume. Part One deals with languages in their social and political context. Part Two deals with the legislative and institutional frameworks within which language policies work. These policies are then assessed in Part Three; whilst Part Four deals with the liberal-democratic norms underpinning the major themes presented in the volume. This review focuses on the chapters that engage more fully with the core ideas presented by Williams, especially those that deal with its six overarching themes. It would be fair to say that not all the chapters in the volume are as incisive in their exploration of the theoretical and practical relationship between language and governance. Nevertheless, they can be read as highly informative accounts in their own right.

The introductory chapter by Colin Williams ('Language, Law and Governance in Comparative Perspective') and the chapter by Colin Williams and John Loughlin ('Governance and Language – The Intellectual Foundations') set the tone for the volume as a whole. They weave together literatures on language and governance which have hitherto had limited cross-fertilization. In the Introduction, the key concepts of governance and globalization are first discussed within the context of the transformation of the nation-state. The point is made that few of the processes of 'new' governance have been discussed within the frame of language policy. In Chapter Four, the authors return to the intellectual foundations of governance and explore language policy in various state traditions. They do this with reference to the reconfiguration from a welfare to a post-welfare state. Williams and Loughlin couch this transformation in terms of 'third-way' reactions to economic and social neo-liberalism. This is in turn related to state traditions, which they identify as belonging to a French, Germanic and Anglo-Saxon genus. They then discuss how these state traditions have dealt with the tension between promotion of the state language and minority-language representation. The authors identify the opportunities and challenges for minority languages in the context of state reconfiguration in twenty-first century Europe, a system that has inherited political and administrative institutions built upon the principles of the Enlightenment. Engaging with these issues in the space of one and a half chapters is ambitious and the reader is left with the impression that Williams and Loughlin have flung down the gauntlet for challenges from those 'leading politicians and commentators, let alone academic specialists' who 'still insist on treating national communities as if they remained self-contained, self-regulating autonomous entities' (p. 37). Although Williams mentions the term 'language governance' (p. 40), he does not actually define what this is, yet we are led to believe that this has to do with opportunities for minority languages within new settings where the weakening of the nation-state leads to distinctive political and institutional forms which will in turn lead to the greater legitimization of non state-wide languages. This would seem to be a precursor to the probability of the politicization of language and the development of new forms of relationship between governance and language. How these forms adapt themselves to the contours of new political situations is partially resolved in the subsequent chapters in Part Three of the edited collection.

Governance for Williams is the governing of society by a wider set of actors including non-elected interest and pressure groups. In the chapter assessing language policy in Wales from 1988 to the present day, critical attention is placed on the Welsh Assembly Government's strategy for a bilingual Wales, *Iaith Pawb*. Interestingly, this discussion frames the possibilities for this strategy in terms of twenty-one key questions (in the space of less than two pages). The opportunities and challenges or 'uncertainies and caveats' (p. 400) related to *Iaith Pawb* can be seen to amount to a 'roadmap' for the future development of the linguistic rights in Wales. Under this conception, language policy focuses less on institutions but rather on individuals' rights, reflecting the way in which global and governance processes have blurred the distinctions between public and private spheres. Williams' chapter grapples with the relationship between state, sub-state, local government and public agencies (including the Welsh Language Board) and their impact upon strategic language policy issues. However, his principal focus is clearly on the Welsh Assembly Government. Is this an acknowledgement that the governance of language in the Welsh polity has still a long way to travel from concept to reality? Or, does is show an uneasiness to apply the politicization of language to its governance processes? The fact that there is no chapter in the volume regarding language planning at the local authority level, such as that by Gwynedd Council for example, could be seen as a missed opportunity to inform readers of the particular mosaic of language governance currently applying in Wales.

Colin Williams's views exert a major influence on this volume and his three contributions offer the reader material with which to begin thinking of the ramifications of how multi-level political systems influence the work of those engaged with language policy. Wales is the locus of this framework in four of the chapters, and the chapters by Rhodri Morgan, Winston Roddick and Rhodri Glyn Thomas add practitioner insight to language policy from both a legislative and government perspective. Federal and provincial Canada is the subject of the majority of contributions (there are eight of these) and whilst they are highly informative in their own right, again with an interesting balance of chapters by academics and politicians, they inevitably overlap with the European chapters, especially around discussion of official languages regimes.

Two chapters stand out from the rest because they engage more fully with the core themes of the volume. The academic Linda Cardinal (chapter sixteen) deals with how neoliberal vocabulary within linguistic governance has affected Canada's commitment to a bilingual nation, while ex-political adviser Jean-François Lisée (chapter seventeen) takes a wider view of how global pressures through governance have impacted upon Quebec's positioning as a *region state*, making itself fiscally competitive especially for US investors, and how, in turn, this impacts upon the use of the French language within the province. Cardinal takes the development of Part VII of the 1988 Official Language Act as the basis on which to introduce the argument that linguistic governance through a federal-provincial-territorial agreement for the promotion of official languages has not managed to break down resistance on the part of specific governmental actors. The thrust of her argument is that, behind multi-level political systems, decisions may be driven upwards to central agencies, thus negating the very expansion of bottom-up transformatory participation that new governance purports to include. Cardinal maintains that governments may still tend to centralize and control in matters of official language minorities and is a useful reminder that interpretations of new governance cut from the hue of efficiency-driven New Public Management may not lead to the legitimizing of minority languages.

In the chapter by Lisée, the linguistic evolution of Quebec, being the cumulative product of macroeconomic decisions in the late 1980s and early 1990s, education policy, economic flows and the continued intervention of linguistic legislation is placed in the context of economic expansion. Connected with this expansion is the diversity and intensity of the paradiplomacy which Quebec conducts. Lisée compares this with the 'extraterritorial relationships' of other Canadian provinces and addresses the reaction to Quebec's desire to see greater economic continental integration. His discussion of the flourishing of the French language within the province and the negation of a 'linguistic border effect' (p. 483) whereby French operates as an internal functional language and English as an interface tool across borders is novel in a setting which brings together the two themes of Williams's worthy volume.

In short, there is much to commend this volume. It is the first of its type that purports to deal with fusing the use of non-statewide languages with a rethinking of political concepts and practices specifically through the prism of new governance. It is inevitable that not all the contributions cling rigidly to the thematic spine that Colin Williams has set out in his contributions, yet this is a mere blemish rather than an impediment to recommending the volume to those interested in the way that the interplay between multi-level institutions in the mosaic between nations and states impacts upon language choice in liberal-democratic settings.

*Patrick Carlin*
*Aberystwyth University*

**Richard Wyn Jones (2007), *Rhoi Cymru'n Gyntaf, Syniadaeth Plaid Cymru*, Cyfrol 1, Cardiff: University of Wales Press**
**ISBN 978-0-7083-1756-3**

This is the first of two volumes exploring the ideas and personalities that have shaped Plaid Cymru, the Party of Wales. The book is timely as it was published in the very year that Plaid Cymru became a party of government for the first time in its eighty plus year history. The focus for Richard Wyn Jones's first volume is valuable, since other work on Plaid Cymru has concentrated more on explaining the party's stuttering electoral development or the cogitations over its rightful status as political party, pressure group or movement. It is astonishing that, despite its longevity, misconceptions of Plaid Cymru's core ideas and root ideologies are rife even among those who, quite frankly, should know better. The first part of Wyn Jones book explains why: modern, post-industrial nationalism has become a relatively elastic concept, frequently mixed in an ideological melting pot with socialism, conservative thinking, fascism and communism, making its specific flavour somewhat hard to identify. Nationalism is usually seen as a 'floating' ideology that can develop a synergy with almost every other defined political ideology – an interpretation that has been closely examined by the likes of Goodwin and Bell. Wyn Jones explores the heritage of theorizing around nationalism as relevant to Wales. He provides a useful digest of the work of Billig, Gellner, Smith, Nairn, Grenfeld and co. which helps contextualize Plaid's own brand. Inevitably, given the book's focus, this part does rather skate over some of the more interesting critiques and counter critiques within nationalism, for example ethnic versus civic nationalism. In the case of Wales, there is also the pervasive influence of British (and previously English) nationalism. This general tension, exacerbated by the Labour Party's traditional hegemony in Wales, explains the ambivalence associated with self-definition of anything labelled 'nationalist' – both British and Welsh. Remember Wayne David M.P.'s rather hysterical take on Plaid's nationalism in a Commons debate in 2002: 'The strong strand of racism and xenophobia in Plaid Cymru's history is well tabulated . . . Saunders Lewis had sympathies for Mussolini, Franco and Hitler.'

Wyn Jones chronicles with authority and some panache the ideas that have underpinned Plaid Cymru's development from a tiny bunch of crusaders into a party of government. The second part of the book takes us on a voyage through the Plaid Cymru leadership journeys, from Saunders Lewis to Gwynfor Evans to Dafydd Wigley and to current National Assembly Presiding Officer, Dafydd Elis-Thomas. This part is split into three chapters – Lewis and Evans are given one each and the two Dafydds share a chapter, interestingly entitled 'Mwy Na Dal Ati . . .' I have to say I was slightly unconvinced as to the logic of lumping them together – for a few reasons: first, the Wigley and Elis-Thomas presidencies straddle a crucial era in Plaid's political and ideological development after what Wyn Jones rightly identifies as the 'trauma' of the 'No' vote in the 1979 referendum. Second, this period was a significant watershed in Plaid Cymru's emergence from the long standing schizophrenia of debates as to its rightful status that framed many of the ideological tensions – was it a pressure group or a movement, and should it focus on becoming a more straightforward political party? The two Dafydds had different interpretations on this matter which, I would contend, go to the very heart of the party's post 1979 political development. Having said this, Wyn Jones counters the argument that each leader, from Lewis to Wigley, presided over a distinctive ideological epoch in Plaid Cymru. There is more to connect the four leaders than some (and they!) would have us believe; interpretations are different but look at their understandings of notions of small scale or decentralist governance, or their views on religion, the third way and the Welsh language. It is also unusual to have such a small number of dominant individuals leading a party in such a lengthy time span.

I am not entirely convinced that a strict personality framework is the best structure for a volume such as this. With the exception of Saunders Lewis perhaps, whose ideological dogma overwhelmed the early development of Plaid (and this says as much about the size and state of the party then as it does about the fervour of Lewis's personal ideology), it does beg the question of what about those behind the scenes – individuals, movements and groups – that advised and influenced the leaders. These are properly documented in the final chapter on the two Dafydds (for example, the socialism and communism of Gareth Meils and Robert Griffiths, and later, the sounding board provided by the group behind the magazine, *Radical Wales*, on Elis-Thomas).

This is a fascinating and rewarding book that collects and analyses material central to better understanding not just Plaid Cymru, but the history of Wales more generally. Wyn Jones writes engagingly and rarely duplicates the flaws in much writing on political ideas of using obfuscating terminology and philosophical riddles to explain rather straightforward concepts. The book's principal achievement is that is poses some very real questions about where Plaid Cymru came from and the likely future direction of travel for a party now in government. I look forward to volume two, which Wyn Jones says will cover the period from 1997 and move away from a focus on individuals, adopting a more thematic perspective. This will square the circle and ensure that we have a better understanding of an odd, slightly idiosyncratic political party that has consistently punched above its weight as a catalyst for change in Wales.

*Laura McAllister,*
*Professor of Governance,*
*University of Liverpool School of Management*

# GUIDELINES FOR CONTRIBUTORS
# OF ARTICLES

## GENERAL POLICY

*Contemporary Wales* is an annual review of economic and social developments and trends in Wales. It provides an authoritative analysis drawing upon the most up-to-date research, and represents the only comprehensive source of analysis across the range of economic and social research about Wales. It is a Board of Celtic Studies journal, published once a year, and contains articles selected for their quality and significance to contemporary society in Wales. Submissions are refereed and are accepted for publication on the assumption that they have not been previously published and are not currently being submitted to any other journal. The normal maximum length for articles is about 5,000 words. An abstract of up to 200 words is required.

## COPYRIGHT

Copyright in the articles in printed and electronic forms will be retained by the University of Wales, but the right to reproduce their own articles by photocopying is granted to the contributors provided that the copies are not offered for sale. Contributors should obtain the necessary permission to use material already protected by copyright.

## PREPARATION OF TYPESCRIPTS

If possible, please email papers as Word attachments to one of the editors:

Paul Chaney: chaneyp@cardiff.ac.uk
Elin Royles: ear@aber.ac.uk
Andrew Thompson: athompso@glam.ac.uk

If email is not possible, please post three copies on single-sided A4 to one of the editors:

Paul Chaney
Cardiff School of Social Sciences
The Glamorgan Building
King Edward VII Avenue
Cardiff CF10 3WT

Elin Royles
Department of International Politics
Aberystwyth University
Aberystwyth
Ceredigion SY23 3AT

Andrew Thompson
School of Humanities and Social Sciences
University of Glamorgan
Pontypridd CF37 1DL

The editors can provide further guidance as to the form and style in which contributions should be submitted, but the following gives a brief guide for potential contributors. Additional general information is available on the UWP website, www.wales.ac.uk/press under the heading 'Guidelines for presentation of texts for publication'.

Articles submitted should be typed using double spacing with wide margins, unjustified on the right. Pages should be numbered throughout consecutively.

## PREPARATION OF TYPESCRIPTS ON DISK

Once a paper has been accepted for publication, it should be sent to the editor in disk form, provided that a hard copy/printout of the full up-to-date text has also been submitted. Authors should retain a back-up copy of both disk and printout of their papers. PC disks using Word are preferred, but other softwares may be acceptable – please contact University of Wales Press for further information.

### Notes and references

Notes and references should be supplied at the end of the article, also in double spacing. Notes should be numbered consecutively. References should be in alphabetical order of author (see below for style).

**Tables, maps and diagrams**
These will eventually appear within the printed page but should be provided on
separate pages in the typescript and their position indicated by a marginal note
in the text. Tables and figures should be provided in separate Excel or tiff files,
not embedded in Word. Some other kinds of software may be acceptable – please
contact University of Wales Press for further information. All figures, diagrams,
maps, charts, etc. must be saved in *black only*, not full colour, and should be saved
at 1,200 pixels per inch.

Diagrams and maps may be submitted in the best possible condition on paper
if the contributor is unable to supply a disk version. References in the text to
illustrative material should take the form 'Table 1', 'Table 2', etc. for tables and
'Figure 1', 'Figure 2', etc. for other illustrations, including maps. Do not use
references such as 'in the following diagram', since there is no guarantee that
pagination will allow this precise positioning. The tables and figures will eventually be labelled 'Table 1.1', 'Figure 2.1', etc. according to the number of the
chapter in which they appear.

## STYLE OF TEXT

Quotations within running text should be in single quotation marks (double for
quotes within quotes). Quotations of more than forty-five words should be
indented without quotation marks and with a line space before and after.

Underline or type in italic any words which are to appear in italic. In English-
laguage articles, single words or short phrases in any language other than English
should be in italic, but longer quotations in another language should be in roman
within single quotation marks.

Dates should be expressed as 1 January 1999; the 1990s; the twentieth century
(but 'a twentieth-century record'); 1988–9; 1914–18 (not 1914–8). Numbers up
to ninety-nine should be spelled out in full except in a list of statistics or in
percentages (e.g. 25 per cent).

Use -ize endings when given as an alternative to -ise, for example, realize,
privatize, organize; but note analyse, franchise, advertise.

Capitalization should be kept to a minimum in the text. For titles, initial capitals
should only be used when attached to a personal name (thus 'President Clinton',
but 'the president of the United States').

Journal style is that 'south' in 'south Wales' should take lower case (also 'north',
'east', 'west' Wales/England, etc.), since this is not a specific political, administrative or geographical region. South America or South Africa would take upper

case since the term refers to the name of a continent or political entity respectively. When referring to a specific area for economic assessment, e.g. the South West of England, upper case may be used for clarity.

## REFERENCES

References in the text should be given in the Harvard system in the following format:

(Dower, 1977), (Welsh Office, 1986), (White and Higgs, 1997), (Gripaios et al., 1995a).

The form of references listed under the heading 'References' at the end of the text should be as follows:

Ambrose, P. (1974). *The Quiet Revolution*, London: Chatto and Windus.

Buller, H. and Hoggart, K. (1994b). 'The social integration of British home owners into French rural communities', *Journal of Rural Studies*, 10, 2, 197–210.

Dower, M. (1977). 'Planning aspects of second homes', in Coppock, J. T. (ed.), *Second Homes: Curse or Blessing?*, Oxford: Pergamon Press.

Note the use of lower case for all initial letters except the first in an article or unpublished thesis title, and capitals for initial letters of all significant words in book and journal titles.

Publications by the same author in the same year should be differentiated by means of a, b, or c etc. after the year of publication, both in the text reference and in the list of references.

## PROOFS AND COMPLIMENTARY COPIES

Checking of proofs will be done by editors, with contributors expected to reply promptly to queries. Upon publication, contributors will receive one complimentary copy of the issue of the journal in which their article appears.